War Without Fronts
The American Experience in Vietnam

D0840486

Westview Special Studies

The concept of Westview Special Studies is a response to the continuing crisis in academic and informational publishing. Library budgets are being diverted from the purchase of books and used for data banks, computers, micromedia, and other methods of information retrieval. Interlibrary loan structures further reduce the edition sizes required to satisfy the needs of the scholarly community. Economic pressures on university presses and the few private scholarly publishing companies have greatly limited the capacity of the industry to properly serve the academic and research communities. As a result, many manuscripts dealing with important subjects, often representing the highest level of scholarship, are no longer economically viable publishing projects--or, if accepted for publication, are typically subject to lead times ranging from one to three years.

Westview Special Studies are our practical solution to the problem. As always, the selection criteria include the importance of the subject, the work's contribution to scholarship, its insight, originality of thought, and excellence of exposition. We accept manuscripts in camera-ready form, typed, set, or word processed according to specifications laid out in our comprehensive manual, which contains straightforward instructions and sample pages. The responsibility for editing and proofreading lies with the author or sponsoring institution, but our editorial staff is always available to answer questions and provide guidance.

The result is a book printed on acid-free paper and bound in sturdy, library-quality soft covers. We manufacture these books ourselves using equipment that does not require a lengthy make-ready process and that allows us to publish first editions of 300 to 1000 copies and to reprint even smaller quantities as needed. Thus, we can produce Special Studies quickly and can keep even very specialized books in print as long as there is a demand for them.

About the Book and Author

This book is a unique source of information about
U.S. troop involvement in South Vietnam from 1965 to 1972.
A quantitative analysis of the critical dimensions of the
war, it is based on then-classified information collected
from the military command in Vietnam--information that was
examined by Robert S. McNamara's systems analysis team and
then used by decisionmakers in Washington and Saigon. The
author, one of McNamara's key analysts, did the research
during the war. He stresses that Vietnam was a war without fronts or battle lines--a war different from any that
the United States had previously fought. This difference
made it difficult for both the public and the military to
comprehend. According to Mr. Thayer, the flaws in strategy stemming from this lack of comprehension made U.S.
failure in Vietnam inevitable.

Thomas C. Thayer was chief of the operations analysis
division in the Advanced Research Project Agency's research
and development unit, Vietnam, for over three years. He
returned to Washington, D.C., and joined the assistant
secretary of defense for systems analysis as head of a team
studying intelligence and force effectiveness in Vietnam.

War Without Fronts
The American Experience in Vietnam

Thomas C. Thayer

Westview Press / Boulder and London

Westview Special Studies in Military Affairs

Published in 1985 in the United States of America by Westview Press, Inc.;
Frederick A. Praeger, Publisher; 5500 Central Avenue, Boulder, Colorado
80301

Library of Congress Cataloging in Publication Data
Thayer, Thomas C.
   War without fronts: the American experience in Vietnam
   (Westview special studies in military affairs)
   Includes index.
   1. Vietnamese Conflict, 1961-1975. I. Title.
II. Series.
DS557.7.T453 1985   959.704'3   85-17892
ISBN 0-8133-7132-5

Composition for this book was provided by the author
This book was produced without formal editing by the publisher

Printed and bound in the United States of America

6   5   4   3   2   1

To those who were permanently disabled
in a physical or mental way by serving in the war,
with special empathy for anyone who
must spend the rest of life in a wheelchair as a result

Contents

PART ONE
BASIC PATTERNS OF THIS WAR WITHOUT FRONTS

PART TWO
THE "MAIN FORCE" WAR

PART THREE
THE CASUALTY TOLL

Tables and Figures

FIGURES

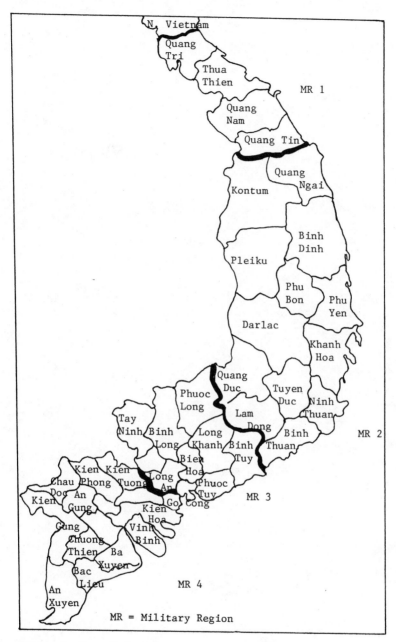

Figure 1   Map of South Vietnam

Foreword

Amid all the renewed attention to the Vietnam War, one dimension remains sadly neglected--systematic analysis of our actual performance in the field. Rightly or wrongly, we had at peak over 540,000 men in Vietnam and paid a price of 58,000 dead over the eight years between when we intervened directly in 1965 and finally withdrew by end-1972. But all too little attention has been paid to what they did--or did not--or could or could not--accomplish.

Perhaps the key reason why so little coverage has been given to what actually happened in Vietnam is the sheer difficulty of assessing that atypical conflict in all its complex dimensions. Indeed, almost the first thing that struck me when I became involved with Vietnam was how different it was from most U.S. wartime experience. Compared to World War II or the Korean War, for example, it was so different as hardly to be explicable in conventional military terms. Instead it was a multidimensional politico-military conflict encompassing not only out-of-country bombing and a "main force" war of more or less conventional forces, but a guerrilla struggle, a clandestine terror campaign, and the like.

Another sharp departure was the relative lack of any battle line which could be drawn on maps, or of the conventional large scale battles and maneuvers by which military victories are usually won. It was, as Thomas Thayer says, a "war without fronts."

Also striking was the fragmentation of the Vietnam conflict. It took varied forms in over 10,000 different hamlets, 260 districts, and 44 provinces. The forces engaged ranged from divisions down to individual terrorists or guerrillas. Thus the usual means of assessing what was happening usually proved unsatisfactory, if not misleading. For example, conventional order of battle analysis hardly sufficed to assess the effect of the attrition strategy which our side pursued or the real impact of insurgency war.

This situation spurred a series of efforts, mostly by Americans, to find better ways of analyzing what was going on. It gradually became apparent, particularly to Secretary of Defense McNamara, that by far the most useful insights came from quantitative analysis of the accumulating mass of field data by a handful of civilian and military analysts in the Southeast Asia Division of the Office of the Assistant Secretary of Defense for Systems Analysis. I thought at the time that their periodic Southeast Asia Reports were the best single source available on how the conflict was really going, (even though on occasion my staff and I vigorously questioned their conclusions). I still think so.

Their analyses often had direct impact on the Washington decision process, notably on the issues of whether the attrition strategy could succeed, on the impact of our bombing, and on how U.S. withdrawals might best be conducted. Perhaps most significant, they contributed to Secretary McNamara's growing conviction that we couldn't "win" the Vietnam war, at least not the way we were fighting it. Their analyses helped lead him and his successors, Clark Clifford and Melvin Laird, to press for U.S. disengagement from the war.

Thomas C. Thayer was the Director of the Southeast Asia Division during 1967-1972, and the only one who served in it from its beginning almost to its end. His analytic recapitulation of the key trends in the Vietnam conflict, drawn in large part from the bimonthly **Southeast Asia Analysis Reports** written at the time, provides an indispensable window on the real course of the Vietnam war. While Thayer's book makes no claim to analyze all facets of that tortuous conflict, without it no historian or analyst can begin to grasp how the war was actually fought.

It is a prime source for "lessons" to be learned by our defense establishment, however uncomfortable some of these might prove to be. Equally useful, it deflates many of the pervasive myths still common, even ten years later, about our Vietnam involvement. For example, its evidence as to the extent and causes of war damage, civilian casualties, and refugee flow is quite different from that so often alleged. In my judgement, Thayer's splendid book is something long overdue--a systematic and dispassionate reconstruction, based on the best available wartime evidence, of the key military and insurgency trends which so largely determined the outcome of the Vietnam War.

R. W. Komer

Preface

This book is written from the perspective of my ten years of active involvement with Vietnam and the war, including three and one-half years spent in the country.

It has two key characteristics. First, it focuses on what actually happened in South Vietnam while American troops were fighting there from mid-1965 through 1972. It does not deal with events in Washington, Hanoi, Paris, or other places important to the outcome of the war.

Second, the analysis is quantitative but written for a layman (like the author) to read and understand without extra effort. It focuses on the critical dimensions of the war, using formerly classified information from the American military command in Vietnam during the war, and the studies of that information performed by our group for the Secretary of Defense and other key decision makers in Washington and Saigon **while** American troops were fighting in Vietnam.

No hindsight or Monday morning quarterbacking will be found here because all basic analysis was performed during the war. In fact, the original drafts of this book were classified. They were declassified at my request by the Office of the Secretary of Defense in cooperation with the Joint Staff which supports the Joint Chiefs of Staff.

Two themes run through the work. First, the war in Vietnam was a war without fronts or battle lines, different from the wars we fought in Europe or Korea. This made it difficult for Americans, including our generals, to understand. Second, to understand this war, one must define the patterns (not the lines) of movement that describe it. A small group of systems analysts in the Office of the Assistant Secretary of Defense for Systems Analysis found those patterns.

They are presented in this book and explain why we could not possibly have won the war in Vietnam with the poor strategy we chose.

Thomas C. Thayer

Acknowledgments

Any written work having its roots in ten years of full-time effort and taking three more years of spare time effort to write owes much to many people. Unfortunately, I cannot hope to acknowledge all the debts, but I would like to start with the late James W. Johnson, an operations research veteran of three wars, who told me in Vietnam in 1963 that we had to start looking for patterns if we were ever to understand what was going on.

None of this work could have ever been done without the able leadership of Robert McNamara, Alain Enthoven, Ivan Selin, Victor Heyman and Philip Odeen, all of whom fostered a spirit of free inquiry despite the problems it brought them.

Some of my compatriots who made notable contributions are (in no particular order): W. James Eddins, USA; James Blaker; Dale Vesser, USA; Frederick Leutner; Matthew P. Caulfield, USMC; Mrs. Sylvia Bazala (who was in Vietnam when it fell); and James Boginis.

As to the writing of this book, it would not have been done without the encouragement of Robert W. Komer, Raymond Tanter, James Blaker and Alexander Tachmindji, who were kind enough to struggle through the initial manuscript and provide many ideas, comments and suggestions for improving it.

Finally, this book's publication was greatly aided by Robert S. McNamara and Robert W. Komer. My sister, Lyn Thayer, played a critical role by doing the final editing and putting the entire manuscript into a word processor.

While the book could not have been written without the contributions of all the people mentioned above as well as countless others who gathered data, made reports to Washington, and furnished computer support over the years, I am fully and solely responsible for everything said in the pages that follow.

Having written this volume, I have come to the conclusion that no one can write a book without the full support and encouragement of their family, so I extend extreme thanks to my wife Ginny and to the kids, Jim, John and Tina, who put up with all this and who make such life such a wondrous adventure.

T.C.T.

Chronology

November 1946 . French enter combat in Vietnam
May 1954 . . . Communists defeat French at Dien Bien Phu.
July 1954 . . . Geneva Conference. Vietnam was divided
                into North Vietnam and South Vietnam.
July 1959 . . . First American soldiers killed
                by communists.
February 1962 . MACV formed. Rapid expansion of American
                Advisory effort began.
November 1963 . President Diem of South Vietnam Killed.
November 1963 . President Kennedy killed in the U.S.
May 1964 . . . Joint GVN-US pacification reporting
                system established.
February 1965 . Airstrikes against North Vietnam begin.
March 1965. . . Two U. S. Marine battalions land in Danang.
June 1965 . . . B-52 strikes begin in South Vietnam.
June 1965 . . . American troops committed to combat.
Late 1965 . . . American forces attack the Iron Triangle.
April 1966 . . First B-52 strike against North Vietnam.
June 1967 . . . Hamlet Evaluation System established.
January 1968. . Tet Offensive begins.
April 1968 . . Ceiling of 549,500 American troops in
                Vietnam established.
November 1968 . Bombing against North Vietnam halted.
March 1969 . . Secret bombing of Cambodia begins.
June 1969 . . . First U.S. Troop withdrawal starts.
Early 1971 . . Spraying of crops and use of Herbicide
                Orange stopped.
March 1972 . . Communist Easter Offensive starts.
April 1972 . . Bombing of North Vietnam resumes.
December 1972 . U.S. withdrawal program complete.
January 1973. . Ceasefire Agreement in Paris.
April 1975 . . South Vietnam falls.

Part One

Basic Patterns
of This War Without Fronts

1
Why Was the War So Confusing?

> The public was also confused because it was impossible to follow the war by simple lines on the map as in other wars.[1]
>
> General William C. Westmoreland

It was September 10, 1963. Two presidents would be killed before the end of November. The National Security Council was meeting on the issue of Vietnam. The State Department's man was talking. He had accompanied the general on a four day trip to assess the situation in Vietnam, and was now reporting to the President. The general had already spoken. When the diplomat finished, President Kennedy looked at the two of them and said: "You two did visit the same country, didn't you?"[2]

Confusion reigned. This is not too surprising because war is a game of confusion. When the fighting starts it must often seem to a commander that everything is going wrong. His enemy pulls surprises, messages get lost, missions are misunderstood, supplies disappear, and dozens of other problems arise to hamper the quest for victory. All the while he worries about the progress being made. In Vietnam the worry about progress and the demand for reports on it were incessant.

General William Westmoreland said of Vietnam: "The longest war in our history, it was the most reported and most visible to the public--but the least understood."[3] Even Westmoreland, shortly after his arrival in Vietnam, was heard to complain that he couldn't make much sense out of the briefings he was receiving. He asked this author to develop a new system for him, but this author couldn't make sense of the war either in those early days.

General Lewis Walt, Commander of the Marines and other American Forces operating in the northern area of South Vietnam said: "Soon after I arrived in Vietnam it became obvious to me that I had neither a real understanding of the nature of the war nor any clear idea as to how to win it."[4] Sir Robert Thompson, a leader in the successful British counter-insurgency effort against the Communists in Malaya, adds: "...There has been a lack of understanding of the nature of the war and of what has been happening."[5]

This war was different. In a conventional war, like the two World Wars and Korea, a commander needs only two items to monitor his progress. First, he has to know where the front is and which way it is moving. Second, he needs to know the strengths of friendly and enemy forces.

If friendly forces are stronger than enemy forces and are pushing the enemy back, then friendly forces are winning and the front can be seen on a map to have moved in the enemy's direction. When the North Koreans pushed the United Nations forces down into a small perimeter around Pusan in 1950, even a child could look at the maps and tell that we were in trouble. However, looking at maps of the war in Vietnam never told anybody what was really happening until the very end.

Vietnam was a highly fragmented struggle to influence the population with few large battles, and no decisive ones until the end. Instead, thousands of small actions took place every day on the battlefields of 44 different provinces, 260 districts, and 11,000 hamlets; each involved and playing its own part. The war had no fronts. This is why the war in Vietnam was so difficult to grasp.

The United States, well prepared to fight a conventional war, was simply not ready to fight a war without fronts. Without fronts, our commanders and analysts were unable to deal with the war at first. Major General Harris B. Hollis, Commander of the U.S. Army's 25th Infantry Division in Vietnam, expressed the commander's problem:

> In no other war have we been deluged by so many tidbits of information, for we have been accustomed to an orderliness associated with established battle-lines. Here, though, we have had to make our decisions based not upon enemy regimental courses of action, but rather upon the isolated actions of communist squad-sized elements.[6]

In Vietnam only one of the sets of data needed to keep track of a war was present, namely, the order of battle information on the forces of both sides. But even these data raised severe problems. The highly unusual nature of the communist force structure with its regulars, guerrillas, part time village defense forces, and subversive apparatus, made it difficult to agree on a valid picture of the whole communist lineup. The Westmoreland-CBS liability trial illustrates the point.

To further complicate matters, forces from both sides often operated for years in the same areas at the same time. This is no surprise in view of Mao's dictum that "The most pressing and most important task of a guerrilla unit is to carry out guerrilla attacks without ceasing in the places occupied by the enemy...."[7]

Our commanders and analysts simply had to have some substitute for the front line if they were to understand even the war's military aspects. When the political, economic and social dimensions of the war were added to the problem, the complexities appeared overwhelming.

The answer turned out to be finding the critical patterns of the war. Through quantitative reports to the Joint Chiefs of Staff from the military command in Vietnam about the hundreds of events occurring all over Vietnam every day we found the patterns. Any given action was seldom important by itself, and at first glance no patterns were seen. Analysis, however, revealed them. From these we, in Washington, were able to monitor the war surprisingly well by examining trends and patterns in the forces, military activities, casualties, and population security.

This allowed us to judge the importance of events to the progress of the war. For example, the communist offensive that opened in April 1970 alarmed those in Washington who were unfamiliar with trends that had been under way for at least two years. By the end of the first week we were able to tell the Secretary of Defense that the communists were not escalating the war because the offensive was not as intense as the previous year's offensive. 1969's offensive, in turn, had been less intense than the Tet offensive two years before.

The pattern of statistics suggested that the war was continuing to wind down at that time, even though the annual spring offensive had just been launched. The Secretary responded by asking us to prepare two papers a week for the President telling him how the offensive was going.

The quantification of the war was often criticized as excessive and misleading. The body count was a prime example. The problem was that quantification became a huge effort but analysis remained a trivial one. This was unfortunate because the limited analysis that was done produced much useful insight into the war and lots of questions during the war about the prospects for winning, given the way it was being fought.

The following chapters present what we found in doing classified analysis for The Secretary of Defense and other senior officials in Washington and Saigon **during the war.** This book does not present hindsight. Everybody with a security clearance knew what we were saying while the war was underway, although many strongly disagreed with us most of the time.

NOTES

1. General William C. Westmoreland, U.S. Army (Retired), **Lectures** (Tufts University, Medford, Mass., December 12, 1973) p. 15.
2. David Halberstam, **The Best and the Brightest** (New York: Random House, 1972) p. 277. See also **The Pentagon Papers, The Senator Gravel Edition,** Volume II (Boston: The Beacon Press, 1971) p. 244.
3. Westmoreland, **Lectures,** p. 25.
4. General Lewis Walt, **Strange War, Strange Strategy** (New York: Funk & Wagnells, 1970) p. 7.

5. Sir Robert Thompson, **No Exit from Vietnam** (New York: David McKay Company, Inc., 1969) p. 8.

6. Major General Harris W. Hollis, Commanding General, 25th Infantry Division, U.S. Army, **MACV Senior Officer Debriefing Rerport September 15, 1969 to April 2, 1970.**

7. Stuart R. Schram, **Mao Tse-tung: Basic Tactics,** (New York: Frederick A. Praeger) p. 123.

2
The Where and When of Combat

The communist habits in combat were well defined and quite repetitive. A clear and detailed knowledge of their patterns of operation might have prevented some of the surprises and saved some American lives.

The communist troops fought in a careful, rigid, doctrinaire fashion with much planning and rehearsal going into each action they launched. This plodding style employed troops who were, by Western standards, peasants with little education and training. The communists overcame this potential shortcoming by training each soldier to perform only one or two specific functions as part of a team. Anyone who has watched a well trained communist sapper move through the barriers around a military base is astounded by how fast he travels. This is the product of narrow training and constant practice of that one function. The result is a soldier who can be a devastating asset in an attack.

These factors generated highly patterned activity at the tactical level year after year. This in turn led to basic patterns for the country as a whole. Three of these patterns need to be described before we plunge into the details of the war. They serve as a backdrop for everything to come and will also give the reader some impression of the shape of conflict in Indochina for the past thirty years.

The first pattern is the "when" of battle. When did the heaviest fighting occur? During the French and American involvements in Vietnam major warfare proceeded in accordance with a well defined annual cycle of combat with peaks and low points.

The second pattern is the "where" of combat. Where did most combat occur? Were the French and American patterns similar?

The third pattern relates only to the American effort and charts the combat deaths for each year of the war from 1965 through 1972, creating a profile of the war's intensity from year to year.

Logic suggests that there ought to be many similarities between the French and American combat experiences in Vietnam. After all we both fought exactly the same enemy in the same place twenty years apart.

Some similarities are obvious. Both countries committed troops to full scale combat in Vietnam for approximately eight years.[1] Both had trouble at home as early support for the war ebbed and began to affect the efforts in Vietnam. Both had to start withdrawing troops from Vietnam long before all of their forces finally were taken out of combat. Both countries began serious efforts to build up the friendly Vietnamese forces only after events placed a ceiling on the availability of French and American troops.[2] Interviews with French officers also suggest that both forces were unable to send units into combat at anywhere near their full personnel strength. Both had terrible problems in finding an elusive foe and in inflicting a long lasting defeat when they did find him. Both even had identical problems with the communists turning their dud artillery shells into deadly mines.

The list of similarities is undoubtedly long but it should not obscure the many differences. For example, the scale of the American effort was probably at least ten times as large as the French effort. The Americans committed ten times as many troops from the U.S. as the French did from Metropolitan France. The French had no more than ten helicopters. The Americans had thousands and the scale of the U.S. air effort was enormous by comparison.

There are many differences and they are significant but the real question here is whether the similarities were important enough to provide lessons that would have helped the Americans adapt to the new kind of war they faced in Vietnam. The approach is quantitative because it allows for the most precise type of statements about the French and American experiences and ought to show with reasonable clarity whether the French experience could have helped the Americans.

The French Experience

American military men criticized the French strategy in Indochina as "lacking in aggressiveness, defensive, and of doubtful value."[3] A four star general once said to the author: "The French haven't won a war since Napoleon. What can we learn from them?" These statements raise the question of how hard the French really fought in Vietnam. If they were not going all out, one could hardly expect the Americans to pay attention to any French advice during the second Indochina war.

This section will provide a rough estimate of the intensity of combat for the average French soldier involved in the French Indochina war, and compare it with American experiences in Korea and Vietnam.

Various data suggest that the average number of full time French and allied forces engaged in the eight year war was about 240,000. Total combat deaths for the force in eight years were about 95,000.[4] Taken together these figures yield an average combat death rate of about five percent of the force each year, or the chances of a person being killed were one in twenty each year. The annual combat death rate of American forces during the Korean War was also five percent.

Approximately 21,000 soldiers from Metropolitan France were killed. In terms of burden on the home country population this many deaths for Metropolitan France would translate into approximately 100,000 American deaths in Vietnam or almost twice as many deaths as actually occurred.[5] The numbers suggest that the French troops fought hard in Indochina.

The number of friendly combat deaths each month are the best way to estimate the combat cycle but they are not available from the French war so this analysis draws from historical narratives. An annual cycle of combat appears in the accounts but cannot be identified with much precision. The cycle of combat seems to be tied to the weather. The weather cycle in Vietnam consists of a dry season from October through April and a wet season from May through September, although some portions of the country may vary from this average.

In view of the difficulties of conducting major military operations during the rainy season, the dry season offered the best opportunity to go on the offensive and both French and communist forces often conducted offensives during this part of the year. Edgar O'Ballance speaks of it as the campaigning season: "During the campaigning season of 1949-1950 the French Military Command let things slide;" and, "When the rains ended in late September 1951, the campaigning season opened cautiously."[6]

Without being too precise, it is probably safe to assume that combat usually peaked from November through May and slacked off somewhat during June through October. But the evidence does not allow a firm conclusion for the French forces because "During the rainy season Gen. Navarre carried out a number of operations designed to improve the French position," and, "...No large scale [French] operations were mounted when the rains did cease in October." Finally, "...By October 1952, the end of rainy season, Gen. Salan was not able to muster any appreciable extra numbers of French troops for offensive operations."[7] The French did sometimes try to go on the offensive during the rainy season and at other times did not go on the offensive during the dry season.

The communist offensives from September 1952 through July 1954 seem to fit the weather cycle better. The data indicate that communist offensive activity clearly peaked during the dry season. Nineteen of the 26 "offensive" months were dry season months.[8] This suggests that the communist cycle of activity may have been well developed by the end of the war even if the French cycle was not. As a final point of interest, the battle at Dien Bien Phu took place from March 13 to May 7, 1954 during the final weeks of the dry season.

The most intense fighting of the French Indochina war took place in North Vietnam but the northern area of South Vietnam saw heavy combat. The most southern part of South Vietnam was quieter but definite pockets of communist strength existed there. Perhaps the best portrayal of the situation in the absence of statistics is shown in Figure 2.1

Figure 2.1 Territory held by Viet Minh after Dien
Bien Phu

The figure shows the territory held by the communists after
Dien Bien Phu fell in 1954. The area of most intense fighting
during the American involvement was under communist control at
the end of the French war although they were not able to gain title
to it at the Geneva Conference. Further south the communists
held the northern part of Tay Ninh province, the southern tip of
the country, and other pockets of people and territory.

In discussing their worst trouble spots the French noted that:

> What we have observed in Indochina confirms a fact already known in our African possessions: there exists a permanence or continuity in the center of unrest. History and geography reveal that certain regions are traditional cradles of insurgent movements, and these later serve as preferred areas for the guerrillas.
> It is in the provinces where the population has always shown itself to be proud, bold and independent that the revolt has taken on the most acute and intense forms.... It is striking to compare some recent engagements with the history of certain battles which occurred during the conquest. The events were often the same and even happened at the same places.[9]

It should be no surprise that the same areas continued to be troublesome to the South Vietnamese and Americans.

The American Experience

> In the past four years, American or ARVN units have fallen into traps at precisely the same places French units did in 1954--traps often laid by the same Communist units, which succeed far more often than they should.[10]

Bernard Fall (1966)

About 1.2 million allied forces were in South Vietnam each year from the beginning of 1965 through the end of 1972, and annual combat deaths averaged about 28,000 per year. Thus, about 2.3 percent of the allied force was killed in combat each year so the chance of being killed was one in forty-three in any year.

The U.S. averaged a 1.8 percent loss of its force each year which translates to one chance in 55 of being killed. The South Vietnamese forces lost an average of 2.5 percent of their force each year, or one chance in 40 of being killed. Vietnamese losses mounted to much higher levels after the Americans departed.

In all cases the death rate of American and allied forces are well below those suffered by the French and their allied forces, probably because those forces averaged one-fifth the size of the U.S. and allied forces 20 years later. (240,000 versus 1.2 million). The American and South Vietnamese support elements were also a much larger proportion of their troop strength and faced less danger from combat.

The Annual Cycle of Combat for the Americans

Friendly combat death statistics from the American involvement are available and they clearly suggest that the first half of each year brought the heaviest combat just as it did in the French war. The combat cycle of the Vietnam war during the American involvement went something like this:

1. The heaviest fighting each year always occurred during February through June. May, on average, had the highest number of American combat deaths, followed by April, February, March and June in that order. June deaths were lower than May's in six of the seven years analyzed because the major communist offensive usually ended about the third week in June.

2. July was always a month of relative lull. American combat deaths in July were always below those in June. In five of the seven years studied, July deaths were also below those of August.

3. In August–September the intensity of combat went up again.

4. October–January was normally a quiet period. October, on average, had the fewest American combat deaths and was nearly always a lull. American combat deaths were below those in September during every year studied. In five of the seven years October deaths were also below those of November.

In summary, the basic pattern was heavy fighting from February through June, a lull in July, renewed combat in August–September, a lull in October, followed by relatively low activity until February when the combat cycle started all over again. Figure 2.2 shows the profile of a typical average year until mid-1973.

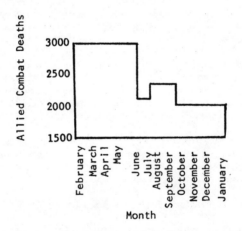

Figure 2.2 The heaviest fighting always occurred during the first half of the year

Weather determined the cycle just as it did in the French war. In the northern part of South Vietnam the rainy season extends from September through January. In the southern part of the Country and in the Laos panhandle where the infiltration roads and trails were located it extends approximately from May through September. The rain closed down the North Vietnamese infiltration routes in Laos and made it difficult for them to continue their major offensive in the South. The terrain got worse and worse as they drew down men and supplies that couldn't be replaced until the infiltration corridors reopened in October.[11]

So, the best time to start a major communist offensive was between January and April when all of South Vietnam was dry, and that is when they all started. Saigon fell on April 30, 1975 to end the last offensive. The cycle is further explained below:

1. By October the communist troops and supplies were low. The rain stopped and infiltration of men and supplies for the spring offensive began.

2. At some point during February–April the Communists got enough rehearsed troops and supplies in position to begin their major offensive of the year. The flow of infiltration continued and gradually the communists went into the final phase of their offensive, ending it about the third week in June.

3. By July the major offensive was over and infiltration through Laos had slowed to a trickle. Much of the terrain in the southern part of South Vietnam was under water.

4. By mid–August the communists had regrouped enough to launch a brief summer offensive lasting into September when it started to rain in the northern part of South Vietnam.

5. October brought the low point of activity and then the cycle started all over again. In November infiltrators and trucks were sighted coming down the trails in Laos and the build–up for next year's winter-spring offensive was underway.

The cycle is important because it lends perspective to analysis of the tempo of combat. If you know that May is usually the toughest month of the year it's easier to remain calm when casualties rise above April's level. By the same token, if you know that the infiltration cycle always starts up again in October–November it is no surprise when fresh North Vietnamese troops are suddenly reported heading down the trails to South Vietnam. Instead the focus in both cases is on the level of activity and how it compares with the same periods of previous years. Trends can be tracked well in this manner if the data are reasonably accurate, or at least of the same quality each year.

14

Where Did Most of The Fighting Occur?

In viewing the war in Vietnam there is some tendency to assume that all parts of the Country were similar and the fighting was evenly distributed throughout the Country. This was not the case as is shown by Figure 2.3. The heaviest fighting tended to be highly localized and the pattern is a familiar one, similar to that in Figure 2.1.

Allied combat deaths in South Vietnam were particularly heavy in a few provinces indicating that combat was much more intense there than in other areas. Five provinces (11 percent of the total) accounted for 33 percent of the allied combat deaths and four out of the five provinces are in the northern part of the Country. The pattern is quite stable. All five provinces ranked among the top ten each year and accounted for roughly a third of the deaths every year. Stated simply, the war in these five provinces was almost four times as intense as it was in the other thirty-nine provinces.

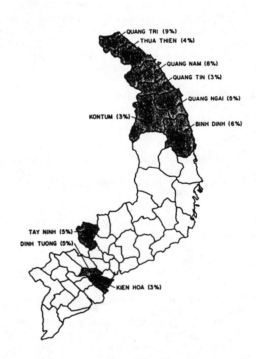

Figure 2.3   Percentage of combat deaths among
Friendly troops, by province, 1967-72.

The top ten provinces accounted for half of the combat
deaths. The other thirty-four accounted for the remainder. All
five provinces of Military Region 1 were among the top ten as were
Kontum and Binh Dinh in Military Region 2.

This is precisely the area considered to be under communist
control in 1954 and where the French fought hardest in South
Vietnam. In the words of Bernard Fall:

> For years communications along the central Annam
> coast had been plagued by Communist attacks against Road 1,
> the main north-south artery along the coast. The principal
> source of trouble was a string of heavily-fortified villages
> along a line of sand dunes and salt marshes stretching from
> Hue to Quang-Tri.[12]

> In the plateau area of the PMS, the war always
> developed favorably to the Viet Minh. Anchored on the
> three provinces of Quang-Ngai, Binh-Dinh, and PhyYen, which
> as Interzone V had been a communist bastion since 1945, Viet
> Minh control had slowly spread to the large Bahnar, Jarai and
> Rhade mountain tribes and smaller groups. Thus, they
> literally "hollowed out" Franco-Vietnamese areas in Central
> Vietnam to the point where they merely covered a few narrow
> beachheads around Hue, Tourane (Danang) and Nha-Trang.[13]

The remaining three provinces are further south and they
also fit the French pattern. Tay Ninh was pointed out in the
French section. Dinh Tuong and Kien Hoa are key provinces
between Saigon and the Delta.

As to the French point that the events were often the same
and even happened again at the same places years later, the
following quotations are offered to suggest that this also
occurred during the American troop involvement in Vietnam.

> Standing in his map tent, the U.S. brigade commander
> was going through the details of the pull-out, for after all
> the blood and the firepower spent here, the Iron Triangle
> would not be held.
> "We just haven't got the troops to stay here, and the
> ARVNs simply won't."
> "In other words," I [Bernard Fall] said, "the VC will
> move right back in again."

> "Sure," said the general. "But they'll find their dug-
> outs smashed, huge open lanes in the forest, and at least
> we'll have helicopter LZ's [landing zones] all over the
> place. Next time's going to be easier to get back in."

> As I walked out of the command post a short,
> whitewashed obelisk caught my eye. Standing at the
> entrance to Lai-Khe it was a monument to the dead of the 2nd
> Moroccan Spahi Regiment, the 2nd Cambodian Mobile
> Battalion, the 3rd and 25th Algerian Rifle Battalions, and
> 3rd Battalion, 4th Tunisian Rifles, who had died for the Iron
> Triangle between 1946 and 1954.[14]

The following account of a major ambush is an even more precise illustration of the point that the same kinds of events recurred at the same time and at the same places.

On July 2, 1964, an ammunition convoy of the Vietnamese Army, shepherded by a U.S. Army helicopter, proceeded on Road 19 from the coastal town of Quang-Ngai to Pleiku. It had passed Ankhe without incident and at 1115 had entered the small valley which precedes the entrance to Mang-Yang pass, when its lead trucks blew up on the well-concealed land mines which barred the road. Within a few minutes the Viet-Cong ambush unfolded fully and the stunned Vietnamese fought for their lives around the remaining trucks while the helicopter, though unarmed, flew low runs over the battlefield in order to confuse the assailants. Armed helicopters which arrived later saved the surviving soldiers from being overrun but could not prevent the partial stripping of the convoy of its cargo and weapons. The communists broke off their attack at 1600.

The ambush had taken place at the foot of the monument commemorating the end of G.M. 100--ten years, eight days and three hours earlier.[15]

Did the Americans Learn Much From the French Experience?

In terms of their casualties the French fought a long, tough war in Indochina with considerable energy and drive. Their strategy was no worse than that of the Americans and they had much less combat support. About five percent of the French and associated forces died in combat each year, equivalent to the American combat death rate in the Korean War and more than double the rate of the American and South Vietnamese combat deaths twenty years later. It was twice as dangerous to serve for a year with French forces as it was to serve in the later war. Moreover, the Americans served in Vietnam for only 12 months, but the French tour of duty was 26 months, which further increased the odds of being killed. The French fought hard in Indochina.

The evidence also suggests that striking similarities occurred in some of the basic patterns of the French and American experiences in Vietnam. Several of the similarities have been mentioned and two have been analyzed. The annual cycles of combat in both wars appear to be similar with both keyed to the weather.

The regularity of the cycle during the American experience is noteworthy. If it had been well known at the time by the American troops who served only one year in Vietnam and were usually unaware that a repetitive cycle existed, there might have been fewer waves of optimism and pessimism which turned out to be patterns keyed to normal, predictable fluctuations in the tempo of the war. Major offensives or waves of communist activity did not occur during the last three months of the year and this was when the year-end reports of progress were being written. (The author has yet to find one American who served in Vietnam who knew about the cycle.)

The most important and startling similarities emerge when the locations of major combat are examined in both wars, and they are supported by quotations from experienced observers and participants. The areas that caused the most problems for the French in South Vietnam were also the worst trouble spots for the American and South Vietnamese troops twenty years later. The Americans surely could have profited from the detailed French knowledge about the conditions in those areas, and about the character of the communist forces and organization opposing them there.

However, in the words of Sir Robert Thompson:

...The French experience in Indo-China was almost totally written off and disregarded. So much so that it came as a complete surprise to many Americans to learn that the situation in a particular district or province in which they were stationed was exactly the same in the 1960's as it had been under the French in the early 1950's.[16]

Other experienced observers agree. Colonel V. J. Croizat, USMC (Ret), who has worked extensively with the French and had access to their accounts of the Indochina war, stated in 1967:

While Mao Tse Tung, Vo Nguyen Giap, and even Che Guevara are avidly read and liberally quoted, the French, who were among the first of the western nations to gain practical experience of modern revolutionary war, are seldom heard from outside of their own country. Moreover, after the United States began the rapid expansion of its advisory effort in South Vietnam in 1962, the British experience in Malaya was often cited by Americans in Saigon as a model of how to handle an insurrection, but little if anything was ever said of the French experience in Indochina.[17]

What is of even greater significance is that today the United States if fighting essentially the same enemy and is doing this over much the same terrain and under the same climactic conditions. Finally, and most important of all, is the fact that the present leadership of North Vietnam is the very same whose determination and tenacity helped it to prevail over the French. The lessons that the French learned in the course of their prolonged conflict should, therefore, offer something more than simple historical data.[18]

Mr. Michael Elliott-Bateman, Lecturer in Military studies at the University of Manchester, adds that the Americans':

...first mistake was a product of military arrogance, i.e., their complete rejection of any lessons that may have emerged from the French experience up to 1954. By 1954, particularly at the Colonel and Major level, the French had realized what kind of war they were fighting and it was a great pity and a tragedy that the Americans didn't start from that point in their military development.[19]

It seems clear that the Americans learned little from the French experience, although there was much to be learned, particularly at the tactical level. Why did they ignore it? The answer may lie in the relationship between the U.S. and France in the 1960s and also in the attitude expressed earlier: "The French haven't won a war since Napoleon. What can we learn from them?"

U.S.-French relations became quite strained after the Geneva Convention of 1954 as the U.S. increased its role in Vietnam. Americans became much more active in the Vietnam scene making "...life in Vietnam difficult for France."[20] In the words of the Pentagon Papers:

> That France and the United States would eventually part company over Vietnam might have been predicted in August 1954, when US policy toward Vietnam was drawn. Formulae for economic, military and especially political courses of action were different from—often antithetical to—French objectives and interests.[21]

Although remnants of the French Expeditionary Corps remained until 1956 France was out of Vietnam to all intents and purposes by May 1955, ten months after Geneva. Those ten months were characterized by professions of Franco-American cooperation but demonstrations of Franco-American division characterized by conflicts of words and actions on several levels. Paris said one thing but did another. Washington activities were not always in line with Washington pronouncements. The gulf between the thoughts and the deeds of Ngo Dinh Diem only compounded an already sensitive situation. It was during this period that Diem established his rule, against French advice and best interests but with almost unwavering support from Secretary of State John Foster Dulles.[22]

After considering these problems and attitudes, it is perhaps understandable that the U.S. was no more eager for French advice in the 1960s than the French were for the U.S. advice in the 1950s. But the French clearly had much to offer in the way of details and experience that could have accelerated the U.S. learning curve in Vietnam.

It is also fair to ask whether the French, after the problems of the 1950 and the strains of the 1960s, would have been willing to help the U.S. by sharing the details of their experience and lessons learned. Some evidence suggests that if asked they would have shared. Their military attache in Saigon circa 1964 was handpicked by the French Government because of his exceptional knowledge of the English language and distinguished record in Indochina and Algeria. He was told to help the Americans in whatever way he could. During the first 18 months of his assignment the only American who visited him to ask about the war was an American defense contractor of French origin from the author's unit in Vietnam.[23]

Combat Intensity During The American Involvement

The best way to measure the intensity of combat in a war without fronts is to examine the levels and fluctuations of "friendly" combat deaths. They were among the most accurate data reported from the war in Vietnam and by their very nature they reflected the tempo of the fighting. To seek converging evidence, the analysis here also looked at the fluctuations in the estimates of communist combat deaths.

Figure 2.4 shows the basic profile of the war's intensity. Combat in Vietnam grew every year until 1968, and then declined until 1972 when the North Vietnamese launched a final round of intense fighting to gain territory before signing the cease fire agreement of January 1973. Then combat continued at a very high level during the "cease fire."

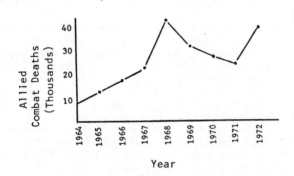

Figure 2.4 Combat Intensity peaked in 1968 and 1972.

The allied and the communist combat death figures both fit the pattern (Table 2.1) as do the numbers of communist military forces and their battalion sized attacks. The pattern seems self-evident now but in 1969-1971 great concern was repeatedly expressed at communist "escalation" of the war each time they opened their Winter-Spring campaign. Fortunately we were able to point out quickly that each new campaign opened weaker than the year before. In 1972 real escalation was obvious. Unfortunately the high level of combat during the "cease fire" was not so obvious--until the author was brought back into the problem in October 1974 and set the record straight.

In summary, three basic patterns of the war without fronts in South Vietnam consisted of: (1) the annual cycle of combat; (2) a stable concentration of the most intense combat in five provinces; and, (3) an increase in combat every year from 1964 to a peak in 1968, followed by a decline each year until 1972 when

TABLE 2.1
Combat Intensity Peaked In 1968 and 1972

		Combat Deaths in Thousands									
	1964	65	66	67	68	69	70	71	72	73	74
Allied[a]											
Deaths		8	13	18	23	43	32	28	25	40	28	31
VC/NVA Deaths	17	35	55	88	181	157	104	98	132		

Source: Table 6, **Southeast Asia Statistical Summary,** Office of the Assistant Secretary of Defense (Comptroller), April 1973, pp. 1-9.
[a]RVNAF-US-3rd Nation.

combat peaked again and remained high until the South Vietnamese collapsed in 1975.

Anyone trying to understand a war without fronts would be wise to determine the history of combat intensity, check the weather cycle and carefully examine whether the fighting historically concentrates in a few areas. The history of combat intensity will indicate whether the war is building up or winding down and will enable an observer to "calibrate" the war's intensity for comparisons over time and with similar wars elsewhere (e.g., South Vietnam versus Cambodia).

If a cycle of combat exists it will tell when the most intense fighting and lulls can be expected and will serve as a useful planning aid. Close monitoring of the cycle will provide accurate trends and highlight any significant changes in the enemy's timing which, in turn, may give clues to his intentions and the state of his forces.

If the fighting is concentrated in a few areas, plans can be developed accordingly, and any changes in the patterns can be monitored, even if change occurs at a snail's pace, as it so often does in a war with fronts.

NOTES

1. The French combat lasted from November 1946 through July 1954. American troops were committed to combat from July 1965 through January 1973.

2. By an act of the French Parliament in 1950, the French Army could not send draftees to fight in an undeclared war which limited the French effort to the military professionals. In the American case the Tet Offensive of 1968 led to a ceiling on the number of U.S. forces that could be sent.

3. **The Pentagon Papers. The Senator Gravel Edition** (Boston: The Beacon Press, 1971, Volume 1), p. 188.

4. Bernard Fall, **Street Without Joy,** (Harrisburg: Stockpole Co., 1964), 4th Edition, p. 385.

5. C. Cooper, L. Legere and others, **The American Experience With Pacification in Vietnam, Volume II: History of Pacification.** Institute for Defense Analyses R-185, March 1972, p. 67. Quoting from Colonel Nemo, "La Guerre dans le Milieu Social," **Revue de Defense Nationale,** Vol. 22 (1956), pp. 610-623.

6. Edgar O'Ballance, **The Indochina War 1945-1954.** (London: Faber and Faber, 1964), p.110 and p. 157.

7. **Ibid.,** pp. 87, 175 and 200.

8. Calculated from data found in Bernard Fall's **The Two Vietnams,** (New York: Praeger, 1966), p. 123.

9. V. J. Croizat, COL USMC (Ret), **A Translation From the French: Lessons of the War in Indochina, Volume 2,** (The Rand Corporation, RM-5271-PR, May 1967), p. 33.

10. Bernard Fall, **Viet-Nam Witness 1953-1966,** (New York: Praeger, 1966), p. 340.

11. After the 1973 cease fire agreement, the communists developed corridors inside of South Vietnam and were able to resupply and fight all year round.

12. Fall, **Street Without Joy,** p. 144.

13. Fall, **The Two Vietnams,** p. 120.

14. Bernard Fall, **Last Reflections on a War,** (New York: Praeger, 1967), p. 259.

15. Fall, **Street Without Joy,** p. 249.

16. Sir Robert Thompson, **No Exit,** pp. 133-134.

17. For a succinct account of the Malayan effort see R. W. Komer, **The Malayan Emergency in Retrospect: Organization of a Successful Counter-insurgency Effort,** (R-957-ARPA, The Rand Corporation, Santa Monica, California February 1972).

18. Croizat, **Lessons,** p.iii.

19. **Lessons from the Vietnam War,** (Whitehall, London: The Royal United Service Institution, February 19, 1969), p. 4.

20. Henry James Kenny, **The Changing Importance of Vietnam in United States Policy: 1949-1969,** Unpublished doctoral dissertation (Washington, D.C.: The American University, 1947), p. 7.

21. **The Pentagon Papers: The Senator Gravel Edition,** Volume 1, p. 212.

22. **Ibid.,** p. 211.

23. Personal recollection of the author.

3
Where Did the $150 Billion Go?

Our search for basic patterns now carries us to how the United States spent $150 Billion ($300 Billion in 1983 dollars) in Vietnam. The patterns of Chapter 2 were generated by conditions existing in Indochina long before the Americans arrived and they seem to tell us more about communist operations than they do about allied operations. A look at how the U.S. spent its money in the war yields some insight into how the allies chose to fight while American troops were in Vietnam.

Besides the tragic cost in lives, the Vietnam war was costly to the U.S. in resource terms, partly because we used firepower to save casualties. According to the official Department of Defense estimates, the Vietnam war cost $145 Billion (1974 dollars) through June 1974. These are not the full costs to the Department but the incremental costs (i.e. expenditures over and above what would have been spent on the forces in peacetime). The full costs exceeded $180 Billion. As Sir Robert Thompson points out, in the peak year the annual dollar cost was "over two-thirds of the total revenue of the British Government."[1]

Why did it cost that much?

The answer lies in the way we chose to fight the war, American style, with expensive forces.[2] An examination of how the dollars were spent in Fiscal Years 1969 and 1971 shows why the war cost so much. An examination of the pattern of spending reveals much about how the war was fought, essentially in a conventional style ill suited to winning a war without fronts.[3] This may have happened because large American and South Vietnamese organizations became involved in the war and tended to play out their institutional repertoires instead of making major adaptations to meet the situations they faced.[4] The pattern of resource allocation seems to reflect this phenomenon.

The U.S. Department of Defense estimates that the incremental cost of the war in Fiscal Year 1969 was abut $21.5 Billion, the highest cost for any single year of the war (shown in Table 3.1). In terms of total costs, more than 95 percent of that money was spent for military operations with less than five percent going for pacification and civil operations. American military activities accounted for more than 80 percent of the overall total and the South Vietnamese military accounted for most of the rest. The Americans paid almost all of the bill, including most of the costs for the South Korean and other third country forces involved in the conflict.

TABLE 3.1
Program Budget Cost of Vietnam
Activities - FY 1969-1971

	(In Billions of U.S. Dollars)		
	FY 69	FY 70	FY 71
Military Operations/Investment			
U.S	17.6	14.8	11.3
Vietnamese	2.6	3.1	3.8
Third Nation	.5	N/A	.5
Total	20.7	17.9 .	15.6
Civil Operations/Investment			
U.S.	.4	N/A	.3
GVN	.4	N/A	.5
Total	.8		.8
Grand Total	21.5		16.4
Cost to U.S.	20.4		14.7
Cost to GVN	1.0		1.6
Cost to Third Nations	.1		.1
Total	21.5		16.4

N/A = Not available
Source: "Where the Money Went," **Southeast Asia Analysis Report,** August-October 1971, p. 28.

In terms of forces the American air elements, including combat and support activities, cost more than $9 Billion in Fiscal Year 1969 (Table 3.2). This was 50 percent more than the money spent on all allied ground forces and twice the amount spent on American ground forces to fight a "land war in Asia." Territorial forces that provided security for the population received only about two percent of the total American and South Vietnamese resources in Fiscal Year 1969.

In terms of activity the emphasis in Fiscal Year 1969 was on main force operations and interdiction of communist forces. These two kinds of actions accounted for more than 70 percent of the total costs. Main force operations cost $9 Billion and interdiction operations by air and land forces cost more than $6.5 Billion. More than half of the interdiction costs went for air interdiction operations outside of South Vietnam.

TABLE 3.2
Cost Of U.S./RVNAF Forces - FY 1969-1971

	(In Billion of U.S. Dollars)			
	FY 1969		FY 1971	
	$	%	$	%
U.S. Forces				
Land forces	4.6	23	3.7	25
Naval forces	.4	2	.1	1
Air forces	9.3	46	5.3	35
General support	3.3	16	2.2	14
Total	17.6	87	11.3	75
RVNAF				
Regular land forces	1.5	7	1.8	12
Territorial forces	.4	2	.7	4
Naval forces	*	*	.1	1
Air forces	.2	1	.3	2
General support	.5	3	.9	6
Total	2.6	13	3.8	25
Total U.S. & RVNAF				
Land forces	6.1	30	5.5	37
Territorial forces	.4	2	.7	4
Naval forces	.4	2	.2	2
Air forces	9.5	47	5.6	37
General support	3.8	19	3.1	20
Grand Total	20.2	100	15.1	100

*Less than $.05 Billion or .5%.
Source: "Where the Money Went," Southeast Asia Analysis Report, August-October 1971.

In Fiscal Year 1971, two years later, Vietnamization was well established as the American strategy, and a large portion of the Americans had left South Vietnam. The total costs of the war dropped and the emphasis changed slightly, but the allocation of costs indicates that there was no fundamental change in how the war was being fought.

The impact of Vietnamization does appear in the Fiscal Year 1971 figures however. They show the Vietnamese consuming a bit more of the costs and paying a larger share of the bill than they did in Fiscal Year 1969, before U.S. withdrawals began. But almost all of the money continued to be spent for American air forces and for American and South Vietnamese regular land forces who carried out main force and interdiction operations. Pacification and civil efforts showed some gains but still received few of the resources that were available.

In terms of resources, then, it was an American war in which the costs of American forces were much higher than those of South Vietnamese forces. As to type of war, it was first and foremost an air war although Vietnam was billed as a land war in Asia, and second, a ground attrition campaign against communist regular units. Pacification was a very poor third.

It is difficult to break out the pacification expenditures from civil and military costs (the latter included territorial security), but it is clear that even the greatly expanded pacification program of Fiscal Year 1969 received only a fraction of the outlays, even though it was supposed to be a major dimension of the combined effort. For example, in Fiscal Year 1969 artillery support alone cost about five times as much as all of the territorial forces who benefited little from it.

In the words of one high level participant, "If we had ever realized at all levels where the money really went in relation to what impact it had, it is a least questionable whether the U.S. would have fought the war the way it did."[5]

The American expenditures in the Vietnam war unbalanced the South Vietnamese economy, and helped lead to unprecedented inflation in the United States, adding still another kind of cost that can be attributed to the war. All the bills are not in yet. Veteran's benefits of all kinds will continue to be paid for the next fifty years or so further adding to the cost.

There may have been yet another intangible cost. According to Sir Robert Thompson, "The enormity of the cost itself accounted for some of the optimism; if so much money was being spent and so much material being expended, it must be achieving some results."[6] We who were questioning progress ran into this attitude every day.

The disparity in resources between the allies and the communists suggests that the outcome ought to have been different. General Maxwell D. Taylor summed up the situation succinctly, "When one considers the vast resources committed to carrying out our Vietnam policy, the effective power generated therefrom seems to have been relatively small."[7]

NOTES

1. Sir Robert Thompson, **No Exit,** p. 62.
2. Operating a South Vietnamese Division in 1969 cost about one twentieth as much as operating a U.S. Division.
3. Much of the material in this chapter is from "Where the Money Goes," **Southeast Asia Analysis Report,** (November–December 1969), pp. 50–59, and "Where the Money Went," **Southeast Asia Analysis Report,** (August–October 1971), pp.26–34.
4. For a full discussion of this facet of the war effort see R. W. Komer, **Bureaucracy Does its Thing: Institutional Constraints on U.S. Performance in Vietnam,** R–967–ARPA (California: The Rand Corporation, August 1972).
5. Interview with the author.
6. Sir Robert Thompson, **No Exit,** p. 143.
7. Maxwell D. Taylor, **Swords and Plowshares,** (New York: W. W. Norton & Company, Inc. 1972), p. 402.

4
Goliath Versus David:
The Forces Involved

In conventional military terms it was truly a struggle between a Goliath and a David. The allies always outnumbered the communists by at least three to one and often by six to one. Moreover, the allies had enormous firepower, combat support and the ability to move forces quickly. But the communists won.

In any war each combatant must learn as much as he can about the other side's forces and each spends a lot of time and energy on the effort to do so. The war in Vietnam was no exception to this so the forces on each side are discussed here, beginning with the communists and moving on to the allies.

It is particularly important to develop a meticulous and detailed record of the other side's forces in a war without fronts. The government's greatest problem is likely to be how to describe, identify and locate scattered insurgent units who spend much of their time dispersed and in hiding. The insurgent likewise has to keep track of the government units so that his forces, usually smaller and outgunned, don't get caught by surprise.

Since the insurgent units are usually scattered and have great mobility it is doubly important for the government to maintain a detailed historical analysis of the trends and patterns of insurgent movement. This enables the government to anticipate and head off insurgent actions before they affect the civilian population. It must constantly be reemphasized that the communist troops in Vietnam weren't lined up behind a front. They were scattered and moving in the areas where allied forces were present and they were hard to find. Detailed analysis of the sizes, trends and movement of their units was needed if they were to be kept out of populated areas.

Communist Forces

The communist forces in the Vietnam war were difficult to count for several reasons. First, they were structured in a way that was unfamiliar to U.S. troop commanders and their order of battle analysts. Also, North Vietnamese and Viet Cong forces were often mixed together and it was difficult to know who to count and how to count them. Should the nebulous secret self

27

defense forces be counted? How about the communist cadre? What about units outside of South Vietnam who could and did enter at any time?

Second, the communist forces fought differently than units in a conventional war. Most of their combat actions were hit-and-run raids conducted by small units scattered around the country. Few such actions each year involved as much as a battalion. The communist units spent most of their time hidden away somewhere, not out fighting. Battalions, for example, usually fought only two or three times a year and always tried to move in secrecy until the very moment they attacked.

Third, the adoption of an attrition strategy by the United States ("destroy the enemy forces faster than they can be replaced") complicated the process by making the number of communist forces a prime measure of success or failure. If force levels rose it was difficult to claim success. For a time this created resistance to estimates that suggested higher communist force levels than before. In addition, analysts often disagreed in their estimates of the force levels and the whole order-of-battle process involved much controversy, many conferences, and lots of compromises. General Westmoreland's lawsuit against CBS in 1984-1985 illustrated these points.

Finally, as noted in Chapter 1, detailed historical analysis is essential to understanding a war without fronts and that includes estimates of force levels. Commanders, analysts and policy makers needed to know what the major communist force trends were. Until 1968 the estimates depended mostly on prisoner interrogations and captured documents and there were time lags in updating them. For example, a document captured in June might indicate that a given communist unit was twice as large in the previous January as the allies had thought.

This meant the intelligence analysts not only had to update the current estimate, they also had to go back and correct the listing for last January and the intervening four months so as to show the correct force level trend. Having been trained in the concept that current estimates are sufficient (that is all that is needed in a conventional war), they were reluctant to retroactively adjust their past estimates and had to be prodded to do so. Eventually the employment of additional means of intelligence from 1968 onward eliminated some of the need for retrospective adjustments.

The communists' highly unconventional force structure had four basic components: combat forces; administrative service forces; irregulars; and, the politico-military infrastructure.[1]

The combat forces consisted of the maneuver and combat support units. The maneuver units were infantry, armor, security, sapper and reconnaissance elements at the platoon level and upward. The combat support units were the fire support companies and battalions, as well as the air defense and technical service battalions.

Administrative Service personnel consisted of the military staffs of the Central Office for South Vietnam (COSVN) and the communist headquarters at the military region, military subregion, province and district levels, as well as the rear technical units of all types that were directly subordinate to the COSVN headquarters for directing the communist campaign in South Vietnam.

The irregulars were organized forces composed of guerrilla, self defense and secret self defense elements, which were subordinate to the village and hamlet level communist organizations. These forces carried out a wide variety of missions in support of communist activities and provided a training and mobilization base for the combat forces. Guerrillas were full-time forces organized into companies and platoons which did not always stay in their home village or hamlet. Typical missions for guerrillas involved collecting taxes, protecting village party committees and conducting terrorist, sabotage and propaganda activities.

Self defense forces were a part-time paramilitary structure which defended hamlet and village areas controlled by the communists. These forces, which did not leave their home area, conducted propaganda, constructed fortifications and defended their homes. The secret self defense forces were a clandestine organization whose general functions in villages and hamlets controlled by the Government of Vietnam (GVN) were the same as those of the self defense forces in communist controlled areas, but their operations involved intelligence collection in addition to sabotage and propaganda activities.

The politico-military infrastructure was the apparatus through which the communists controlled their entire effort in South Vietnam, including their military forces (except the North Vietnamese divisions). It embodied the Peoples Revolutionary Party control structure which included a command apparatus at the national level (COSVN) and the leadership of a parallel front organization, the National Front for the Liberation of South Vietnam (NFL), which extended from the national down through the hamlet level.

These descriptions in themselves suggest some of the problems involved in estimating communist force levels. The combat and combat support units were probably the easiest to count because they spent much of their time inside South Vietnam although they didn't show themselves very often. Much of the administrative service force was outside the country in Laos or Cambodia. The COSVN was the most important headquarters but it stayed out of the country, as did the units that supported the infiltration routes.

Much of the logistical support for the North Vietnamese forces remained in North Vietnam. The allied forces had little or no access to any of the communist support areas until very late in the war so the difficulties of estimating forces there were formidable. There was great interest in knowing how much of the force was composed of Viet Cong personnel from the south and how much of it consisted of North Vietnamese troops who came down the infiltration trails. It was seldom possible to tell them apart although gross changes in the mix of the forces were discernable.

The irregulars and subversive infrastructure posed additional problems. Even if an accurate count was possible, were they military forces that should be counted in the same way as the regulars? After counting them all for a while Military Assistance Command Vietnam (MACV) finally decided in October 1967 to retain the guerrillas in the military order of battle but not the self defense forces, secret self defense forces and the covert infrastructure. One effect of this change was to lower the estimated force level as shown in Table 4.1

Briefly, the old estimate (first column) includes all of the categories. The new estimate (second column) no longer includes the self defense forces and Viet Cong infrastructure, but it does show large increases in administrative service and guerrilla personnel. The net result is about 58,000 fewer communist forces. The third column shows what would have happened to the force level had all the elements been included in a single total; it goes up by at least 100,000. This didn't necessarily mean that the forces had recently increased that much but simply that newly captured documents revealed additional forces that had been there all along, a retrospective adjustment. The example and the Westmoreland trial illustrate the order of battle problems associated with the unconventional communist force structure. Table 4.1 is fairly elaborate with all footnotes included because it shows what the Westmoreland lawsuit against CBS spent so much time arguing about in court.

Other problems arose as a result of making the destruction of communist forces the primary allied military objective in the war. Until Vietnamization began in earnest during the summer of 1969, the main American military objective was to destroy communist forces faster than they could be replaced. This generated pressure to hold the force levels down and to lower them, if possible. During 1967 the intelligence estimates showed a steady drop in guerrilla strength, reportedly the result of heavy combat losses and mounting recruiting problems.

However, the intensity of the 1968 Tet Offensive led to questions about that decline, and an analysis of the guerrilla data reported separately in the Hamlet Evaluation System (HES) also cast coubts upon it. Instead of a decline from 116,000 guerrillas in March 1967 to 81,000 in December, a HES-based estimate suggested a guerrilla force of 155,000 which remained nearly constant all year.[2] This is not to assert that the HES estimate was correct but simply to make the point that all estimates of guerrilla strength should be viewed with strong skepticism.

By now the reader may be asking whether the estimates of communist forces have any validity at all. The estimators were aware of the great uncertainties in their estimates and did their best to furnish a reasonably accurate picture of the communist forces, although their reluctance to provide good retrospective estimates for accurate trends persisted. But a lot of effort went into the estimates and they probably improved as the years passed. Uncertainties were recognized by stating the estimates in ranges instead of as single figures. On December 31, 1972 for example, the spread was 65,000 troops. Despite the problems the figures are useful and they must be addressed in any attempt to describe what happened in Vietnam. Table 4.2 presents figures published in 1973.

TABLE 4.1
MACV Changed Communist Force Estimates[g]

	(In Thousands)		
	Old Estimate[a] Total Force	New Estimate[b] Military Force	Postulated Combined Estimate[c] Total Forces
Combat Strength[d]			
VC	62,852	62,852	62,852
NVA	53,700	53,700	53,700
Total	116,522	116,552	116,552
Administrative Service	25,753	38,000	38,000
Irregulars[e]			
Guerrillas	37,587	81,300	81,300
Self Defense and Secret Self Defense	75,173	f	75,173–162,600
Total	112,760		156,473–243,900
VC/NVA Infrastructure	39,175	f	84,000
Total	294,240	235,852	395,025–482,452

[a]Presentation and strength estimates used by MACV before 31 October 1967.
[b]MACV's new presentation without self defense, secret self defense and political cadre and with his new strength estimates of administrative service, and guerrilla strengths.
[c]The pre–31 October 1967 total OB presentation with the new estimates of administrative service, guerrilla, self defense and political cadre strength.
[d]Includes confirmed, probable and possible.
[e]"The old data divided the 100,000 to 120,000 irregulars, roughly putting one-third of them into the guerrilla and the other two-thirds into self defense and/or secret self defense personnel." **MACV Briefing on Enemy Order of Battle,** 24 November 1967.
[f]"The self–defense forces provide a base for recruitment as well as for political and logistical support, but are not a fighting force comparable to the guerrillas. Although secret self–defense forces cause some casualties and damage, they do not represent a continual or dependable force and do not form a valid part of the enemy's military force. The political cadre (infrastructure) has no military function." **MACV Briefing on Enemy Order of Battle,** 24 November 1967.
[g]Source: "Revised Estimates of VC/NVA Order of Battle," **Southeast Asia Analysis Report,** December 1967, p. 4.

TABLE 4.2
Communist Force Estimates 1965 - 1972

(In Thousands)

	1965	1967	1968	1969	1970	1972
Communist Forces	226	262	290-340	240-290	220-270	243-308

Source: Estimates for 1964-1967 are from Table 105, **Southeast Asia Statistical Summary,** Office of the Assistant Secretary of Defense (Comptroller), January 10, 1973, p. 4, and are based on summary information in the MACV-J2, JGS-J2, Order of Battle Summary, retroactively adjusted. Estimates for 1968-1972 are from "Adjusted DIA Estimates for VC/NVA Forces in RVN/Cambodia-Retro-OB Strengths," a statistical table prepared by Defense Intelligence Analysts on March 13, 1973, based on all-source data.

The 1964-1967 period and the 1968-1972 period were estimated differently and intelligence analysts warned that they would not track. They considered all the figures to be rough estimates (note the wide range in the 1968-72 figures), but would put more credence in the later figures than in the earlier ones. According to Table 4.2 the total communist force fluctuated somewhat from year to year but remains quite stable. The difference between the 1965 estimate and the low end of the 1972 estimate is only eight percent. The high estimate for 1972 is 36 percent higher.

About two-thirds of the communist forces after 1968 were estimated to be North Vietnamese troops, including North Vietnamese fillers in Viet Cong units. These percentages didn't change much until 1972 when the North Vietnamese share climbed to 80 percent. Again, the reader should not impute any precision to the communist force mix estimates.

It is important to note that the reduction in guerrilla strength from 1968 through 1972 accounted for 75 to 100 percent of the total force decline during that five year period. Estimating the size of the guerrilla forces was difficult and this generated much controversy within the intelligence community. Disagreements about the estimates probably exist even today so they should be used with care, if at all.

Table 4.3 suggests that the total number of communist maneuver and combat battalions fluctuated in the same way as the combat strength except in 1969 when troop strength fell but the number of battalions reportedly increased

This suggests that the average size of the communist battalion fell in 1969, which appears to be what actually happened. Calculations of average strength per battalion can be misleading, but in this case the data do seem to suggest that the average

TABLE 4.3
Communist Battalions

	1965	1967	1968	1969	1970	1972
North Vietnamese	55	146	174	203	175	403
Viet Cong	105	112	142	149	138	64
Total	160	258	316	352	313	467

Source: Table 105, **Southeast Asia Statistical Summary,** Office of the Assistant Secretary of Defense (Comptroller), January 10, 1973, pp. 1-4.

battalion size was between 500 and 600 troops at the end of each year from 1964 through 1968. Then with heavy losses having occurred in the 1968 Tet offensive, the average battalion size dropped to between 300 and 400 by the end of 1969 and remained in that range.

Incidentally, Table 4.3 shows what happens when a current estimate was changed but no retrospective adjustment was made to clarify the trend. In 1972 the North Vietnamese battalions increased to 403 while the Viet Cong battalions declined sharply. A good portion of the increase stemmed from a decision to shift all Viet Cong battalions with 70 percent or more North Vietnamese into the North Vietnamese category. This doubled the North Vietnamese battalions while cutting the number of Viet Cong battalions in half. Actually the situation didn't change that much at all but without retrospective adjustment it is impossible to figure out what the trends really were. For example, Table 4.3 shows a decline in 65 Viet Cong battalions. Were these all shifted to the North Vietnamese category of did they disappear in the Tet offensive? There is no way to tell from the table without a retrospective adjustment and one is not available. This suggests that only the total figures be used for any analysis.

Allied Forces

Six nations contributed military forces to fight the communists in South Vietnam: The United States, Republic of Vietnam, Republic of Korea, Australia, New Zealand and Thailand. South Vietnam furnished most of the forces, followed by the United States and then Korea.

The Koreans provided most of the Third Nation Forces. All of the countries furnished ground forces, while the naval and air forces were contributed by South Vietnam and the United States. To simplify, the data are presented here in three categories: RVNAF (Republic of Vietnam Armed Forces), United States, and Third Nation.

TABLE 4.4
Allied Troops Tripled By 1969 Then Declined
25 Percent As U.S. And Third Nation Troops Withdrew

(End of Year Strength in Thousands)

	1964	1965	1966	1967	1968	1969	1970	1971	1972
RVNAF[a]	514	571	623	643	819	969	1047	1046	1090
U.S.	23	184	385	486	536[c]	475	335	158	24
3rd Nation[b]	.5	23	53	59	66	70	68	54	36
Total	538	778	1061	1188	1421	1514	1450	1258	1150

Source: Table 3, **Southeast Asia Statistical Summary,** Office of the
Assistant Secretary of Defense (Comptroller), February 14, 1973.
[a]Includes regular, regional and popular forces, but not paramilitary
forces such as CIDG, national police, RD cadre, People's Self Defense
Forces, etc.
[b]Includes military forces of Korea, Australia, New Zealand and
Thailand, plus a few civilians from the Philippines, Republic of China
and Spain.
[c]U.S. troop strength peaked in April 1969 at 543,400.

Allied military strength almost tripled between the end of
1964 (538,000) and the end of 1969 (1,514,000). But by the end of
1972 (1,150,000) it had declined back to the 1967 level (1,188,000).
It is interesting to note that the South Vietnamese troop
buildup did not begin in earnest until after U.S. troops strength
had almost peaked. The major U.S. buildup was in 1965, 1966 and
1967, but the RVNAF buildup came later in 1968, 1969 and 1970.
During the period 1965-1967 the U.S. forces increased by 465,000
but only 130,000 troops were added to the RVNAF. In the three
years after the 1968 Tet offensive the South Vietnamese added
405,000 troops, a U.S. forces declined by 150,000. (Figure 4.1
shows the patterns).
The South Vietnamese military forces had three major
components: Regular Forces, Regional Forces and Popular Forces.
The Regular Forces were composed of army (ARVN), marine corps
(VNMC), Navy (VNN) and air force (VNAF) and these were all
designed to perform the functions one would expect of such forces.
Theoretically they could be used anywhere in South Vietnam but
actually only a few of them operated throughout the country.
Most confined their operations to one of the four Military
Regions.
Regional Forces started out as infantry companies that
stayed within a district of province of South Vietnam and never
operated outside of it. Later in the war the Regional Forces

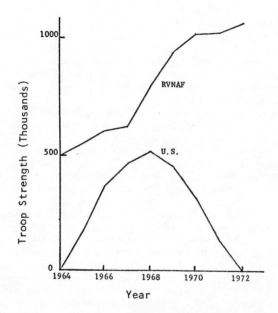

Figure 4.1   The Vietnamese troop buildup did not begin
             until the American troop strength had peaked.

were upgraded to battalions and they began to operate in adjoining
provinces when needed, particularly during the 1972 offensive.
The Popular Forces were local platoons assigned to specific
villages.[3] They manned the outposts, guarded the bridges and
attempted to maintain security in their villages, and they were
not supposed to be used in any other area.

RVNAF doubled between 1964 (514,000) and 1972 (1,090,000).
Within the total the regular forces also doubled with the army
dominating, while the Regional Forces tripled.   After a decline in
1965 the Popular Forces eventually increased by 50 percent to
reach their peak and then began to decline in 1971, falling more
noticeably in 1972.

The impact of Vietnamization began to show in the regular
forces in 1969 and 1970 with sharp increases in the navy and air
force.   The navy in 1972 was three and one-half times as large as
it was in 1964, and the air force was about five times as large.
The army buildup started in 1968 with the Tet Offensive, and it was

36

fairly complete by the end of 1969 although there was an additional spurt in 1972. The figures reflect the Vietnamization program's emphasis on building up the ground forces first while waiting for slower, more technical programs for the Air Force and Navy to take effect.

The mix of the RVNAF force structure (regulars on the one hand and Regional and Popular Forces on the other) did not change much but the combination of rapid growth in the Regional and Popular Forces and later U.S. withdrawals had the effect of shifting emphasis in the remaining allied forces toward territorial operations. For example, the Regional and Popular Forces accounted for 27 percent of the allied forces in 1968, before U.S. withdrawal, but by the end of 1972 they accounted for 45 percent of the allied forces.

The personnel strengths of the South Vietnamese paramilitary units tripled between 1964 and 1972 from 50,000 to 150,000. These data are often displayed with the RVNAF totals and call for a brief mention at this point. A detailed discussion of each force and its performance appears in Chapter 14.

Four major groups made up the paramilitary units. First, the Civilian Irregular Defense Groups (CIDG, usually Montagnards) were advised by U.S. Special Forces Teams along the South Vietnamese borders of Laos and Cambodia. Their mission was primarily to provide border security. They really should be included in the RVNAF totals from the beginning because they performed military missions and because they were incorporated into the RVNAF in 1969 and 1970 as border defense units.

Second, the National Police quadrupled, showing particularly rapid growth in 1971 as the importance of developing an effective police force was recognized. They accounted for 121,000 of the final paramilitary total of 150,000 in 1972.

The third group was the Revolutionary Development Cadre (RD Cadre) which was the cutting edge of the pacification program. After a modicum of security was established in an area, the RD Cadre went in to bring government programs to the people and to organize support for the GVN. This program was phased out as the need for it diminished.

The fourth major group of paramilitary units included Kit Carson Scouts who operated in villages where security was tenuous. Both groups drew their people from communist defectors who surrendered to the GVN through the Chieu Hoi Program (see Chapter 16). Finally the Peoples Self Defense Forces (PSDF) added several hundred thousand villagers to the local troops charged with village security.

The U.S. had 23,310 troops in South Vietnam in December 1964. The total peaked in 543,400 in April 1969 and by the end of 1972 had returned to the 1964 level (24,172).[4] Table 4.5 shows the pattern and how the strength of each U.S. military service in Vietnam changed over time. The army and marine corps accounted for 80 percent of the forces.[5]

TABLE 4.5
U.S. Forces in South Vietnam

(End of Year strength in Thousands)

	1964	1965	1966	1967	1968	1969	1970	1971	1972
Army	15	117	239	320	360	331	251	120	14
Marine Corps.	1	38	69	78	81	55	25	(.6)	1
USAF	6	20	53	56	58	58	43	29	8
Navy & Coast Guard	1	9	24	32	37	31	17	8	1
Total	23	184	385	486	536	475	336	158	24

Source: Table 103, **Southeast Asia Statistical Summary,** Office of the Assistant Secretary of Defense (Comptroller) February 7, 1973.

It has already been noted that the bulk of the U.S. forces arrived in Vietnam during 1965-67, then redeployed to the United States in 1970-72. The air force built up the fastest and remained in Vietnam the longest. It reached 90 percent of peak strength by the end of 1966 and 14 percent of its peak strength remained at the end of 1972. The marine corps arrived early and left early. It reached 85 percent of peak strength by the end of 1966 and then virtually withdrew by the end of 1971. The army and navy built up at slower rates, not reaching their peak strengths until the end of 1967. This is not surprising because the army deployed four times as many troops as any other Service.

Table 4.6 displays the stages of the U.S. force buildup in South Vietnam and the subsequent withdrawal. The buildup was in six steps, culminating in a peak authorized U.S. force level of 549,500 spaces. The actual strength peaked at 543,400 or 6,100 below the authorized level.

The withdrawals, or redeployments, took place in fourteen increments which for convenience be grouped into four major steps. In the first step the President made three separate announcements authorizing the withdrawal of 115,500 U.S. troops, reducing their number to a level of 434,000 on April 15, 1970. In the second step the President announced a force reduction of 150,000 by May 1, 1971, dropping the authorized level to 284,000. Then, in another single announcement the President reduced the forces by 100,000. This resulted in an authorized force level 184,000 on December 1, 1971. The final step, prior to the cease fire agreement, consisted of five separate presidential announcements that reduced forces by 157,000, to a level of 27,000 by December 1, 1972. The cease fire agreement then provided for the withdrawal of the remaining American forces.

TABLE 4.6
Build-Up And Withdrawal Of
U.S. Force Levels in Vietnam

Sea Program Number	Approval Date	Force Force Level Authorized	Effective Date	Increase/ Decrease
Build-up				
1 (Phase (I)	July 31, 65	190.1	June 67	–
2 (Phase II, IIA, IIIR)	Dec. 11, 65	393.9	June 67	+203.8
3	July 2, 66	437.0	June 67	+43.1
4	Nov. 18, 66	470.0	June 68	+33.0
5	Aug. 14, 67	525.0	June 69	+55.0
6	Apr. 4, 68	549.5	June 69	+24.5
Withdrawal				
7 (Increment 1)	June 8, 69	524.5	Aug. 31, 69	-25.0
8 (2)	Sept 16, 69	484.0	Dec. 15, 69	-40.5
9 (3)	Dec. 15, 69	434.0	Apr. 15, 70	-50.0
				-115.5

On April 20, 1970 president Announces reduction of
150,000 U.S. spaces. To be done in three stages.

10 (4)	June 3, 70	384.0	Oct. 15, 70	-50.0
11 (5)	Oct. 12, 70	344.0	Dec. 31, 70	-40.0
12 (6)	Mar. 1, 71	284.0	May 1, 71	-60.0
				-150.0

On April 7, 1971 president announces reduction of
100,000 U.S. spaces. To be done in three stages.

13 (7)	Apr. 9, 71	254.7	June 30, 71	-29.3
14 (8)	Apr. 9, 71	226.0	Aug. 31, 71	-28.7
15 (9)	Apr. 9, 71	184.0	Dec. 1, 71	-42.0
				-100.0
16 (10)	Nov. 12, 71	139.0	Jan. 31, 72	-45.0
17 (11)	Jan. 13, 72	69.0	May 1, 72	-70.0
18 (12)	Apr. 26, 72	49.0	July 1, 72	-20.0
19 (13)	June 28, 72	39.0	Sept. 1, 72	-10.0
20 (14)	Aug. 28, 72	27.0	Dec. 1, 72	-12.0
				-157.0

Australia, Korea, New Zealand and Thailand all contributed military forces to fight in Vietnam. Their troop strength peaked at 70,000 in 1969. The Philippines sent a civilian contingent. The ROK (Korean) forces comprised 80 percent of the third nation contribution. The Koreans quickly built up to a force of about 45,000 by the end of 1966, increased to 50,000 in 1969 and were still in Vietnam at the end of 1972. The Korean units operated primarily in Military Region 1, the area of South Vietnam that was so noticeable in Figures 2.1 and 2.3 shown in Chapter 2.

Conclusions

At least two patterns and a question emerge from the data presented in this chapter.

The first pattern reflects the shift in force composition on both sides. As the years passed the communist forces consisted of less Viet Cong and more of the North Vietnamese Army. The decline in Viet Cong strength and compensatory increase in North Vietnamese Army troops (even as fillers in ostensibly Viet Cong units) was notable. In contrast, the allies relied increasingly on outside forces (United States, South Korean and other third nations) during the early years of 1965-68 and then reverted mostly to RVNAF. The communists relied increasingly on North Vietnamese Army troops from outside of South Vietnam while the allies relied more on the RVNAF troops from within South Vietnam.

A second pattern is the gradual change in the kind of war both sides fought. This will become clearer after reading chapters 5 and 6. To oversimplify, the communists built up from primarily Viet Cong guerrilla operations and forces to progressively greater emphasis on main forces. This trend accelerated as regular North Vietnamese Army units were brought in; first for the kill in 1964-1965, and then to counter the U.S. buildup. Gradual allied attrition of the Viet Cong also made the communist effort more and more a main-force war, culminating ironically in their most conventional effort of all, the Easter 1972 offensive that made use mainly of the regular North Vietnamese Army with artillery and armor.

The allies were predominately regulars all along, including Vietnamese regular forces but the 1967-1972 pacification effort gradually built up the allied counterguerrilla and anti-Viet Cong infrastructure effort. Meanwhile, gradual U.S. withdrawal reduced the allied main forces. Hence the allied style and force structure were becoming somewhat less conventional as the communists became notably more conventional.

The question emerging from the chapter is why couldn't the allies destroy the communist forces since they outnumbered them by substantial margins throughout the war. A comparison of the allied and communist forces shows that from 1965 on the allies always outnumbered the communists by at least three to one. Despite this advantage the allies could not destroy the communist forces and their force level at the end of 1972 was in fact slightly higher than in 1965.

Communist forces seemed to be considerably weaker by 1972 but their army remained intact. If the additional allied advantages of mobility, firepower and combat support are taken into account it is even more difficult to understand how the communist army survived. But survive it did, despite the allied attempts to destroy it. Chapter 9 suggests some possible reasons why the communists were able to hold out and why they finally accepted the stalemate and signed the cease fire agreement in January 1973.

NOTES

1. **MACV Monthly Order of Battle Summary,** 31 August 1967.
2. "Enemy Guerrilla Forces in 1967," **Southeast Asia Analysis Report,** March 1968, p. 6.
3. Villages in Vietnam have boundaries similar to a township in the U.S. A hamlet is a specific geographical concentration of people.
4. Table 103, **Southeast Asia Statistical Summary,** Office of the Assistant Secretary of Defense (Comptroller), February 7, 1973.
5. The cumulative number who had served in Vietnam from January 1, 1965 through September 30, 1972 is: army – 1,641,696; navy – 144,062; air force – 356,724; marine corps – 447,425; for a total of 2,590,480.

Part Two

The "Main Force" War

5
The Name of the Communist Game:
Small Unit Actions

In guerrilla warfare, we must observe the principle, to gain
territory is no cause for joy, and to lose territory is no
cause for sorrow."[1]

Mao Tse-tung

In accordance with Mao, the communists fought a war of small
unit actions with no fronts evident. This chapter is based on all
the reports of communist-initiated actions in South Vietnam.
Many incidents probably weren't reported but those that were
recorded are sufficient to show the style, patterns and trends of
communist actions. The analysis examines the various types of
communist operations, their levels and trends over time, where
they were concentrated, and how the targeting of allied forces
changed over time.

In a war without fronts it is particularly important to keep a
detailed historical record of the other side's pattern of action.
As with the forces, the actions will be scattered about the
country and may appear random and individually unimportant at
first glance. However, if the other side is well organized and
operating seriously, analysis will reveal that its actions are far
from being random and follow well defined patterns. These
patterns are extremely important since they provide concrete
evidence of what the other side is doing, sometimes contrasting
with what it says it is doing and sometimes supporting it.
Incident patterns yield many clues about intent, strategy,
strength and weakness.[2] The annual cycle of combat should be kept
in mind as a key facet of the communist style of operation. It
continued year after year as a basic background to the patterns
explored here.

Table 5.1 displays the official U.S. Department of Defense
statistics concerning communist initiated actions in South
Vietnam. These data present several problems. One is that the
reporting categories were changed without retrospective
adjustment so the time series was disrupted as it was for
communist forces. Incidents involving indirect fire of 20 rounds
or more were not counted as attacks until late 1966 when inclusion

43

TABLE 5.1
Communist Battalion Sized Attacks
and Other Actions In South Vietnam

	1965	1966	1967	1968	1969	1970	1971	1972
Attacks								
Battalion size								
or larger	73	44	54	126	34	13	2	106
Other	612	894	2422	3795	3787	3526	2242	6478
Sub-Total	685	938	2476	3921	3821	3539	2244	6584
Other Incidents								
Harassment	–	10288	19231	18233	18640	19148	10648	11997
Terrorism	0730	14585	1963	1047	1375	1904	2333	819
Sabotage	4132	2212	1443	1609	199	185	101	134
Propaganda	1974	1504	801	102	43	73	367	24
Anti-aircraft								
Fire	4008	8128	13290	13078	10167	8734	6846	817
Total	31519	37655	39204	37990	34245	33583	22599	20375

Source: Table 2, Statistics on Vietnam by Month, **Southeast Asia Statistical Summary,**   Office of the Assistant Secretary of Defense (Comptroller), April 11, 1973, pp. 1-8.   (Based on summary data from the MACV-OPREP reports.)

of these incidents boosted the total number of attacks in a major way after 1966 as shown in Table 5.2.   The same problem is seen in the harassment and terrorism date for 1965-1966.   In mid-1966 the harassment category was established without a retrospective adjustment and here, too, the trend is disrupted.

The most serious problem in dealing with the official U.S. figures is that they do not include communist actions reported by the Vietnamese National Police and other civilian authorities. These data started to become available in the final quarter of 1967 but are not included in Table 5.1.   This table includes only information from the military reports and therefore omits some of the terrorism, sabotage and propaganda incidents that were reported.   Finally, the summary data from the military reports limit analysis of communist action to the types of action by military region.   To analyze incidents by casualties, provinces, targets and detailed types (e.g., ground assaults and standoff fire attacks) one must turn to two computer files, which taken together, record the details of individual actions reported by the military or civil authorities and provide data for detailed analysis.

Table 5.2 displays the complete data in summary form.   It contains all the data shown in Table 5.1 plus the additional civilian data collected from late 1967 on, so the totals are much higher.   The attack data and the anti-aircraft data agree with Table 5.1 because they were reported only through the military channel.   The additions lie in the areas of harassment, terrorism,

TABLE 5.2
Communist Actions In South Vietnam

(Computer Data Including Military and Civilian Reports)

	1965	1966	1967	1968	1969	1970	1971	1972
Attacks								
Ground Assault	685	906	1538	1500	1615	1770	1615	2429
Indirect fire only		32	992	2410	2237	1630	1009	4074
Subtotal	685	938	2530	3910	3852	3400	2624	6503
Harrassment								
Harassment by fire			15502	13435	13812	12927	7682	8939
Other harassment			7566	9716	10638	12056	9973	8906
Subtotal			23068	23151	24450	24983	17655	17899
Political & Coercion			1756	3237	2776	3844	3552	5658
Anti-aircraft Fire			12066	12646	9706	8081	6794	774
Total Actions			39420	42944	40784	40308	30625	30834
Difference from								
Table 5.1 Total			216	4954	6539	6725	8026	10459

Source: VCIIA and TIRS Computer Files, Department of Defense, National Military Command Systems Support Center.

sabotage and non-violent political coercion (propaganda, etc.). The effect of adding indirect fire (20 rounds or more) to the attack category in late 1966 shows up clearly. Such incidents accounted for more than half of the total attacks during the 1967–1972 period.

Table 5.2 shows clearly the unconventional style of the communist brand of war. Most of their actions took the form of standoff attacks, harassment and terrorism which did not involve direct contact between their ground forces and those of the allies. The communist ground assaults where their troops came in contact with allied forces accounted for less than five percent of the total actions during 1965–1972. More than 95 percent of those assaults were attacks by communist units smaller than a battalion. Incessant small unit actions truly was the name of their game.

The various categories of action shown in Table 5.2 are different enough to require separate analysis. A ground assault is usually a much more serious action than an indirect attack by fire so it doesn't make much sense to add them and then look only at the total. The analysis here regroups the incidents into ground assaults, standoff attacks, harassment, coercion and anti-aircraft incidents.

TABLE 5.3
More Than 95 Percent Of The Communist
Ground Assaults Were Conducted By Small Units

Communist Ground Assaults By	1965	1966	1967	1968	1969	1970	1971	1972	Total
Battalion Sized or larger units	73	44	54	126	34	13	2	106	452
Small Units	612	862	1484	1374	1581	1757	1613	2323	11596
Total Ground Assaults	685	906	1538	1500	1615	1770	1615	2429	12058

Source: Tables 5.1 and 5.2.

The communist ground assaults are shown in Table 5.3. The figures probably understate the actual rate at which ground attacks took place because communist attacks in reaction to allied operations were seldom, if ever, included in the data. Such actions were normally reported as allied operations not communist attacks on the assumption that allied units, not the communist units, were on the offensive in such situations. The figures in the Table probably represent the minimum communist attack rate.

Table 5.3 also presents the evidence that the communists fought a small unit war. As noted above, more than 95 percent of their ground assaults during the eight year period were conducted by units smaller than a battalion. Even in the peak combat years of 1968 and 1972 small units accounted for more than 90 percent of the reported ground assaults.

The total number of ground assaults doubled between 1965 and 1967, remained stable for the five year period 1968-1972 and then leveled off at about 1600 per year from 1968 to 1971. Only in 1970 was there as much as a ten percent deviation. Then the 1972 offensive brought a 50 percent increase in ground assaults. After 1966 the fluctuations in battalion sized attacks became a fairly good guide to the intensity of the war. Battalion size ground assaults peaked in 1968, declined steadily in 1969-1971 and then rose sharply in 1972.

As would be expected communist ground assaults were concentrated in the same provinces where allied combat deaths were highest. The ten provinces showing the highest allied death rates included eight of the provinces with the highest communist ground attack rates.

Attacks by indirect fire (referred to as standoff attacks) are considered in two categories here. The first category includes indirect fire of 20 rounds or more (mortar, rocket or artillery shells) which, along with ground assaults, were classified as attacks in the official statistics. The second category consists of harassment by indirect fire of less than 20 rounds or fire from small arms. These are grouped with other types of harassment in the official figures. Since the two types of action are alike except for the number of rounds fired they are analyzed together here.

An attack by fire typically consisted of about 30 rounds. Although an attack required advanced planning, logistical support and was military in style, the target was not assaulted. A standoff attack was generally a means of exerting military pressure on a target which the communists could not hope to or did not desire to defeat. The communists inflicted an allied combat death for every 50 to 60 rounds they fired[4] and, while they sometimes suffered casualties from allied counter-battery fire, they usually escaped unharmed.

Harassments by indirect fire were usually isolated incidents not coordinated with other types of military action. They were essentially an extension of terrorist activity. The communists would fire six or seven rounds using a small mortar (81 mm) and for every 25 rounds fired an allied soldier or civilian would be killed, usually at no cost to the communists except the ammunition.[5]

Table 5.4 indicates that the annual average of indirect fire incidents was quite stable at about 15,000 per year except for 1971, although a slight declining trend is evident. More than 85 percent of indirect fire incidents consisted of harassing fire until 1972 when the high rate of artillery fire introduced into Military Region 1 altered the balance. The Table also suggests that harassments by fire were almost level during 1967-70.

TABLE 5.4
More Than 85 Percent Of The Indirect Fire
Incidents Were Harassments Every Year Until 1972

	1967	1968	1969	1970	1971	1972	Total
Attacks by fire[a]	992	2,410	2,237	1,630	1,009	4,074	12,352
Harassment by fire[b]	15,502	13,435	13,812	12,927	7,682	8,939	7,2297
Total	16,494	15,845	16,049	14,557	8,691	13,013	84,649

Source: SEAPRS Computer File Department of Defense, National Military Command Systems Support Center.
[a]Twenty rounds or more.
[b]Less than twenty rounds.

TABLE 5.5
Harassment And Political Coercion Incidents

	1967	1968	1969	1970	1971	1972	Total
Harassment	7,566	9,716	10,638	12,056	9,973	8,960	58,909
Political Coercion	1,756	3,237	2,776	3,844	3,552	5,658	20,823

Source: SEAPRS Computer File, Department of Defense, National Military Command Systems Support Center.

Table 5.5 displays communist acts of a political or coercive nature and incidents of harassment other than indirect fire. Harassment includes acts of sabotage and terror. Terror is defined as incidents against civilians that resulted in casualties such as assassinations, abductions or wounded. The political and coercive category includes actions directed against civilians that did not result in casualties (such as propaganda, holding meetings, entering hamlets, etc.).

Table 5.5 indicates that harassments averaged about 10,000 per year for the six year period of 1967-72. Harassments peaked in 1970 but the level was fairly constant throughout this period.

Acts of a political or coercive nature without casualties ranged from 1756 in 1967 to 5658 in 1972, the year of a major communist offensive. This type of incident was probably reported less accurately than any of the others because it was less serious (no casualties) and therefore more likely to escape the notice of authorities. The political-coercion figures should not be taken too seriously although the figures for 1968 and 1972 reflect the communists' major increases in other activities during these two years.

Figures dealing with terrorism are included in the harassment category of Table 5.5 but terrorism was such an important communist activity that it needed special coverage. Terror is a traditional weapon of the insurgent and in South Vietnam the communists began using terror in 1957 as part of their renewed campaign to unite Vietnam under a communist government. General Giap, the communist commander, recognized the value of terror as a guerrilla war tactic and the communist use of terror in South Vietnam was aimed at several important goals:

1. Intimidation of The People. The communists assassinated, abducted, threatened and harassed the population in order to force its cooperation, to obtain laborers and porters when needed, to collect taxes, food and other supplies, and to prevent the local inhabitants from giving intelligence to allied forces.

2. Elimination Of Enemies. Certain individuals, particularly South Vietnamese officials (e.g. hamlet and
village chiefs), National Police, RD Cadre, school
teachers and individual citizens who defied communist
threats were specifically marked for elimination. If
the individual was unpopular so much the better since
the communists could claim credit for removing an
"enemy of the people."

3. Propaganda. Within Vietnam the communists pointed to
their terror tactics as signs of their strength and
presence throughout the country, even in the cities
that traditionally were government strongholds. The
communists also tried to influence external factors
such as the Paris Peace Talks and world public opinion
by terror attacks on well-known U.S. and Vietnamese
personalties. Such actions gave the communists
publicity and helped boost their morale.

According to Bernard Fall and Jay Mallin, terror was used as a
tactic to isolate the rural areas from the cities since the people
had not been provided security by the GVN in the past. Rural
areas were easier for the communists to control since the
elimination of a few key people (the hamlet chief, police chief,
local school teacher, etc.) was usually all that was necessary to
intimidate the rest of the rural population. Once rural bases
were set up, according to the communist theory, the cities would
be isolated and would eventually fall to communist control through
economic pressure, terror tactics and lack of popular support for
the government.

The rural terror campaign was complemented by terror in the
cities. The communists sought to discredit the government and
to undermine the economy by discouraging business activity
causing investment capital to flee and disrupting transportation
and communication.

The communists explained the function of terror in
formulating a three pronged military, diplomatic and political
strategy in the COSVN Resolution No. 9 of July 1969. Military
force was to exert pressure to make the United States speed it
withdrawal, shorten the time available for strengthening the GVN
and to keep the government on a wartime footing. Diplomacy was
to marshal world opinion in the communists' favor and the
political struggle was to be accelerated in order to lay the
communist groundwork within South Vietnam itself.

An integral part of the political struggle would be the
liberal use of terror to weaken and destroy local government,
strengthen the party apparatus, proselytize among the populace,
erode the control and influence of the GVN and weaken the South
Vietnamese armed forces. If positive benefits could not be gained
COSVN No. 9 indicated the communists would then settle for
creating "fiercely contested areas." They intended to motivate
the peasants in all rural areas regardless of whether they were
contested or were controlled by either side. One experienced
observer noted that they sometimes settled for simply teaching
peasants how to remain neutral.

In summary, terrorism was the means by which the communists entered or reentered populated areas in South Vietnam. Provinces that experienced high levels of terrorism had fairly large populations and were historically the sites of communist bases. In these areas the communists felt they could rekindle the sympathy for their cause, nullify the effect of GVN presence and make inroads into government control. In contrast, terrorism in areas traditionally opposed to the communists (e.g. Catholic or Hoa Hao) generally stiffened the peoples' resistance.

Incidents of terror were reported individually from South Vietnam for several years and before mid-1968 two sets of terrorism data were collected and used separately. One set consisted of Vietnamese National Police data which were reported to Washington in the U.S. Agency for International Development (USAID) monthly report of assassinations and abductions, and the other set was reported through U.S. and Vietnamese military channels which arrived in Washington in the military reports. In late 1967 the pacification advisors in Saigon consolidated the two sets of information into the Terrorist Incident Reporting System (TIRS) which then took over the job of reporting incidents of terrorism for the duration of the war.

Table 5.6 shows the reported number of terrorist victims in South Vietnam. When reading the table it is important to remember that the figures showing persons killed do not include the entire toll exacted by the communists. Many additional civilians were killed in communist attacks and other actions not included in the terrorism report.

Table 5.6 suggests that government officials were twice as likely to be killed as kidnapped, with an average of 340 officials being killed each year as opposed to 170 being kidnapped. Officials accounted for eight percent of the civilians killed but only two percent of those kidnapped. The pattern is the exact opposite for other civilians. Other civilians were twice as likely to be kidnapped as killed and more of them were kidnapped in years of large communists offensives such as 1968 and 1972, probably because of the large communist demand for porters and other logistics support during those years.

In August 1971 after estimating that one South Vietnamese person in a thousand would be a terrorist victim in 1971, we attempted to place the terrorism data in perspective by comparing the South Vietnam data to Bureau of the Census statistics on U.S. crime rates.[6] Based on 1971 Vietnam terrorism rates the analysis found that:

> ...the communists are assassinating people in Viet-Nam at a rate which is about 50 percent higher than the murder rates of the three worst U.S. cities (28 per 100,000).
> ...woundings occur at a rate of 50 per 100,000, about one-third the aggravated assault rate in the U.S. (152 per 100,000).[7]

Anti-aircraft incidents are not analyzed in detail here although the data were shown in Table 5.1. An anti-aircraft

TABLE 5.6
Officials Were Most Likely To Be Killed And
Other Civilians Were Most Likely To Be Kidnapped

	1965	1966	1967	1968[a]	1969	1970	1971	1972	Total
Officials									
Killed	209	168	285	362	342	464	352	518	2700
Kidnapped	323	176	192	172	119	160	67	134	1343
Other Civilians									
Killed	1691	1564	3421	5027	5860	5483	3419	3887	30352
Kidnapped	7992	3643	5177	8587	6170	6771	5322	12985	56638
Total Killed	1900	1732	3706	5389	6202	5947	3771	4405	33052
Total Kidnapped	8315	3810	5369	8759	6289	6931	5378	13119	57970

Source: Table 2, **Southeast Asia Statistical Summary,** Office of
the Assistant Secretary of Defense (Comptroller), April 11,
1973, pp. 1-9.
[a]Prior to August 1968 includes terrorist incidents reported by
the GVN National Police. Beginning August 1968 also includes
those incidents reported through military channels.

incident requires the flight of an aircraft and someone on the
ground able and willing to fire at it. The number of such
incidents tended to fluctuate with the level of allied air sorties.
As the number of sorties went up so did incidents of anti-aircraft
fire. In 1972, however, while the number of air sorties tripled
the number of anti-aircraft incidents fell from 6,800 in 1971 to
800 in 1972. Such a drastic change in the face of intense combat
suggests that pilots simply stopped reporting anti-aircraft fire,
not that the fire itself had stopped.

Anti-aircraft incidents were a sure sign that the
communists were on the ground. Analysis of the pattern of such
incidents, particularly if they cluster over periods of time,
provides a good guide to the location of insurgent camps or bases
during the early stages of an insurgency when intelligence about
them is usually sparse.

Communist Target of American Forces

Table 5.7 presents evidence that the communists
increasingly targeted American forces from 1966 through 1969.
The American proportion of allied combat deaths resulting from
communist actions increased each year, from 11 percent in 1966 to
37 percent in 1969. This targeting trend is indicated mainly by

TABLE 5.7
The Communists Increased Their Targeting of U.S. Forces:
U.S. vs. RVNAF Share of KIA From VC/NVA Initiated Actions

(Monthly Average)

Combat Deaths	1966	1967	1968	1969
U. S.	57	102	215	231
RVNAF	443	463	483	400
Total	500	565	698	631
U.S.%	11	18	31	37

Sources: "Enemy Emphasis on Causing U.S. Casualties,"
Southeast Asia Analysis Report, April 1969, p. 30, and "Enemy
Targeting of U.S. and RVNAF Forces," Analysis Report, February
1970, p. 2.

the fact that South Vietnamese military deaths from communist
incidents remained fairly constant while American deaths
increased every year shown. The lone exception is 1969 when
Vietnamese deaths from communist incidents declined slightly
while American deaths increased relatively little. However,
American combat deaths resulting from other types of actions
dropped 35 percent in 1969 which further accents the thrust of
communist targeting.

The rising number of American forces during the period might
seem to explain the increased communist tendency to target
American troops simply because of an increased number of American
targets. This explanation does not work, however, because the
South Vietnamese forces grew much more than the American forces
during the period shown. The increasing proportion of American
combat deaths from communist incidents was most likely the result
of intentional communist
concentration on Americans to keep U.S. casualty rates as high as
possible. The communist guidance for the summer offensive in
1969 supports this interpretation:

> In short, during the 1969 spring offensive we killed
> many Americans. The most significant success of the 1969
> spring offensive was that it boosted the anti-war movement
> in the United States, which seriously affected the American
> plan of aggression.
>
> What we should do: for each additional day's stay, the
> United States must sustain more casualties. For each
> additional day's stay they must spend more money and lose
> more equipment. Each additional day's stay, the American
> people will adopt a stronger anti-war attitude while there
> is no hope to consolidate the puppet administration and
> army.[8]

Conclusion

The large numbers, small size and dispersed nature of the various types of communist incidents clearly suggest the need to perform quantitative analysis to seek the patterns of activity which yield clues about the communist strategy and mode of operation. Essentially, the strategy called for constant small scale harassment, punctuated by a few high points of activity, particularly during the first half of the year.

Battalion sized attacks were rare, as were ground assaults in general. Continual indirect fire, harassment and terror were the name of the communist game and the data show how much they used them year after grinding year as a good substitute for conventional tactics throughout the country. The communists' war was truly a war without fronts.

NOTES

1. Stuart R. Schram, **Mao Tse-tung: Basic Tactics,** (New York: Praeger, 1966). p. 67.

2. A. I. Schwartz, **Selected Characteristics of VC Incidents,** W.S.E.G. Staff Study, N. 137, September 1967.

3. Duplication between the military and civilian reports has been screened out: incidents are counted only once even if they appeared in both reports.

4. "Standoff Attacks: A Major Element of VC/NVA Strategy in RVN," **Southeast Asia Analysis Report,** (January-February 1971), p. 47.

5. **Ibid**

6. Bernard Fall, **The Two Vietnams,** (New York: Praeger, 1967) and Jay Mallin, **Terror in Vietnam,** (Princeton: D. Van Nostrand, 1966).

7. "Terrorism in South Vietnam," **Analysis Report,** (August-October 1971), P. 15.

8. "Enemy Emphasis on Causing U.S. Casualties: A follow-up," **Analysis Report,** (May 1969), pp. 16-17.

6
Allied Ground Operations
Are Difficult to Analyze

The statistical reporting to Washington of Allied ground operations in South Vietnam, particularly the reporting by the U.S. Army, was so unsystematic that no table of data can be presented here because the figures are not useful for even simple analysis of trends and comparisons. The reporting by the U.S. Marines was far better but analysis of those data will be left to them. Vietnamese reporting of ground operations was more consistent than that of the U. S. Army. This chapter explains a few of the problems that arose in dealing with the data and presents some of the major themes that emerged from analyses of the fragmentary information that we received during the war regarding allied ground operations.

The confusion in reporting data about ground operations may have resulted from a persistant inability to understand a war without fronts. It was difficult to figure out what to report and then even more difficult to figure out how to report that. The problem was compounded by the American military command's reluctance to enforce uniformity of reporting.

Basically the reporting system divided the allied ground operations into large operations and small operations. A large operation was defined as one conducted by an allied force of three companies or more.[1] The number of such large operations was a statistic often displayed as an indicator of the tempo of allied operations. But this statistic in itself gave no clue to the size of the operations or how long they lasted.

The size and lengths of large operations were supposed to be described by a statistic called battalion days of operation. The title suggests that each day a battalion spent on a combat operation counted as one battalion day. But comparing the battalion days to the number of battalions supposedly involved often showed more battalion days than were theoretically possible with the battalions on hand.

This apparent disparity stemmed from two factors. First, battalion days often weren't really battalion days, they were aggregations of company days. Three company days equaled one battalion day, but many battalions had four companies and so generated four company days or 1.33 battalion days per day.

Second, the battalion day measurement came to cover every day of a battalion's or company's existence. After correcting for company days most of the battalions still showed up as operating at something virtually every day and this degraded the concept of battalion days as a measure of combat effort.

Another common statistic was operational day of contact. A contact was an action which resulted in the application of firepower by either side. An operational day of contact for a large unit operation was credited for each 24-hour period in which contact during that operation had been made.[2] As the army staff pointed out, the operational day of contact was not a good measure of allied military activity "...because an operation qualified under this category if it has one or more contacts in a day (it could have had a dozen and be enumerated as one operation with contact)."[3]

Aside from the problems inherent in the statistics there were problems of inconsistent and misleading reporting. In 1968 American operations in Military Region 3 were reported as a single large operation (Toan Thang -- Resolved to Win) after April. All of the battalion days were reported as accumulating in Tay Ninh province although U.S. forces operated in other Military Region 3 provinces.[4] Military Region 3 also reported all American operations in 1968 as combined U.S.-Vietnamese operations whether both nations participated or not.[5] Further, the allied operations reporting from Saigon did not provide a realistic breakdown of different types of operations. For example, in Military Regions 1 and 2 practically all operations in 1969 were reported as Search and Clear. In Military Region 3 they were called Reconnaissance in Force.[6]

Similar problems occurred in the statistics regarding small unit actions. The first problem was the incompleteness of the American reporting with the exception of that done by the Marines in Military Region 1. Ninety percent of all small unit actions reported by our forces were conducted in Military Region 1 where most of the U.S. Marines were.[7] Military Region 2 simply didn't report small unit actions by U.S. units until 1969, while Military Region 3 stopped reporting them that same year despite evidence from outside the official reporting system that small unit actions remained prevalent there.[8] In contrast, the Vietnamese reported practically everything as a small unit action (bridge guards, check points, routine patrols, etc.).[9] Any analysis of small unit actions from the official data is extremely difficult and any results quite uncertain. Analysis of the small unit actions that involved actual contact is of some use.

The futility of attempting systematic analysis with the available statistics of allied ground operations should now be fairly evident to the reader.

Given the problems in handling data covering operations on the ground, we had to focus on the efficiency of the various allied forces in killing communists in most early studies of allied ground force effectiveness. Later, as pacification data and methods of analyzing it developed, a broader view of the effectiveness of allied forces came into being. Here the focus is on inflicting casualties on the communists.

The American and third nation forces tended to take over the mission of fighting the communist main forces when they entered the conflict. From 1965 through 1968 there was a tendency to assign the Vietnamese regular units to security missions in all the military regions except Military Region 4 where few U.S. forces were present. After the buildup of the Vietnamese Regional and Popular Forces in 1969 and 1971 and the initial withdrawals of U.S. forces, the emphasis shifted to freeing the Vietnamese battalions from security duties and committing them to offensive combat against the communist main forces.

If these two points are kept in mind an analysis of the statistics through 1969 yields some tentative conclusions about the operations of American and Vietnamese forces on the ground in South Vietnam. The conclusions must remain tentative, given the data problems and the inadequacy of using communist combat deaths as the primary index of effectiveness.

There is some evidence that actions by the South Vietnamese troops slackened in 1966 as the American and third nation troops went into full-scale offensive combat. The RVNAF killed 20 percent fewer communists in 1966 than in 1965 although total combat deaths among communist forces rose 50 percent during 1966.[10]

Analysis of data for the period from 1966-1969 indicated that man for man the Vietnamese regular battalions were 50 to 60 percent as effective as American battalions in killing communist troops. In other words, each man in a Vietnamese battalion got credit for killing about half as many communist troops as each man in a U.S. Battalion.[11] By this measurement, the Vietnamese consistently exceeded the U.S. command's calculation that a Vietnamese battalion was equivalent to only 31 percent of an American battalion.[12] And they did it during a period in which they were receiving only one-tenth of the artillery and tactical air support per man in a maneuver battalion that a soldier was receiving in a U.S. maneuver battalion.[13] The Vietnamese did receive more support in later years. Considering the amount of support they received the Vietnamese were not doing too badly compared to American units if they were reporting with roughly the same accuracy as the American units.

If judged by the reporting artillery unit, with the exception of the Tet offensive in 1968 some 70 percent of the American artillery rounds were fired in situations of light or inactive combat intensity.[14] Expenditures of artillery ammunition in Vietnam remained fairly constant between June 1967 and June 1970, and in the latter month they were only six percent below the highest monthly rate ever recorded (February 1968). Variations in the intensity of the main-force conflict (trending downward from 1968 until 1972), the considerable pacification gains during 1969-1970, and U.S. redeployment all had little apparent effect on artillery consumption during the three-year period.[15]

Clearly, analysis of allied operations on the ground in Vietnam is an essential requirement for a full understanding of that war, or any war without fronts. Unfortunately a systematic analysis of the ground operations and their effectiveness will

58

probably require at least as much effort as went into the rest of
this book and will have to await the patient efforts of historians.

NOTES

1. "Combat Performance of U.S. and ARVN Divisions,"
Southeast Asia Analysis Report, (February 1969), p.21 and "RVNAF
Effectiveness," **Analysis Report,** (May 1967), p.22
2. "RVNAF Status – CY 1967," **Analysis Report,** (February
1968), p. 23.
3. "Army comments of September 1968 Articles," **Analysis
Report,** (October 1968), pp. 53–54.
4. "U.S. Combat Deaths in Vietnam," **Analysis Report,**
(April 1969), p. 23.
5. "ARVN Performance in Combined Operations," **Analysis
Report,** (December 1968), p. 6.
6. "U.S. Combat Deaths in Vietnam," **Analysis Report,**
(September 1969), pp. 11 and 13.
7. "RVNAF Effectiveness," **Analysis Report,** (August
1967), p. 30.
8. "U.S. Combat Deaths in Vietnam," **Analysis Report,**
(September 1969), p. 13.
9. "RVNAF Effectiveness," **Analysis Report,** (August
1967), p. 30.
10. "GVN Regular Force Effectiveness," **Analysis Report,**
(June 1967), p. 18.
11. "RVNAF Effectiveness," **Analysis Report,** (August
1969) p. 9, and "RVNAF Effectiveness," **Analysis Report,** (August
1967), p. 26.
12. **MACEVAL Study No. 2–68,** "Capability Study of U.S. and
ARVN Infantry Battalions."
13. "Artillery Support of RVNAF," **Analysis Report,**
(November 1968), p. 19, and "Air Support for RVNAF," **Analysis
Report,** (November 1968), p. 36.
14. "Artillery Fire in Vietnam," **Analysis Report,** (August
1970), p. 9.
15. **Ibid.**

7
South Vietnamese Forces

> I guess you can take men from any nation on earth, give
> them leadership, time to train, and produce an effective
> combat force.[1]

General Matthew B. Ridgeway, USA (Ret)

Wars without fronts tend to occur mostly in the less
developed countries of the world, and several of them have seen
the participation of forces from outside of the country, usually
assisting the government. One of the lessons that seems to have
emerged from these wars is that indigenous troops are the ones
that win, not the outsiders helping them. If the government is to
win the military side of the war, its troops have to be good enough
to do it.

Developments in South Vietnam indicated that the South
Vietnamese forces and their government would determine the
outcome of the war. Therefore it is fitting to look at some of the
problems the South Vietnamese had and the progress they made
toward solving them before American forces withdrew. Chapter 6
noted that even before Vietnamization took hold the Vietnamese
regular force battalions, man for man, were about half as effective
as American battalions, even without the tremendous firepower
and other support enjoyed by our troops. Not bad, considering
the South Vietnamese problems which occur in varying degrees in
most armies, including ours.

This chapter concentrates on the problems that the South
Vietnamese armed forces had in trying to become a fully effective
combat force and on what the U.S. did or did not do to help them.
The focus is on leadership, training and shortages of troops in
combat units.

How The Korean Army Improved[2]

After Vietnamization became U.S. policy in early 1969 we
interviewed General Matthew B. Ridgeway, USA (Ret), as part of
our search for ways to improve the South Vietnamese armed forces.

59

General Ridgeway had been successful in transforming a weak and demoralized South Korean Army into an effective fighting force. We sought his views for their possible application to the South Vietnamese forces. General Ridgeway noted that the two wars were more different than alike. He also said: "From this distance I wouldn't presume for a minute to judge the Viet-Nam situation. I have never been there." Nonetheless, his views were quite pertinent to the upgrading of the South Vietnamese Army, although they were not applied with much vigor.

General Ridgeway's advantage in Korea was that he commanded the South Korean Army. Backed by the powerful and strong willed President of South Korea, Syngman Rhee, General Ridgeway and his subordinates fired incompetent Korean commanders freely, replacing them with the best ones they could find. This was an enormous advantage in upgrading the South Korean Army, and General Ridgeway "never could understand why they have a dual command in South Viet-Nam. Why in hell didn't they put the ARVN under Westmoreland?"

The principles applied by General Ridgeway in Korea are best stated by him:

> The building of any military establishment into an effective combat force rests on several basic principles which are the same the world over. In general, a military establishment's effectiveness is dependent primarily on its officer corps and secondarily on its noncommissioned officer corps. Of course, weaponry is an essential, time to train is essential, but the focus must always be on the officer corps. It takes time to produce an effective combat force and there are a multiplicity of functions which have to be carried out before an armed force is effective. No amount of equipment or numbers of personnel can be substituted for the basic ingredient of leadership.
>
> What I want to stress above everything else is the foundation of an Army—its officer corps. With one, any problem can be overcome; without one all other efforts are in vain. This is the one principle I never stopped stressing when we were building the Korean Army.

and:

> I told President Rhee in the presence of his Minister of Defense, "we aren't going to get anywhere with your Army until you get some leadership. You haven't got it from the Minister of Defense on down and until you get it, it's just hopeless. Don't you ask me to arm any more of your people. You've lost enough equipment now to equip six of our divisions."
>
> This wasn't just carping criticism. These fellows had a division commander with the experience level of a U.S. Army Captain and a young one at that. They just hadn't had the training and the experience. Regardless, President Rhee was tough on them. He even fired his Minister of Defense.

Besides leadership, General Ridgeway emphasized that continuous training is critical:

Oh, yes, training is a continuing function. It should go on at all times, even during combat. In some ways, it is the finest training you can get because that is your ultimate reason for existence--to be effective in combat. Every chance we had in World War II and Korea, we trained. Started at the bottom and worked up. We took advantage of every opportunity to leave the lines and train. Some of those combat exercises in Korea were great. We put officers of ROK divisions up on a hillside there to observe the exercise taking place in the valley. This had a tremendous effect.

Leadership

Throughout the war in Vietnam U.S. reports cited poor leadership as the South Vietnamese Army's major deficiency, but progress in resolving this problem remained poor. The main problem was that Vietnamese officers, especially in the field grade ranks, often owed their promotions more to political than to battlefield performance and were difficult to remove because of their family and political ties.

Other factors also contributed to the problem. Between 1967 and 1970 the South Vietnamese forces grew by 60 percent creating an even stronger demand for leaders but they remained scarce. Combat losses and the diversion of military officers into essential civilian jobs further aggravated the situation. Finally, the American command was never willing to put enough pressure on the South Vietnamese to replace their poorest military leaders with better ones. This was in sharp contrast to the pacification advisors' success in getting the South Vietnamese to put better leaders into key pacification jobs.

The main key to the effectiveness of a South Vietnamese unit was the competence of its commander. He set the tone of the unit because his subordinates were usually reluctant to take any initiative without his lead. Also, leadership in a Vietnamese unit was uneven compared to that in an American unit. If a U.S. commander was killed or disabled in combat, his second in command was expected to take command and was trained to do so. The unit continued to fight. When a Vietnamese commander was killed his unit sometimes fell apart immediately, even though the other officers survived, because they often were not trained to take over.

Studies in April 1969 and February 1970 indicated that the ability of an ARVN division commander was a key factor in the performance of all Vietnamese forces in the area under his command.[3] Unlike American military commanders the Vietnamese division commander retained tight control of all operations and activities in his division tactical area, allowing little leeway for the initiative of his subordinates. The studies suggested a close relationship between ARVN leadership and ARVN performance and that Regional Force/Popular Force (RF/PF) combat performance in the division area was also affected. Divisions with good commanders had good overall leadership and good performance, while poor divisions had mediocre performance. An example of this correlation was General Truong who commanded the ARVN 1st Infantry Division and was widely recognized as an excellent combat leader by both Vietnamese and Americans. The performance rating and indicators showed that his division ranked first or second in almost every category when compared with all other ARVN divisions. On the other hand, the 5th and 18th ARVN divisions had the worst performance rating and in August 1969, as a result of American pressure, the commanders of those divisions were finally removed.

In March 1970 further evidence of the association between leadership and combat effectiveness was found through analysis of the relationships among three ratings of ARVN units: combat effectiveness, leadership, and quality of personnel.[4] The main result was a strong relationship between combat effectiveness and leadership in ARVN infantry divisions, but only a moderate one between combat effectiveness and the rated quality of ARVN troops. This suggested that improving leadership and giving it authority was more likely to increase combat effectiveness than trying to improve the quality of the troops without concentrating on leadership. Additional evidence from a regression analysis suggested that improvement of leadership would yield four times as much improvement in combat effectiveness as an equivalent increase in the quality of the troops. These results were not precise but the statistical relationships between the rated quality of leadership and the rated quality of performance were fairly strong. More important, the results agree with General Ridgeway and the doctrine of the U.S. Army. Good leadership is critical to combat performance.

If the quality of ARVN division commanders was so important it follows that the American evaluation of each commander should have been as candid and accurate as possible. Unfortunately, as the comments included in Table 7.1 indicate, the American advisors' assessments gave the impression that all of the ARVN division commanders were capable. Experienced observers disagreed. It is clear that the advisors' reports were not too helpful and that they must be read as one reads personnel efficiency reports. An "able" commander was probably inferior to an "excellent" and "aggressive" commander. Worse, one "highly respected and admired ...competent general officer" appears to have been nothing of the sort and to those who knew him best he was a "coward and military incompetent (Table 7.1)."

The ARVN 7th Division in 1969-1970 provides an example of what can happen to an ARVN division when a good leader takes command.[5] Withdrawal of U.S. Army 9th Division units from Military Region 4 in the summer of 1969 left the ARVN 7th Division in charge of the area where the American units had operated. It soon became apparent that the division was not up to the task it faced. Recognizing the problem, President Thieu relieved the division's commander and appointed an aggressive brigade commander from the ARVN airborne division to the job. No other measures were taken nor was additional support furnished. The new commander quickly turned the division into an effective fighting unit, furnishing strong evidence that replacing a poor commander with a good one was the best way to improve a poor ARVN Division. Here is how it went.

In the second half of 1969 the performance of the ARVN 7th Infantry Division deteriorated rapidly as it faced a difficult task for which it was ill-prepared. The U.S. 9th Division had dominated the 7th Division's tactical area for two and one-half years, leaving the ARVN division to carry out defensive missions. The 7th Division had spent only 30 to 40 percent of its time on offensive combat missions during the American division's tenure, about the same proportion as the regional forces in the division tactical area. Only one or two 7th Division battalions had participated in joint operations with U.S. forces for a few days each month, accounting for only one percent of the division's battalion days of operation.

Just before the U.S. forces left the communists began sending reinforcements to the division tactical area, including a north vietnamese regiment and refillers for some Viet Cong battalions. The result of all this was a dismal performance for the 7th Division during the second half of 1969. The division killed only 125 communists troops per month, 42 percent below the number killed by the Regional forces and barely more than those killed by the Popular Forces in the division tactical area. An entire battalion was badly mauled by the Viet Cong late in the year.

American advisors attributed many of the division's problems to poor leadership. Brigadier General Hoang was known for being conservative and his subordinates for lacking initiative. By the end of 1969 U.S. advisors rated the 7th Division seventh in leadership and ninth in operational effectiveness among the ten ARVN divisions.

Seeing the problem, President Thieu relieved General Hoang in January 1970 and installed Colonel (later Brigadier General) Nguyen Khoa Nam, the dynamic and aggressive commander of the 3rd Airborne Brigade, as the new 7th Division Commander. At the time Colonel Nam's U.S. advisors indicated that he had "outstanding leadership ability" and judgement, and that "his services are sought all over Viet-Nam; he has excelled in all areas." This was the only significant change made in the situation. Support from the Vietnamese marines and other ARVN units in the division tactical area remained about the same. Tactical air support and helicopter airlift sorties declined in 1970. Helicopter gunship sorties and artillery rounds increased but they remained below the countrywide average for South Vietnamese regular battalions.

Colonel Nam's arrival had two immediate effects on the 7th Division's performance. Its tempo of operations picked up, and its motivation and leadership improved. The division ceased its "9 to 5" pattern of operations and moved its base of operations out from My Tho and Ben Tre cities into the field. Offensive combat operations increased to 60 percent of the division's effort, up from 30 to 40 percent during the American 9th Division's tenure and 45 percent after its departure.

TABLE 7.1
Comments on ARVN Division Commanders

Commander	Dia and Advisor Comment	Experienced Observer Comment
MS Ngo Quang Truong (1st Infantry Division) 43 months as CG	"One of the hardest working and most professionally competent officers in the Vietnamese Armed Forces... an excellent and aggressive commander...."	1. "Outstanding, aggressive commander." 2. "Terrific. Better than most US. On the go and out with units all the time. Tough on subordinates. 'In' with JGS so he gets good people and is able to promote them and hold them.
BG Nguyen Van Toan (2nd Infantry Division) 24 months as CG	"An excellent leader and intelligent, decisive, and conscientious officer who is concerned for the welfare of his troops...consistently displays his personal courage under fire to encourage his troops." (US source) "unwilling to use his troops in any way that would endanger them... rumored to be corrupt and a playboy." (Vietnamese source).	1. "Grossly overrated. Division performance is marginal. Lacks aggressiveness. Would relieve him. 2. "Super defensive. Lacked aggressiveness. Looking upward rather than down--not good to his people. Couple of very bad reports from province advisors in his area."
MG Nguyen Van Hieu (5th Infantry Division) 6 months as CG	"One of the ablest senior Vietnamese officers." Former CG of the 22nd Infantry Division.	1. "Poor as 22nd Division commander. Americans are over-impressed by his fluent English, which he learned in Malaysia." 2. "When Hieu was in the 22nd Division it was like 2nd Division in performance-- non-innovating and careful, even when enemy forces were depleted. Insufficient concern with the RF and PF while in the 22nd and conflicts with province officials."
BG Lam Quang Tho (18th Infantry Division) 6 months as CG	"He exudes self confidence and has a noticeable influence on the actions of his junior officers. He is highly respected and admired...a competent general officer.	1. "Coward and military incompetent, despite his six foot height and bearing. Was the armor commander at the crucial battle at Ap Hao, which ARVN lost."

BG Nguyen Thanh Hoang
(7th Infantry Division)
19 Months as CG, relieved
in January 1970

"a professional military officer who is highly intelligent, extremely shrewd, quick to apprehend, and is deliberate in thinking and speech. He commands the attention of his subordinates." Replaced in Jan. 1970 by Col. Nguyen Khoa Nam, former commander of the 23rd Airborne Brigade.

1. "Relieving him was a good move. He was a lousy province chief. Super defensive, indecisive. Didn't replace poor officials. Tried to do all the work himself, didn't use his staff.

BG Nguyen Khoa Nam
(7th Infantry Division)
1 month as CG

"Outstanding leadership ability. His full devotion seem to be being a full time soldier. His serives are sought all over Vietnam...one of the great leaders in this country...one of the most competent officers I have ever known."

1. "Good reputation."
2. "Don't know him."

Col. Tran Ba Di
(9th Infantry Division)
19 months as CG

"Colonel Di clearly commands the division, however his leadership is weak dealing with significant failures by some of his commanders and sometimes with poor staff performance...this lack of force and aggressiveness extends to combat operations in that his units seldom take full advantage of enemy contacts by exploiting them effectively. In other respects his competence as a commander is far above average."

1. "Better than before, but only fair."
2. "As a province cheif he made such effective use of RF-PF in 1963-64 that no ARVN battalions were needed in Phong Binh or to protect Can Tho, despite the presence of substantial VC forces. The Vietnamese say he is doing a good job, but the Division is in a tough area and the problems of operating the division tactically seem beyond him. Lacks the necessary experience at Division level. Would do well if he had an absolutely first rate advisor who could help him with the tactics of employing the Division."

BG Nguyen Vinh Nghi

"Very intelligent. He replace MG Nguyen Van Minh...under Minh the 21st Division was one of South Vietnam's finest combat units."

1. "Poor commander in the 21st Division but excellent staff officer as chief of staff in I CTZ. Super defensive posture--put barbed wire around Bac Lieu. The Division lost alot of its old steam--I attribute this to Gen. Nghi's domineering--scares his commanders. Overrated."

The division achieved this by passing some of its pacification and security duties to the Regional and Popular forces. During the first half of 1970 the 7th Division achieved its highest number of communists killed (190 per month) and its highest kill ratio (3.5 communists to one ARVN) since the Tet Offensive of 1968. For the first time since 1968 the Division killed about as many communist troops and achieved a better kill ratio (3.5 versus 2.4 to 1) than the regional forces did in the divisional tactical area.

Colonel Nam quickly gained the respect and admiration of the American and ARVN officers who worked with him. He delegated authority to his regimental commanders and encouraged them to do the same in directing the battalion commanders. One of his first acts was to relieve the commander of the 12th Regiment and replace him with a newly promoted ARVN Lieutenant Colonel who had a good record as a ranger unit commander in Military Region 1. In May Colonel Nam replaced the weak commander of the 11th Regiment. The U.S. advisors reported that the commander of the 10th Regiment turned out to be a real gem after Colonel Nam gave him more authority. By June 1970 all three commanders were competing in a useful way.

In 1970 the 7th Division took the initiative against the same communist forces that had mauled it the year before. It prevented further inroads into the populated areas and provided security for significant pacification gains, despite a shift of communist emphasis to terrorism instead of attacks against military targets. The HES/70 (Hamlet Evaluation System-1970) suggests that population security increased by 9 to 17 percent in the division tactical area during the first half of 1970, compared to a 3 to 8 percent increase countrywide. At the end of June 45 percent of the rural population was controlled by the GVN, compared to 36 percent six months before.

While the operational success of the 7th Division had not yet reduced the overall threat to the division area, HES/70 suggests that the communist forces in populated areas were steadily being reduced. On June 30 they reportedly affected only 46 percent of the population in the division tactical area, compared to 66 percent the previous December (1969). The U.S. Senior Advisor to Kien Hoa Province, where most of the increase in terrorism had occurred, stated in June 1970 that the civilian population's reaction to armed incursions by the communists into populated area "is encouraging," and that "it is clear that the enemy is fast losing what little voluntary popular support he may once have had."

The evidence clearly indicates that Colonel Nam turned the division around. The lone action of putting a competent commander in charge produced these favorable effects. No other changes were necessary.

Shortage of Senior Officers

The South Vietnamese officer corps was bottom heavy during 1967-1970 and probably later, with too many junior officers (aspirants and lieutenants) and not enough senior officers (captains through colonels). The persistent shortage of senior officers resulted partly from the increased need for officers to fill out the expanding South Vietnamese force structure (up 60 percent from 1967 through 1970), as authorized billets increased faster than officer promotions.

But the main reason for the shortfall was South Vietnamese reluctance to promote officers to the important grades of captain and above. The South Vietnamese Joint General Staff failed to carry out their announced 1968 and 1969 promotion objectives and fell short of their 1970 objectives too. The Vietnamese corrected the imbalance in the noncommissioned officer corps much better than they did in the officer structure. Finally, the officer corps was bottom heavy even before the rapid buildup began early in 1968. Only half of the authorized billets for captain through colonel were filled in April of that year.[6]

The evidence suggests that the South Vietnamese reluctance to promote officers into the senior grades was the major reason for the shortfall in these important grades.[7] This was the product of a promotion system that responded more to the politics of the senior generals than to the needs of the military service. As a result, the system was unable to respond to the requirements for professional officers and to the war itself. For example, by 1970 the South Vietnamese still had not loosened the educational requirements for a commission, nor had they ever used their quotas for battlefield promotions. The steady expansion in the size of the force overtook army politics in the sense that the need for more senior officers and promotions outstripped the capacity of the political system to sanction such promotions.

In 1970 the South Vietnamese promotion system provided two general types of promotions, annual and special. Annual promotions were made on the basis of selection lists similar to those used in the U.S. Army, while special promotions were made on the basis of commander's recommendations. A few were granted as special battlefield promotions but most went to individuals who had served meritoriously in non-combat positions.[8] Promotions to second lieutenant (from aspirant) and first lieutenant were automatic after the required times in grade. The views of senior officers did not come into play until promotions to captain and above were considered.

As already noted, in April 1968 the South Vietnamese armed forces had only about half of their authorized captains and above. Moreover, the number had dropped by 10 percent (800) during the previous year despite a 20 percent increase in the regular forces.[9] Some progress is evident by the end of 1969 as the South Vietnamese doubled the number of senior officers (7,000 to 14,000) while total personnel of regular and regional forces increased only 50 percent. However, the South Vietnamese were still able to fill only 62 percent of the authorized billets.[10]

Meanwhile the category of aspirants and lieutenants remained overstrength as new entries almost kept up with new authorizations although some progress in correcting the imbalance was seen. The category was about 25 percent above its authorized strength in April 1968.[11] It fell to 20 percent above

68

at the end of 1969.[12] Also, the noncommissioned officer imbalances were on the way to correction.[13]

Thus, despite the great increase in Captains and above, these ranks remained the lagging category. There is no way to evaluate the validity of all of the increased authorizations and it is conceivable that they were inflated, but the evidence suggests that by U.S. standards the South Vietnamese had a significant shortage of senior officers.[14] At any rate morale could not have been high in a service where, in June 1968 if all authorized jobs were held, 62 percent of the lieutenant colonels were holding colonel's jobs, 48 percent of the majors were holding lieutenant colonel's jobs, and 47 percent of the captains were holding major's jobs.[15]

Performance In Combat Was Not The Way To Get Ahead

The most difficult hurdle in developing combat leadership was that South Vietnamese officers had no incentive to seek combat commands because commanders in the field were least favored for promotion. In November 1969 only 12 percent of the battalion commander billets were filled by lieutenant colonels, but more than half of all the lieutenant colonel billets authorized were filled by lieutenant colonels. This suggests the extent to which staff officers were promoted ahead of combat commanders.[16]

Most battalion and regimental commanders were officers who were one or two ranks below the rank authorized for the job. In November 1969 two battalions were led by first lieutenants. Elite units such as airborne and cavalry battalions did better, even though the infantry battalions in army divisions bore the brunt of the fighting. The typical infantry battalion commander in an army infantry division was a captain filling a lieutenant colonel's slot. He had 12 years of commissioned service and 13 months on the job. Airborne and cavalry units were usually led by lieutenant colonels with more experience.[17]

The pattern of promotions also shows the lack of emphasis on combat performance. Battlefield commissions were rare and the American command noted that the criteria for them were too stringent.[18] The figures support the contention. In 1966 only two battlefield promotions were granted and the following years saw little improvement. In 1967 four percent of the total advancements were battlefield promotions,[19] while the figure for the first half of 1968 was five percent and for 1970 it was two percent.[20]

The staff favorites did better: 19 percent of the promotions in 1966; 26 percent in 1967;[21] and, 59 percent in the first half of 1968 were special non-battlefield promotions.[22] In 1967 the promotions boards selected for promotion only 33 percent of the officers eligible for annual promotions.[23] The emphasis on special non-battlefield performance is clear. No wonder that South Vietnamese performance in combat wasn't better.

Civil Operations and Rural Development Support (CORDS) Replaced Poor Pacification Leaders

In October 1970 a memorandum to the Secretary of Defense observed that:

> Some progress has been made in improving RVNAF combat leadership during the past year. These changes should lead to improvements and MACV undoubtedly played a significant role in bringing them about.... However, aside from the pacification effort, there is little sign of a systematic and continuous MACV effort to have the GVN replace poor combat commanders with good ones. The MACV-CORDS system for having better provincial and district officials appointed works quite well, but no other MACV staff section uses it.[24]

The CORDS system had the following elements:[25]

(1) A CORDS agreement with President Thieu gave CORDS the right to call his attention to officials who should be replaced. The President delegated authority in such matters to Prime Minister Khiem.

(2) A MACV directive written by CORDS spelled out how an advisor could try to get a Vietnamese official relieved, but it applied only to CORDS. It told the advisor how to prepare a dossier, who had authority to relieve each type of official and what channels to use.

(3) Once a year each CORDS advisor prepared a dossier on his counterpart's ability and performance and sent it to an automated central file in Saigon.

(4) If an advisor wished to have his counterpart relieved he started the following procedure:

    (a)   He prepared a dossier, citing a least three or four specific instances that justified replacement of the official.

    (b)   He passed the dossier to his U.S. province senior advisor, who checked with the Vietnamese province chief to see if he agreed and who expanded the dossier to include the official's basis of power, political and family connections, etc.

    (c)   The dossier then moved up to the military region level for discussion with the military region commander.

    (d)   It was then passed to Saigon where CORDS conducted an investigation. If CORDS decided the advisor was correct the head of CORDS sent a letter to the Prime Minister citing the CORDS-Thieu agreement and asking that the man be relieved. Often, he was.

This system enabled CORDS to pressure the GVN to replace virtually all of the worst province and district chiefs in 1969-1970. Moreover, CORDS developed dossiers on all Vietnamese officers who had served in key pacification jobs during that time. It used them not only to fire incompetents, but to identify capable leaders for key jobs. It is difficult to understand why MACV did not develop a comparable set of dossiers for South Vietnamese combat leaders.

On October 13, 1970 the Secretary of Defense wrote to the Chairman of the Joint Chiefs of Staff saying: "I want to stress again the high priority and extreme importance I place on our efforts to improve RVNAF leadership in Vietnam." He then went on to ask "...do you think that the MACV-CORDS system for replacing poor province and district chiefs could be adapted to improve the leadership of RVNAF military units?"[26] Apparently the U.S. command believed it could not be adapted for there is no evidence that it ever was.

Training

The following analysis concentrates primarily on the training of South Vietnamese regular ground forces: the ARVN (Army) and VNMC (Marine Corps) during 1968-1970.[27] The focus here is limited to regular ground forces because: (1) the success of Vietnamization depended primarily on the ground forces; (2) detailed data are readily available for 1968-1970 but not for later years; and, (3) the Regional and Popular forces are later covered in Chapter 14.

Table 7.2 shows the proportion of time that the maneuver battalions spent on training during 1969-1970. After spending about three percent of their time on training in the first half of 1969, the average rose to about six percent for the rest of the

TABLE 7.2
Vietnamese Maneuver Battalions Did Not Train Much

	(Percent of total time)							
	1969				1970			
	1Q	2Q	3Q	4Q	1Q	2Q	3Q	4Q
ARVN Infantry Battalions	3.2	3.4	6.5	6.9	5.9	4.8	7.7	5.7
Cavalry, Airbourne Rangers & Marine battalions	N/A	N/A	4.9	6.0	4.6	4.1	11.2	7.9

Source: **MACV SEER Report,** Part I (ARVN, VNMC, NVV, last quarter of 1969 and all four quarters of 1970, PPC-18 or 19.

period. The annual cycle of combat is reflected in the figures which show a smaller proportion of time spent on training during the first half of the year when the fighting was at its yearly peak, than during the last half when fighting subsided to lower levels.

Thirty-five percent of all regular South Vietnamese battalions spent no time on training in 1969, 18 percent conducted ten or less days of training and 27 percent received more than 30 days of training.[28]

Training programs for the maintenance of unit combat proficiency were conducted at training centers as unit refresher training (a four week course for infantry battalions), or as command-supervised in-place training. Each unit was supposed to complete refresher training once every three years.[29] The 1st and 2nd Divisions and the ranger units in Military Regions 1 and 2 were the only units who completed all of their refresher training during the three year period.[30] An accelerated program to provide refresher training was planned for 1970 but "increased combat activity" led to cancellation of about half of the proposed training.[31] Combat activity in 1970 was well below that in 1968 or 1969.

There is little agreement on how much unit refresher training is best but General Ridgeway stated and experienced observers agree that it is essential for maintaining and improving the leadership, morale, spirit and effectiveness of an army. In the Korean War South Korean units were taken out of combat and sent to a center for systematic training, starting with the individual soldier and working up to division level exercises with live fire. Unfortunately the frequency of this training is not known. Experienced observers indicated that a refresher training period each year would be ideal, with the follow-up training conducted regularly at the unit.

The evidence suggests that the average South Vietnamese maneuver battalion trained a average of about three hours per week at most. Some units did not train at all, some trained less than three hours per week and some trained more. Compared to accounts of the Korean experience the South Vietnamese training during 1968-1970 appears deficient.

One of the main problems was the emphasis on necessary recruit training due to the force buildup after 1968 and the high loss rates from casualties and desertions. Recruit training tended to fill up the national and divisional training centers and set back the schedule for refresher training. It does not, however, entirely explain the lack of emphasis on refresher training as the Secretary of the Army reported that South Vietnamese use of training centers during the first half of 1969 was 29,000 below what was programmed (most of the shortfall occurred during the first quarter of 1969 when the post-Tet offensive occurred).[32]

In addition to the above, the record of follow-up training at the unit to improve combat skills was not good either.[33] Advisors reported that approximately 17 percent of the units trained for an average of less than 20 minutes per week during 1970. Approximately 50 percent trained for less than two hours per week or an average of less than one day per month. Obviously not much time was devoted to the training of South Vietnamese maneuver battalions during 1969 and 1970.

To compound the problem further, about half of the training conducted was not very effective. In 1969 advisors rated about one-half of the training to improve combat skills as ineffective or marginal.[34] In 1970 the rating system changed and advisors rated about 22 percent of the training as poor, and an additional 40 percent as being only fair.[35] So, some units didn't train at all and half of the training conducted was considered ineffective or marginal.

American advisors also reported on the training of company grade officers and non-commissioned officers in South Vietnamese units. These ratings are not a direct measure of battalion training effectiveness but they help fill in the picture of training conditions.

Thirty-three percent of the company grade officers were rated below average in training during 1968 and 1969. About 25 percent were rated poor in 1970, after the rating system changed (another 45 percent were only fair). About half of the non-commissioned officers training was rated below average in 1968 and 1969, with 33 percent rated poor and another 40 percent fair in 1970. No trends, favorable or unfavorable, were evident.

Finally, 20 to 30 percent of the advisors consistently reported that the operations staffs of the divisions, regiments and battalions were ineffective when it came to planning and implementing training programs in 1969 and in 1970. A trend toward lower ratings was evident during 1970.

On paper the South Vietnamese ground forces had an impressive military school and training system by 1969. Pressed on them by the American command, it was generally patterned after the American system and consisted of formal schools, individual training, and unit training programs. But the system had major deficiencies.[36] The Central Training Command was not staffed to control the training effort.

The system for rotating training cadre into and out of training centers did not work. Poor instructors remained in training centers for as long as seven years. Key officials at training centers and service schools had no combat experience. Combat experience or lessons learned in combat were not being related to the training programs.

Training facilities were inadequate. To further compound the problems, corruption was alleged to be widespread in the training centers with consequent effects on the recruits. To complete the picture, there was a tendency to assign incompetent division commanders to training commands after they had been fired from commanding their divisions.[37]

Early in 1970 a U.S. plan for the RVNAF improvement and modernization program indicated that approximately three percent of the program's 1970 funds were for training. Of this three percent most (2.7 percent) were for training the South Vietnamese Air Force and the remaining (.2 percent) was allocated to training the ground forces.[38]

Training during the Vietnam war obviously did not get anywhere near the priority it got in the Korean war despite the impetus of the Vietnamization program.

Combat Units Were Short of Troops

The inability of the South Vietnamese to keep the troop strength of their maneuver battalions and other combat units up to authorized levels was a chronic problem. True, it was also a problem for the U.S. and French armies in Vietnam,[39] but it was compounded in the case of South Vietnam by the lack of a system for replacing casualties and other losses in combat. High desertion rates, particularly in the regular force combat units, contributed to the problem and rapid expansion of the South Vietnamese forces hurt also. Yet, at the same time, headquarters and other rear area units were generally at much higher strength levels, suggesting that some Vietnamese were avoiding combat duty.

In September 1969 the assigned strength of the South Vietnamese regular forces as a whole was five percent above their authorized strength, but the army and marine maneuver battalions were 13 percent below this.[40] MACV calculated the shortage as equivalent to 30 infantry battalions.[41] But the problem was worse that that. Delays in replacements and other problems reduced the number of soldiers actually present for duty in the maneuver units to 35 percent below that authorized.

A year later, in September 1970, the assigned personnel were 26 percent below the number authorized and the maneuver units of the 9th and 21st Divisions were 37 percent below their authorized strengths. The 25th Division was in the best shape with only a 17 percent shortfall.[42] After two more years (September 1972) the maneuver units had worked their way back up to a 16 percent shortfall, while the regular forces as a whole remained five percent overstrength. The troops actually present for duty in the maneuver units were 28 percent below the authorized level.[43]

Little progress in bringing the maneuver battalions up to full strength was evident, despite considerable U.S. concern about the problem. A South Vietnamese battalion normally went into combat with less than 75 percent of the troops to which it was entitled. To add to the problem, once the unit got into a major fight for any length of time, casualty reports were neither timely nor accurate, and the system did not furnish replacements fast enough to keep up with losses. This occurred repeatedly in the highlands of MR 2[44] and in the Lam Son 719 operation into Laos during 1971.[45] But desertions were the worst problem.

Desertions

The problem of RVNAF desertions received considerable attention throughout the war and all sorts of measures were proposed and adopted in efforts to curb the flow. Table 7.3 suggests that the desertions problem was endemic, and that the measures simply had the effect of maintaining the status quo. In the four normal combat years shown, 12 to 13 percent of the troops

TABLE 7.3
The RVNAF Desertion Rates Were Stable

	(In thousands)					
	1967	1968	1969	1970	1971	1972
Net loss to desertions	78	116	108	127	140	176
Average RVNAF Troop strength	617	747	887	1017	1052	1078
% of strength lost to desertion	13	16	12	12	13	16

Source: Table 2, **Southeast Asia Statistical Summary,** Office of the Assistant Secretary of Defense (Comptroller), April 1973 and other dates, pp. 1-6.

deserted. In the two years of heavy combat (1968 and 1972) the rate went up to 16 percent. The percentages suggest great stability. No trends of any kind are apparent.

Desertions were a serious problem. In the normal years they outnumbered RVNAF combat deaths about six to one, while in the two peak years they outnumbered deaths by about 4.5 to one. Again, the relationship is quite stable, as might be expected from the stability of South Vietnamese combat death rates as discussed in Chapter 10. In terms of loss of personnel desertions were more serious to a unit than the combat deaths.

The regular forces accounted for about 60 percent of the desertions, with the Regional and Popular forces accounting for about 23 and 17 percent respectively. More important, the ground combat units (20 percent of the force) accounted for 50 percent of all desertions and for 80 percent of the desertions from the regular force.[46]

The data indicate that 30 percent of the average ARVN combat strength deserted every year.[47] Some returned but most did not. At least no records of their return exist. In December 1971 only nine percent of the deserters from combat units returned (27 percent of the deserters from non-combat units returned) A year later, December 1972, only three percent returned.[48]

Where did they all go? Many of them apparently left the regular combat units, went home, and enlisted in the regional or popular forces to be closer to their homes. How many went from the ARVN to the territorial forces is not known because the RVNAF did not develop any way to identify deserters who joined other units.[49]

Although the desertion rates of combat units were higher than other forces, a comprehensive statistical analysis covering a two year period (1968-1969) failed to show any statistical relationship between casualties suffered in a unit and the desertion rate.[50] A study of American advisors' responses to questions about the causes of desertion support the finding because it indicates that family connected matters were the principal cause of desertion. Only four percent of the advisors' responses identified combat intensity as a cause for desertion.[51]

Several Vietnamese studies, including interviews with 520 deserters, identified the following causes of desertion:[52] (1) deficiencies in leadership; (2) homesickness; (3) concern for welfare of the family; (4) inability to make the transition from the civilian to military way of life; (5) fear of hardship and danger; and (6) leniency in the treatment of deserters which made desertion preferable to the rigors of military life. Homesickness and family hardship were the causes cited most often by the deserters. The relationship of leadership to desertions was especially apparent in combat units. Generally, units which had good leaders and good combat records had low desertion rates.

The ARVN and marine combat units had the real desertion problem within the South Vietnamese forces. Taken as a group these units experienced desertions at four to five times the rate for non-combat ARVN units and the popular forces, and at about three times the rate for the regional forces. Family problems generated most of the desertions, not fear of combat. Whatever the cause, most desertions were apparently permanent and they hurt the effectiveness of the regular combat units. One can only hope that this was balanced by the deserters who went into the regional and popular forces and may have increased the effectiveness of those important units because of their experience with the regular forces.

Comparing South Vietnamese desertion rates to American rates of unauthorized absence gives some useful perspective. An American was carried as Absent without leave (AWOL) for 30 days and became a deserter after that. The Vietnamese became a deserter after 15 days. If the American Army had used the 15 day criteria for deserters, Vietnamese desertions probably would have run only 30 to 40 percent higher than U.S. desertions.

However, the crux of the Vietnamese problem was the permanence of desertions. During 1969 to 1971 only about 14 percent of the Vietnamese deserters returned to military control. About 60 percent of the U.S. Army AWOL returned to military control. As mentioned before, there is no way of determining how many of the vietnamese deserters signed up with the territorial forces near home.

Conclusions

It seems clear in retrospect that the United States could have profitably put more emphasis on improving South vietnamese forces from the very beginning of the large American involvement in 1965. Really serious efforts did not get underway, except in the area of pacification, until the Vietnamization program began in earnest early in 1969. The South Vietnamese armed forces made some progress in solving their problems, but Vietnam's leaders never really got serious about it. They were a fairly good fighting force of more than 1 million troops by the time the last American troops pulled out, but they were not good enough.

NOTES

1. "How the Korean Army Improved: Interview with General Matthew Ridgeway, USA (Ret)," **Southeast Asia Analysis Report,** (October 1969), p. 55.

2. The entire discussion of how the South Korean Army improved is taken from the interview with General Matthew Ridgeway cited in note 1, pp. 44–56.

3. "ARVN Division Commanders," **Analysis Report,** (February 1970), and "ARVN/RF/PF Combat Performance and Leadership," **Analysis Report,** (April 1969), pp. 11–16.

4. "Leadership and ARVN Combat Effectiveness," **Analysis Report,** (March 1970), pp. 21–27. SEER (The System for Evaluating the Effectiveness of RVNAF) included a quarterly report in which the U.S. advisors of battalions and higher units responded to 157 questions on various aspects of the unit, its personnel, and its operations.

5. Unpublished paper of August 28, 1970, Office of the Assistant Secretary of defense (Systems Analysis).

6. "RVNAF Leadership," **Analysis Report,** (June 1968), p. 43.

7. "RVNAF Officer and NCO shortage," **Analysis Report,** (March 1970), p. 16.

8. **Ibid.,** p. 19.

9. "Leadership," **Analysis Report,** (June 1968), p. 43.

10. "Shortage," **Analysis Report,** (March 1970), p. 15.

11. "Leadership," **Analysis Report,** (June 1968), p. 43.

12. "Shortage," **Analysis Report,** (March 1970), p. 15

13. **Ibid.**

14. "Leadership," **Analysis Report,** (June 1968), p. 46.

15. "Leadership," **Analysis Report,** (August 1969), p. 29.

16. **Briefing Note,** "RVNAF Leadership," Office of the Assistant Secretary of Defense, (Systems Analysis), February 4, 1970.

17. **Ibid.**

18. "Leadership," **Analysis Report,** (August 1968), p. 29.

19. "Leadership," **Analysis Report,** (June 1968), p. 48.

20. Memorandum for the Chairman, Joint Chiefs of Staff, from the Secretary of Defense, Subject: "RVNAF Leadership," June 23, 1971.

21. "Leadership," **Analysis Report,** (June 1968), p. 48.

22. "Leadership," **Analysis Report,** (August 1968), P. 29.

23. "Leadership," **Analysis Report,** (June 1968), p. 28.

24. Memorandum for the Secretary of Defense from the Assistant Secretary of Defense (System Analysis), Subject "RVNAF Leadership," October 7, 1970.

25. **Ibid.**

26. Memorandum for the Chairman of the Joint Chiefs of Staff from the Secretary of Defense, Subject: "RVNAF Leadership," October 13, 1970.

27. This analysis is based on "RVNAF Ground Forces Training," **Southeast Asia Analysis Report,** (October 1969), pp. 30–43. "RVNAF Training," **Southeast Asia Analysis Report,** (February 1970), pp. 55–58 and **MACV SEER Reports** for each quarter of 1969 and 1970. As noted on page 31 of the October analysis, it is also based on data derived from

MACV training programs; reports on RVNAF schools and training centers; U.S. Army reports of U.S. training support for Vietnamese; comments made by the Secretaries of the Military Services and the Chairman, Joint Chiefs of Staff in their review of the RVNAF Improvement and Modernization Program; and observations contained in U.S. Army senior officer debriefing reports. In addition, General Matthew B. Ridgeway, USA (Ret), and Brigadier General Arthur S. Champany, USA (Ret), were contacted to obtain background information on Korean War training programs.

28. "RVNAF Training," **Analysis Report,** (February 1970), pp. 55-56.

29. **MACV SEER Report,** Part I, 4th Qtr. CY 70, p. 86.

30. **Ibid.**

31. **Ibid.**

32. "RVNAF Ground Forces Training," **Analysis Report,** (October 1969), p. 32.

33. **MACV SEER Report,** Part I, 4th Qtr. 1970, p. 85.

34. **MACV SEER Report,** Part I, 4th Qtr. CY 69, p. 84.

35. See **MACV SEER Reports,** Part I for 4th Qtr. CY 70; 3rd and 4th Qtrs. CY 69, pp.84-85, 80-82, and "RVNAF Ground Forces Training," **Analysis Report,** (October 1969), pp. 33 and 35.

36. "Training," **Analysis Report,** (February 1970), p. 56.

37. **Ibid.**

38. **Ibid.,** p. 58.

39. The French problem is cited in : Croziat, V.J., COL. USMC (Ret), **A Translation From the French: Lessons of the War in Indochina,** Volume 2 (The Rand Corporation, RM-5271-PR, May 1967) p. 196. The American problem is stated by any company or battalion commander who took his unit into combat.

40. "ARVN/VNMC Problem Area Progress Report," **Analysis Report,** (November-December 1969), p. 22.

41. **MACV SEER Report,** Part I, 3rd Qtr. CY 69, p. 2.

42. **SEER Report,** Part I, 3rd Qtr. CY 70, p. 72.

43. **Army Activities Report: Southeast Asia,** (Final Issue, as of: 20 December 1972), pp. 45-49.

44. "Battle Prospects in the MR2 Highlands," **Analysis Report,** (November-January 1972), p. 15.

45. "Lam Son 719 - Preliminary Evaluation," Office of the Assistant Secretary of Defense (Systems Analysis), April 2, 1971, p. 1.

46. Calculated from the date in (1) "Selected RVNAF Personnel Data," **MACV Monthly Report** (data for October 1967-December 1972), and (2) Table 4B, Southeast Asia Statistical Tables, OASD (Systems Analysis), May 1968.

47. **Army Activities Report: Southeast Asia,** (Final Issue, as of: 20 December 1972), p. 47.

48. "Selected RVNAF Personnel Data," MACV, for December 1971 and December 1972.

49. "RVNAF Desertions," **Analysis Report,** (June-July 1971), p. 12.

50. "Desertions from ARVN/VNMC Ground Combat Forces," **Analysis Report,** (February 1970), p. 47.

51. "Causes of RVNAF Desertions," **Analysis Report,** (March 1970), p. 14.

52. **Ibid.,** p. 11.

8
Did Airpower Work?

> If it is accepted, as on the evidence it must be, that
> the bombing had a minimal effect on infiltration and on the
> capacity of North Vietnam to wage this type of war, which
> were the only two advantages the Americans might have got
> out of it, then all the benefits have been derived by Hanoi.
> The first benefit was that it enabled the North to organize
> the whole country on a war footing with the full support of
> all the people.[1]

> Sir Robert Thompson

Americans seldom realize how large a role the U.S. and South
Vietnamese air operations played in the allied attrition strategy.
The program budget in Chapter 3 suggests the heavy emphasis on
air power. Most of these operations were directed at targets
within South Vietnam and along the Ho Chi Minh Trail in Laos, not,
as commonly believed, at North Vietnam.

This chapter focuses on the American and South Vietnamese
operations by fixed-wing combat aircraft in Southeast Asia,
including the B-52 bombers. It does not cover helicopters or
other aircraft carrying troops or supplies.

Allied air operations in combat were enormous in size and
cost. U.S. and South Vietnamese aircraft flew about 3.4 million
combat sorties in South Vietnam, North Vietnam, Laos, and
Cambodia during the period 1965-1972. In five years, 1965-1969,
the U.S. dropped nine times the tonnage it dropped in the Pacific
during World War II. This averages out to 70 tons of bombs for
every square mile of Vietnam and about 500 pounds of explosives
for every man, woman and child in the country.[2]

The total costs of this effort are not readily available, but
the cost estimates given in Chapter 3 are enough to indicate that
this was the largest and costliest air effort in the history of
warfare. Fortunately, less than 3 percent of the American combat
deaths resulted from these operations. However, virtually all of
the American prisoners of war were pilots or from air crews.

Where The Combat Sorties Were Flown

Table 8.1 displays the numbers of combat sorties flown by the U.S. and South Vietnamese Air Forces in Southeast Asia. After the U.S. buildup in 1965, the two forces together averaged 465,000 sorties per year. The final total was about 3.4 million sorties, as noted above. The U.S. flew more than 90 percent of them. The total number of sorties grew each year to their peak of 615,000 in 1968, and then declined, as the American forces withdrew, until 1972 when U.S. and South Vietnamese sortie rates increased to meet the communist offensive that year.

The impact of Vietnamization began to show in 1970 when South Vietnamese (VNAF) tactical air sorties showed a significant increase for the first time, and then continued to increase in 1971 and 1972. In 1968 the Vietnamese flew only four percent of the sorties, but in 1972 they flew 13 percent. The B-52 sorties were emphasized more and more as time passed. As a percentage of American attack sorties they increased every year, from two percent in 1966 to 15 percent in 1972.

TABLE 8.1
About 3.4 Million Combat Sorties Were
Flown in Southeast Asia 1965–1972

	Thousands of Sorties							
	1965	1966	1967	1968	1969	1970	1971	1972
U.S. Attack:								
Tactical Aircraft	103	254	320	372	300	193	122	167
B-52	1	5	10	21	19	15	13	28
Other combat tactical Aircraft Sorties[a]	54	135	177	197	217	177	125	116
Sub-Total	158	394	507	590	536	385	260	311
VNAF								
Attack	23	32	30	23	33	38	43	53
Other combat tactical aircraft sorties[a]	1	1	4	2	1	1	15	11
Sub-Total	24	33	34	25	34	39	58	64
Total								
Attack	127	292	360	416	352	246	178	248
Other[a]	55	137	181	199	218	178	140	127
Total	182	427	541	615	570	424	318	375

[a]Other sorties include combat air patrol, escort, reconnaisance and other non-attack sorties.
Source: Tables 8.3 and 8.4, which follow.

Table 8.2 shows the locations of the targets. South Vietnam received the largest number of sorties. Approximately 45 percent of all combat sorties were flown there while 22 percent were flown in North Vietnam, 28 percent in Laos, and four percent in Cambodia.

The results of the interdiction campaigns are best shown by the U.S. air operations in North Vietnam and southern Laos. These two target areas accounted for about half of the sorties, but they shifted from one country to the other each time the rules of engagement changed. When political decisions allowed us to bomb North Vietnam, most of the sorties went there. When they didn't these sorties shifted to Laos.

The shift to Laos is seen clearly in 1969 when sorties almost doubled there after the November 1968 bombing halt in North Vietnam. When bombing in North Vietnam was allowed again in 1972, the sorties shifted back into that area from Laos. In 1973, when Laos and North Vietnam were both off limits, the sorties simply swung into Cambodia until the bombing was halted there too.

Which country got the interdiction sorties apparently depended more on the number of planes ready to fly than on any judgements about effectiveness. The sorties were like a fire hose pointed with full pressure at whichever target was allowed. Senator Stuart Symington commented: "...as the general just said,...orders were that if you do not need the planes against Vietnam, use said planes against Laos."[3]

Table 8.3 shows the combat sorties flown in South Vietnam for 1965-1972. After U.S. troops arrived in 1965, U.S. and South Vietnamese aircraft flew about 210,000 combat sorties per year in South Vietnam for the next seven years, almost half of the total flown in all of Southeast Asia.

The U.S. flew 93 percent of all the sorties flown in South Vietnam, but this share went down as combat declined between 1968 and 1971, and Vietnamization began to take hold. The U.S. flew 92 percent of the sorties in 1968, compared to 54 percent in 1971. U.S. sortie rates had dropped 70 percent while South Vietnam rates rose about ten percent. South Vietnamese improvement really shows in 1972 when U.S. sorties tripled but still were able to account for only 68 percent of the total.

The Vietnamization program increased South Vietnamese sortie rates earlier, but the gain did notshow up in South Vietnam until 1972. The early increases had become sorties to Cambodia instead of to South Vietnam as shown in Table 8.4

B-52 Strikes

Interest in B-52 strikes during the war was high enough to call for separate treatment here, before moving on to look at tactical air operations. The ARC LIGHT program started on June 18, 1965 with 27 sorties against targets in South Vietnam. About 220 sorties a month flew during the rest of 1965. In December 1965 targets were struck in Laos for the first time. North Vietnamese targets near the Demilitarized Zone (DMZ) were struck in April 1966, and the DMZ was first hit in July 1966.

TABLE 8.2
Almost Half Of The American and VNAF
Combat Sorties Were Flown In South Vietnam

Sorties in Thousands

	1965	1966	1967	1968	1969	1970	1971	1972
South Vietnam	105	203	261	307	289	159	74	175
North Vietnam	61	147	191	172	37	37	24	106
Laos	16	77	89	136	242	186	159	69
Cambodia	–	–	–	–	2	42	61	25
Total	182	427	541	615	570	424	318	375

Source: Tables 8.3 and 8.4 which follow. Cambodia totals include the secret sorties previously reported as being in South Vietnam.

TABLE 8.3
The Americans Flew More Than 80 Percent Of The
Combat Sorties Flown In South Vietnam

Sorties in Thousands

	1965	1966	1967	1968	1969	1970	1971	1972
American								
Attack:								
Tactical Air	66	125	170	205	155	76	16	80
B-52	1	4	7	17	11	4	2	19
Other	14	41	50	60	89	50	22	20
Total	81	170	227	282	255	130	40	119
VNAF								
Attack	22	32	30	23	33	28	31	49
Other	2	1	4	2	1	1	3	7
Total	24	33	34	25	34	29	34	56
Total								
Attack	89	161	207	245	199	108	49	148
Other	16	42	54	62	90	51	25	27
Grand Total	105	203	261	307	289	159	74	175

Sources: Table 1304, October 3, 1974, and Table 1322, May 13, 1974, both prepared by the Department of Defense, Office of the Assistant Secretary of Defense (OASD) (Comptroller), Directorate for Information Operations.

TABLE 8.4
Vietnamization Improvement Showed Up
As VNAF Sorties In Cambodia

Sorties in Thousands

	1969	1970	1971	1972
American				
Attack:[a]				
Tactical Air	–	15	17	7
B-52	2	3	1	2
Other	–	14	19	8
Total	2	32	37	17
VNAF				
Attack	–	10	12	4
Other	–	0	12	4
Total	–	10	24	8

[a]Includes secret sorties in 1969 and 1970.
Source: Table 1304, October 3, 1974 and Table 1323, July 19, 1974, both prepared by the Department of Defense, OASD (Comptroller), Directorate for Information Operations.

Table 8.5 shows B-52 sorties by target country for 1965-1972. They increased until 1968 and then declined slowly until 1972, when they rose to the highest level ever. The increased use of B-52s as a proportion of the total air effort was noted above. South Vietnam received 58 percent of all the B-52 sorties flown. North Vietnam was the target of six percent of them, and two-thirds of those were flown in 1972.

Tactical Air Operations In South Vietnam

The tactical air operations performed two primary missions, close air support and interdiction of troop and supply movements.
The objective of close air support was to furnish fire support to the troops on the ground quickly when they needed it, but few sorties were used for this purpose. Table 8.6 indicates that approximately ten percent of the tactical air strikes in South Vietnam were flown to support allied forces in contact with communist forces (four percent of the Southeast Asia total). Most of the remaining sorties (two-thirds of the total) were preplanned 24 hours or more in advance, and they struck known or suggested communist locations, roads and supply storage areas.
Taking all these figures into account, it seems likely that 25 percent of all the attack sorties flown in Southeast Asia were closely linked to combat taking place on the ground, or to a freshly sighted target. This suggests that most of the tactical air

TABLE 8.5
B-52 Sorties Peaked In 1972

	1965	1966	1967	1968	1969	1970	1971	1972
South Vietnam	1320	4290	6609	16505	11494	3697	2386	19289
North Vietnam	–	280	1364	686	–	–	–	4440
Laos	18	647	1713	3377	5567	8500	8850	2799
Cambodia[a]	–	–	–	–	2437	2906	1319	1855
Total	1338	5217	9686	20568	19498	15103	12555	28383

[a]Includes the secret bombing in Cambodia during 1969 and 1970.
Source: For 1966 through 1972: Table 1304 (October 3, 1974) and
Tables 1320, 1321, 1322 and 1323, Sorties and Losses, OASD
(Comptroller), Directorate of Information Operations, May 13, 1974
and July 19," 1974. For 1965: "An Appraisal of ARC LIGHT (B-52)
Operations," **Southeast Asia Analysis Report,** September 1967, p. 25.

effort in Southeast Asia concentrated on interdicting supplies
and, occasionally, personnel movements.

The pattern for artillery fire is the same. In fiscal 1968
and 1969, except for the Tet 1968 period, about 70 percent of all
U.S. artillery rounds were fired in a situation of light or inactive
combat, as judged by the reporting artillery unit (See Chapter 6).

Table 8.7 suggests that interdiction took some priority over
close air support for South Vietnamese troops. It shows that
support for both U.S. and South Vietnamese troops in contact used
about ten percent of the total sorties. Vietnamese units in
contact with the communists received about 55 percent as many
sorties per unit as American units did and 23 percent as many per
man killed in action in 1969 and early 1970.

Interdiction Campaign

As already noted, the interdiction campaigns are best shown
by the American air operations in Laos and North Vietnam,
although as just seen, probably 75 percent of the sorties flown in
South Vietnam can be called interdiction. The important
question, however, is not how the sorties were allocated, but how
effective they were.

The communists probably received about 70 percent of their
supplies for operations in South Vietnam from sources inside the
country. Air operations over the Laotian panhandle struck at a
flow of communist supplies from North Vietnam equal to about 15
percent of their supply requirements in South Vietnam. Despite
intensive bombing, they still moved enough supplies to continue
and increase their operations.

TABLE 8.6
Approximately 10 Percent Of The Sorties In South Vietnam
Supported Allied Troops In Contact With the VC/NVA

	Attack Monthly Sorties (Jul 69–Mar 70)	Percentage of Total[a]
Support of Allied Troops in Contact (TIC)		
From strip alert aircraft	722	6
From preplanned strikes	329	3
From armed reconnaissance missions	21	–
Total	1,072	9
Immediate Strikes (Other Than TIC)		
Known VC/NVA locations	1,851	15
Suspected VC/NVA locations	778	6
Preparation of allied positions	203	2
Anti-aircraft sites	222	2
Total	3,054	25
Preplanned Strikes (Not Diverted)		
Known VC/NVA locations	3,470	28
Suspected VC/NVA locations	3,996	32
Preparation of allied positions	708	5
Anti-aircraft sites	164	1
Total	8,338	66
Total Sorties	12,464	100

Source: "Southeast Asia Tactical Aircraft Operations," **Southeast Asia Analysis Report,** June–July 1970, p. 22 (Based on USAF DASCLOG Computer File).

About 75 percent of U.S. air support for Laotian forces in Northern Laos struck logistics targets. Yet the flow of supplies into Northern Laos was always more than communist forces needed. North Vietnamese needs and casualties in this area were not a significant drain on their manpower pool.

Table 8.8 suggests that air operations imposed no critical material costs on North Vietnam since its allies paid for most of the resources destroyed. North Vietnam's foreign aid during 1966-1969 was two or three times as large as the costs of keeping its forces supplied in South Vietnam, Cambodia and Laos and replacing the damage from bombing in North Vietnam.

86

TABLE 8.7
South Vietnamese Troops Received
Less Air Support Than American Units

Jan. 1969 - Feb. 1970

	Support for Troops in contact with VC/NVA	Total Sorties Received
Total Attack Sorties Received Per Month		
RVNAF	514	4,639
U.S.	939	8,130
RVNAF as % of U.S.	55%	57%
Total Attack Sorties Per Person Killed In Action		
RVNAF	0.3	3.0
U.S.	1.3	11.3
RVNAF as % of U.S.	23%	27%

Source: "Southeast Asia Tactical Aircraft Operations," **Southeast Asia Analysis Report,** June–July 1970, p. 24.

The results indicate that Secretary of Defense Robert S. McNamara was correct when he stated in November 1966: "A substantial interdiction campaign is clearly necessary and worthwhile.... But at the scale we are now operating, I believe our bombing is yielding very small marginal returns, not worth the cost in pilot lives and aircraft."[4]

The Bombing Conclusion

When the political impact in the U.S. of the bombing and its effect on North Vietnamese unity is added to its other costs, the effectiveness of the way the air war was conducted is certainly open to question. Indeed, the military themselves kept pointing out how political constraints impeded the optimum use of airpower. But these constraints applied mostly to North Vietnam and Cambodia. No comparable restraints existed in South Vietnam or along the Ho Chi Minh trail in Laos where so many of the sorties were flown. It is relevant for the reader to remember that the strategic bombing survey after World War II showed that the effects of bombing were overstated significantly during that war.

TABLE 8.8
Foreign Aid To North Vietnam Exceeded
The Cost Of Supplying VC/NVA Forces

	($ Millions)		
	Calendar Year		
COSTS	1967	1968	1969
Cost of Supplies Shipped To:[a]			
Northern Laos	53	61	58
Southern Laos	45	63	60
Total	98	124	118
Cost of Trucks Destroyed:[b]			
Northern Laos	1	1	3
Southern Laos	6	44	38
Total	7	45	41
Costs of supplies, equipment and industry destroyed in North Vietnam[c]	139	85	–
Cost of air defense in North Vietnam[d]	235	122	83
Total Costs	479	376	242
AID			
Total foreign aid to North Vietnam[d]			
Economic	380	480	470
Military	650	395	220
Total Aid	1,030	875	690
COMPARISONS			
Total costs as % of Foreign Aid	46%	43%	35%
Total costs as % of Military Aid	74%	95%	110%

Source: "Southeast Asia Tactical Aircraft Operations,"**Southeast Asia Analysis Report,** June–July 1970, p.29.
[a]Computed from CIA estimates of supply shipments and estimated costs per ton of supplies of $1,300 for Northern Laos and $1,100 for Southern Laos.
[b]Computed from DIA estimates of truck attrition and estimated cost of $6,000 per vehicle.
[c]OASD/SA estimates, based on several earlier studies.
[d]CIA/DIA estimates.

The Special Case of the Herbicide Spraying Operations

Two of the most controversial American operations in South Vietnam were the programs to defoliate vegetation and to destroy crops. The controversy reached such a fever pitch by the end of 1970 that the spraying of crops and use of the herbicide called Orange were stopped by order of the Deputy Secretary of Defense early in 1971.

Another result was a directive from Congress to the Department of Defense to fund a study of the effects of herbicides in Vietnam by the National Academy of Science. This study is available to interested readers, and is not dealt with here.[5] Nor is a defense of the herbicide program attempted. The size and dimensions of the defoliation and crop destruction programs are simply described.

The main source of data was a computer file that contained a record of every spray mission flown in South Vietnam. This was used to develop the statistical findings set forth below. Analysis of data on herbicide operations in South Vietnam through 1970 showed that:

(1) Herbicides could not have caused catastrophic devastation through all of South Vietnam, because from 1962 to 1970 herbicide was sprayed on less than ten percent of its land area.

(2) The Hamlet Evaluation System indicated that only about three percent of the population lived in defoliated areas. Less than one percent lived where crops were destroyed. Herbicide operations were conducted under rigid controls involving both U.S. and Vietnamese authorities at all levels.

(3) Crop destruction was confined to the lightly populated rice deficit highlands of Military Regions 1 and 2. At no time were crops destroyed in the country's food producing center (Military Region 4). After 1967 the primary crop destruction targets were plots of mountain rice and vegetables in areas considered hostile. Most (about 90 percent) of all crop destruction was confined to areas in and around known communist base areas.

NOTES

1. Thompson, **No Exit**, p. 139.
2. Samuel P. Ginder, **Moral Imperatives in Foreign Policy** (Final Seminar Paper, Georgetown University, Fall 1983), p.39.
3. U.S. Senate, **Subcommittee on United States Security Agreements and Commitments Abroad Hearings,** October, 20, 21, 22 and 28, 1969, page 713.
4. **The Pentagon Papers, The Senator Gravel Edition** , Volume IV, p. 374. The statement was made in a paper dated November 17, 1966.
5. National Academy of Science, "Effect of Herbicides in Viet Nam."

9
Stalemate:
The Americans Couldn't Win

The pace of fighting was dictated by the North Vietnamese and the Vietcong, not by the United States.[1]

Sir Robert Thompson

The dominant strategic thrust of the allies from mid-1965 through at least 1969 was to destroy the communist military forces by grinding them down. As General William Westmoreland has said: "It was, in essence, a war of attrition." He also stated what became the standard formulation of the attrition objective: "Attrit by year's end, Viet Cong and North Vietnamese forces at a rate as high as their capability to put men into the field."[2] This was always stated as one of several goals, but until at least late 1969 it was the most important one. Corporal Reynoulds stated the method: "Find the bastards and pile on."[3]

But after several years the war was acknowledged to be a military stalemate.[4] Why? What caused the attrition strategy to fail? After all, on the face of it the allies had all the military advantages. They outnumbered the communist forces by as much as six to one and they had far superior mobility, firepower, and combat support. Yet the allied forces could not destroy the enemy. Quite the contrary--the estimated communist forces at the end of 1972 were larger than in 1965. They appeared weaker but there could be no doubt that they were still intact.

It was becoming apparent in late 1966 that the American military strategy of attrition was in trouble. The objective was not being achieved and the prospects did not look good. This theme is evident in Secretary of Defense Robert McNamara's statement of November 17, 1966 in his Draft Memorandum for the President:

...If MACV estimates of enemy strength are correct, we have not been able to attrit the enemy forces fast enough to break down their morale and more U.S. forces are unlikely to do so for the foreseeable future....

...The data suggest that we have no prospects of attriting the enemy force at a rate equal to or greater than his capability to infiltrate and recruit, and this will be true at either the 470,000 personnel level or 570,000.

If we assume that the estimates of enemy strength are accurate, the ratio of total friendly to total enemy strength has only increased from 3.5 to 4.0 to one since the end of 1965. Under the circumstances, it does not appear that we have the favorable leverage required to achieve decisive attrition by introducing more forces.[5]

The North Vietnamese Had The Manpower

By the middle of 1967 it was clear that the availability of North Vietnamese manpower and the willingness to send it south would prevent the allies from winning the war of attrition. After more than two years of American troop involvement, the number of North Vietnamese troops in South Vietnam was less than two percent of the North Vietnamese male labor force, and less than three percent of the male agricultural force. By comparison, the U.S. forces in Southeast Asia at that time amounted to about one percent of our male civilian labor force.[6]

After the 1968 Tet Offensive statistical analysis again suggested that manpower reserves in North Vietnam were sufficient to meet 1968 requirements and could even support a higher level of mobilization without significant shortages, although there would probably be some strains in the labor force. The analysis also noted that if North Vietnam mobilized the same percentage of its population as South Vietnam, its full time military force would double in size.[7]

Another set of calculations after the 1968 offensive suggested that, at first half 1968 loss rates (highest of the war) available North Vietnamese manpower would be exhausted in about 30 years and Viet Cong manpower in three and one-half years. Together they appeared able to last about 12 years.[8] The analysis was crude, but it does give some idea of the communists' potential staying power in the face of loss rates so high that they never occurred again. It also suggests that the Viet Cong forces could be attrited. Indeed, by the end of 1972 most of them may have disappeared; only 20 percent of the communist forces were estimated to be Viet Cong. The rest were estimated to be North Vietnamese troops, even in the traditional Viet Cong units.

The foregoing statements were all very rough estimates based on the best data available in 1967-1968. But they have turned out to be roughly right. They accurately foreshadowed the allied failure to the win the war of attrition.

The Communists Could Control Their Losses

A second major reason the communist forces were able to survive the allied strategy of attrition was that they were able to exercise considerable control over their loss rates and keep them from going beyond the limits they could afford. They did this by deciding when and where large scale combat would occur. They held the initiative in this respect, not the allies.

The vastly superior forces of the allies found it impossible to pin down and defeat an enemy who chose to evade combat. A key aspect of the communist's ability to avoid combat was their use of sanctuaries in North Vietnam, Laos and Cambodia which remained off limits to allied ground forces for political reasons until 1970-71.

Assistant Secretary of Defense Alain Enthoven summed up the problem on March 20, 1968 in his first memorandum about Vietnam to the then new Secretary of Defense, Clark Clifford:

> One important fact about the war in Vietnam is that the enemy can control his casualty rate, at least to a great extent, by controlling the number, size and intensity of combat engagements. If he so chooses, he can limit his casualties to a rate that he is able to bear indefinitely. Therefore the notion that we can "win" this war by driving the VC/NVA from the country or by inflicting an unacceptable rate of casualties on them is false. Moreover, a 40 percent increase in friendly forces cannot be counted upon to produce a 40 percent increase in enemy casualties if the enemy doesn't want that to happen.[9]

A statistical analysis after the 1968 offensives also indicated that the communists had much more influence over fluctuations in American combat deaths than did the allied forces.[10] It concluded that the communists held the basic military initiative in South Vietnam because they could change the level of American battle deaths by changing the frequency and intensity of their attacks.[11] Changing the tempo of U.S. operations had little effect.

A later study used the same correlation technique to see whether the earlier relationship continued to hold after the Tet Offensive in 1968.[12] After Tet 1968 the relationship between communist attacks and allied combat deaths declined substantially and the correlations between U.S. large operations with contact and battle deaths increased as dramatically. This was taken as a sign that the military initiative in terms of control over American combat deaths had been shifting to us after June 1968.

Table 9.1 shows the relationships between combat deaths in South Vietnam and communist attacks. The correlations between their attacks and their own combat deaths did not change much after the 1968 offensives. Before 1968 they could presumably control about 85 percent of the fluctuations. After June 1968 they seemed to have some control over about 75 percent of the changes, enough to frustrate the allied attrition strategy.[13]

Table 9.1 also suggests that the correlation between communist attacks and American combat deaths changed significantly in our favor after the Tet Offensive. Before and during the offensive the communists seemed to control about 85 percent of the fluctuations in American combat deaths. Afterwards they could control only about 20 percent of the variation in U.S. combat deaths. The pre-1968 figure of 63

TABLE 9.1
Correlation Analysis: Communist
Attacks Against Combat Deaths

Communist Attacks	(All figures are the R^2) Combat Deaths		
	VC/NVA	U.S.	RVNAF
Pre-1968 Offensives[a]	.55	.63	.10
Through 1968 Offensives[b]	.84	.87	.68
Post-1968 Offensives[c]	.77	.22	.28

[a]July 1965 through December 1967.
[b]January 1966 through June 1968.
[c]July 1968 through November 1969.

percent indicates that the relationship did not simply drop back
to pre-Tet days. A real change appears to have taken place.

More important, the correlation between American battalion
days with contact and VC/NVA combat deaths rose sharply after
the 1968 offensive as shown in Table 9.2. This would indicate
some improvement in American influence over the fluctuations in
communist and American combat deaths. The results seem to
say that major fluctuations in communist deaths were still
fundamentally determined by their willingness to fight, but that
the American forces learned how to step up their operations and
fight much more efficiently when the communists stepped up their
attacks.

Another reason why the initiative may have shifted toward
the allies is that losses of trained communist cadre and
personnel, particularly during the 1968 offensives, apparently
lowered the fighting effectiveness of the communist forces in
South Vietnam. The results of the accelerated pacification
campaign in the second half of 1968 and the further gains made
without stiff opposition until 1972 also testify to the serious
beating the communist cadre and units took during the Tet
Offensive. Largely because of these losses, Hanoi apparently
elected to conserve and rebuild its forces during 1969-71 while
awaiting American withdrawal.

Manpower In The Foxholes

Even the shift in initiative was not enough for the allies to
drive the Viet Cong and North Vietnamese forces from the field and
win a victory. The communist military forces were weakened
significantly in the years following 1968, but they remained
strong enough to launch a major offensive in 1972 and to win the
war in 1975.

How did they do it? In terms of total military manpower the
allies always outnumbered the communists by at least three and a

TABLE 9.2
Correlation Analysis: Friendly Battalion
Operations with Contact Against Combat Deaths

	(All figures are the R^2) Combat Deaths		
Allied Operations	VC/NVA	U.S.	RVNAF
Pre-1968 Offensives[a]	.05	.02	N/A
Through-1968 Offensives[b]	.07	.10	N/A
Post-1968 Offensives[c]	.66	.63	.19

[a] July 1965 through December 1967.
[b] January 1966 through June 1968.
[c] July 1968 through November 1969.

half to one and the ratio approached six to one during 1969-1971.[14] However, the cutting edge of fighting forces are the troops who actually fight, and allied superiority falls away sharply on this basis because the allied foxhole strength, particularly the American foxhole strength, was much lower than the public realized.

Instead of outnumbering communist forces by almost six to one in 1970, the foxhole advantage falls to 1.6 to one (see Table 9.3). The ratio remains fairly steady during 1965-1971 instead of

TABLE 9.3
The Allied Advantage Declined Sharply When
The Comparison Is Limited To Combat Manpower

	(Manpower in Thousands)					
	1967	1968	1969	1970	1971	1972
Allies[a]	218	240	223	188	145	119
Communists[b]	132	160	130	120	105	152
Allied/Communist force ratio	1.7	1.5	1.7	1.6	1.4	.8

[a] Strengths were calculated by assuming 550 men per RVNAF battalion, and 1000 men per U.S./3rd Nation battalion for the Maneuver Battalions shown in Table 100, **Southeast Asia Statistical Summary,** Office of the Assistant Secretary of Defense (Comptroller, January 24, 1973.
[b] Total regular combat force figures from Table 4.2. Midpoint of range estimates is used here.

rising as the total manpower ratio does. It actually shifts to an allied disadvantage of .8 to one in 1972. The comparison is revealing because the maneuver forces are the principal ones available to each side for combat and their size imposes a limit to offensive activities.[15]

Furthermore, the commitment of some of these forces to defensive missions further reduced allied offensive capabilities. The allies had large and continuing needs for combat forces to secure military bases, lines of communication (roads, canals, etc.), and populated areas. An analysis of force allocations in January 1968 suggests that only 40 percent of the allied maneuver forces were available for offensive operations during that month.

Of course allied offensive forces could be increased by shifting units from security missions back into offensive operations. This happened, particularly during communist offensives but there was always a risk of leaving the population unprotected. The South Vietnamese ability to shift their forces to trouble spots was always severely limited until late in the war when the territorial forces had become numerous. enough and strong enough to take over most of the security missions.

The communists' strategic situation was quite different. They didn't have to use many of their regular forces for defensive missions. They had no cities to defend and their base areas and lines of communication were not held and defended by large numbers of troops. They also had the advantage of sanctuaries up to 1970–1971. Most of their regular forces were free to engage allied forces as they saw fit, as long as they didn't incur heavy losses too frequently.

Given the commitment of regular forces to security missions for much of the war, the remaining allied forces held no significant numerical advantage over the communist forces that could potentially be committed against them. The force ratio in this situation ranged from an allied advantage of 1.2 to one to an allied disadvantage of .7 to one. In other words, the communist potential sometimes outnumbered the allied maneuver forces by 1.4 to one (see Table 9.4).

The two sets of combat force ratios are not precise—far from it. They are based on the best data available, some of which are rough estimates. However, the findings deserve serious consideration because even if the ratios are wrong by 50 percent they still say that the foxhole force ratio did not favor the allies nearly as much as the total manpower figures suggest. The data may be rough but the findings seem roughly right,[16] and they are in accord with Sir Robert Thompson's observation that "...in 1968 it was estimated that, out of a total strength of 500,000 American Troops, only 100,000 were operational and only 80,000 could be deployed in sustained operations."[17]

The comparisons do not tell the whole story because the allies enjoyed overwhelming superiority—or so it seemed—in firepower, logistics support and rapid movements of troops. However, there is evidence that the communists were able to fight in a way that nullified many of the allied advantages.

TABLE 9.4
The Communists Outnumbered The Allies
Half the Time In Terms of Combat Troops
Available For Offensive Operations

	1967	1968	1969	1970	1971	1972
		(Manpower in thousands)				
Allies[a]	111[c]	184	162	131	81	101
Communists[b]	132[c]	160	130	120	105	152
Allied/Communist force ratio	.8	1.2	1.2	1.1	.8	.7

[a]The allied regular force manpower engaged in offensive combat operations was calculated by arriving at the average number of allied battalions engaged in combat operations each day in the month of January for the years 1968 through 1973 and then asuming 550 man RVNAF battalions and 1000 man U.S.- 3rd Nation battalions. The number of allied maneuver battalions on combat operations is available for each day in the "Ground Operations Daily Summary" in the National Military Command Center Operations Summary.
[b]Source: Total Regular Combat force figures from Table 4.2.
[c]Allied figures are for January following the year shown, i.e., 1967 figure is actually January 1968 data. Communist figures are end of year shown.

One such way was for the communists to mass their forces to exploit favorable opportunities while tying down allied forces by using small forces to attack and harass outposts, roads, waterways, and the population. In this way they tied down some of the allied forces in order to gain an edge against the others. Such a strategy, combined with the use of night operations and thousands of standoff attacks by fire, went a long way toward neutralizing allied advantages. The cost in communist lives was high but controllable, and the allies were not able to turn their decisive resource superiority into a decisive military advantage.

By the end of 1968 the futility of the attrition strategy had become evident to all as stated in the summary of responses to National Security Study Memorandum 1--The Situation in Vietnam:

> There is general agreement with the JCS statement, "The enemy, by the type of action he adopts, has the predominant share in determining enemy attrition rates." Three fourths of the battles are at the enemy's choice of time, place, type and duration. CIA notes that less than one percent of nearly two million Allied small unit operations conducted in the last two years resulted in contact with the enemy and, when ARVN is surveyed, the percentage drops to

one tenth of one percent. With his safe havens in Laos and Cambodia and with carefully chosen tactics, the enemy has been able during the last four years to double his combat forces, double the level of infiltration and increase the scale and intensity of the main force war even while bearing heavy casualties.[18]

Finally, late in the summer of 1969 the attrition strategy ceased to be the prime objective stated by MACV. It was superceded by Vietnamization which reflected the American decision to gradually disengage from the war.

"Ceasefire"

If the attrition strategy failed, why did the communists agree to a ceasefire? Why not wait until the American forces finally departed and then attack? The answer is not clear, but yet another set of force ratios may provide a clue. So far the discussion has considered only total manpower and the cutting edge of combat manpower, the regular force maneuver battalions. The communist guerrillas and the South Vietnamese territorial forces have not been highlighted. Adding the combat manpower represented by these forces yields the result shown below. The ratios shown in Table 9.5 do not favor the allies as much as those for total manpower but the trend is better. The force ratio rose every year until 1972 and portrays an increasingly favorable balance of combat forces, even as American troops withdrew. The decline in 1972 stems from the large buildup of communist regular forces in the northern part of South Vietnam for the 1972 offensive.

The key change is the growth of the Vietnamese Territorial Forces, who grew not only in numbers but in improved equipment and other factors which increased their effectiveness. Their growth enabled them to take over security duties from the regular units and to free most of them for offensive combat, even as American battalions left the country.

The effects of this growth on allied manpower available for combat and for security missions are fairly clear. Allied regular troops on offensive combat operations declined from 184,000 in 1968 to 101,000 in 1972, a reduction of 83,000. But 127,000 American and Third Nation troops withdrew from offensive operations during the same period. Thus, the gain of 95,000 Territorial Force troops released 44,000 regular RVNAF regular troops to go into offensive combat against communist forces. An additional benefit was that 95,000 territorial troops, mostly in companies and platoons, could protect more population than could 44,000 regular troops concentrated in battalions. Best of all for the allies, the new posture depended solely on South Vietnamese troops, not Americans or Third Nations. The communists also faced the prospect that the allied posture might get better as time passed.

The patterns, while certainly not conclusive, do suggest that some trends unfavorable to the communists were underway and likely to continue even without the continued presence of American ground and air forces. This may have weighed in the communists' decision to

TABLE 9.5
Growth Of The RF/PF Improved The Allied
Position As American Troops Withdrew

(Manpower in Ground Combat Maneuvers in Thousands)

	1967	1968	1969	1970	1971	1972
Allies						
All regular forces[a]	218	240	223	188	145	119
VN regional forces[b]	98	143	170	184	185	196
VN popular forces[b]	134	155	193	226	223	197
CIDG	38	42	35	–	–	–
Total	488	580	621	598	553	512
Communists						
Regular[c]	132	160	130	120	105	152
Guerrillas	81	65	45	35	30	30
Total	213	225	175	155	135	182
Allied/Communist force ratio	2.3	2.6	3.5	3.9	4.1	2.8

[a]Includes RVNAF, U.S. and 3rd Nation regular forces.
[b]Regional Forces (RF) combat manpower calculated as 65 percent of RF total strength, and Popular Forces (PF) as 90 percent of PF total.
[c]Source: Table 4.2. See "RF-PF Effectiveness," Analysis Report, August 1969.

settle for the cease fire. It must also be pointed out that while the allies couldn't defeat the communists by attacking, the heavy combat losses in the all-out offensives in 1968 and 1972 twice forced them into a strategy of protracting the war and, particularly in 1972, negotiation. Even as late as the end of 1974, five months before Saigon was to fall, the communists had clear doubts about winning the war anytime soon. In January 1975 Robert Shaplen wrote: "A communist member of the moribund International Commission of Control and Supervision commented recently, 'One side is not strong enough to win and the other is notweak enough to lose.'"[19] From 1967 on both sides faced a stalemate. The communists, as they so often predicted, were to outlast the allies.

NOTES

1. Thompson, No Exit, p. 135.
2. Lecture, by General W. C. Westmoreland, U.S. Army (Retired) at Tufts University, Medford, Mass., December 12, 1973, p. 17.

3. James B. Sterba, "Hiepduc: One Man's Victory is Another's Defeat," **New York Times** (September 7, 1969), p. 2

4. According to press reports if returning American prisoners of war asked who won the war their escort officers were to answer: North Viet-Nam didn't win. South Viet-Nam didn't lose." Also see: "U.S. Officials See a Viet-Nam Stalemate," **New York Times,** (May 7, 1974), p. 3.

5. **The Pentagon Papers, The** Senator **Gravel Edition,** Volume IV, pp. 369-371.

6. "Manpower Availability in North Viet-Nam," **Analysis Report,** (September 1967), pp. 3-4.

7. "Manpower Availability in North Viet-Nam," **Analysis Report,** (May 1968), pp. 1-2.

8. "North and South Vietnamese Manpower," **Analysis Report,** (August 1968), pp. 4-7.

9. Alain C. Enthoven and K. Wayne Smith, **How Much is Enough?,** (New York: Harper & Row, 1971), p. 298.

10. "Military Initiative in South Viet-Nam," **Analysis Report,** (September 1968), pp. 6-18.

11. Attacks include all communist attacks (large, small and by fire) and are used here as an indicator of the level of the communist willingness to fight and to take casualties.

12. "Military Initiative in South Viet-Nam: A follow-up," **Analysis Report,** (January 1970), pp. 35-37.

13. All percentages are based on the R^2 coefficients derived from statistical correlation analysis. The R^2 indicates the degree of relationship between the variables; that is, the proportion of total variation in one variable explained by the other. An R^2 of .50 indicated that 50 percent of the variation in one variable can be explained by variation in the other. In the case the R^2 are .84 and .77 respectively.

14. The analysis in this section is based on the methods employed in: "A Comparison of Allied and VC/NVA Offensive Manpower in South Viet-Nam," which appeared in the **Analysis Report,** June 1968, pp. 26-32; and (October 1968), pp. 33-38.

15. This force comparison would be misleading if a large portion of the Allied or VC/NVA enemy offensive forces were committed against forces-- GVN paramilitary or VC guerrillas--not included in the comparison. Evidence from 1967 indicates about 60-70 percent of allied main force activity was probably directed against communist main force units and vice versa. For instance, during 1967 only 33 percent of the communist actions against allied forces were against the territorial forces. (From "A Comparison of Allied and VC/NVA Offensive Manpower in South Viet-Nam," **Analysis Report,** (October 1968), p. 33.

16. For criticism of the approach see the **Analysis Report,** (August 1968), pp. 46-50.

17. Thompson, **No Exit,** p. 53.

18. **Congressional Record,** Volume 118, No. 76 (May 10, 1972), p. E4978.

19. Robert Shaplen, "Letter from Saigon," **The New Yorker,** (January 6, 1975), p. 104.

20. Lest the author ever be accused of arguing from the benefit of 20-20 hindsight, the reader should note that many of the analyses and statements cited in this chapter were written prior to the end of 1968. Doubts were beginning to arise in 1968 but the first clear, unabashed challenge to the attrition strategy came in May 1967 with the publication of "The Strategy of Attrition" in the **Analysis Report,** (May 1967), pp. 13-15.

Part Three

The Casualty Toll

10
Who Got Killed?

Casualties are the tragic byproduct of any war and they loomed large in controversies about the Vietnam war in the United States and elsewhere. This chapter discusses casualty rates on both sides, presenting the statistics available and analyzing the trends and patterns they show. Unfortunately the statistical style seems cold-blooded because numbers can never give the reader any real feeling for the suffering, death, maiming and tragedy they represent, although the enormity of some of them may have impact. The personal tragedy and agony represented by these numbers is an inherent part of the Memorial built in Washington D. C. that is dedicated to the memory of those Americans who died in Vietnam.

Some knowledge of casualty levels, trends and locations is necessary to understand a war without fronts so the data, tragic as they are, must be analyzed. The approach centers on combat deaths or KIA (Killed In Action) because prisoners, although they had a large political impact, were a small portion of the American casualties and every allied force in Vietnam counted its wounded differently so those figures are not comparable among forces. Also, no data are available for communist wounded. For comparative analysis the combat death figures are the best measurement.

Communist Deaths

It is doubtful whether anybody, including Hanoi, really knows how many communist troops died. As with the figures on communist forces there are great uncertainties in the communist KIA estimates. This is not surprising in view of the obvious difficulties encountered in counting communist casualties. The problem is not unique to the Vietnam war but the allied attrition strategy generated emphasis on the body count so the numbers received more attention than they deserved. Indeed, they cast a pall over the American effort in Vietnam.

Allied forces simply could not count communist casualties accurately while the war was being fought because it was too difficult and too dangerous. Many problems existed. Early in the war the communists placed a high priority on reclaiming their dead from the battlefield so bodies were not left to be counted. The terrain in much of Vietnam made it difficult to find all of the communist dead, particularly in the jungles and swamps. If several allied units were involved in the same action with each doing its own body count double counting was possible, even likely. Continuing combat or sniper fire sometimes made it too dangerous to do more than estimate communist losses and it is a safe bet that headquarters was demanding a body count from the unit commander. Some of the communist forces were killed by artillery, tactical air and B-52 strikes in areas where the dead could not be counted. Finally, if the body count made the outcome look bad for the allied unit the temptation to produce an exaggerated estimate was strong.

Other difficulties exist but the foregoing illustrate the problem. They also indicate why it was not possible to count Viet Cong and North Vietnamese dead separately, despite pressure from higher headquarters to do so. Again, the attrition strategy generated the pressure with its concern about trends in the North Vietnamese force structure.

Considerable effort was made to check the validity of the communist loss estimates but the results were not conclusive. One type of analysis tried to extrapolate the losses reported in captured documents. Another used a balance sheet approach which subtracted communist losses from communist recruitment and infiltration and then compared the answer with the changes in estimated force levels.

At least four attempts were made to extrapolate total communist losses from a sample of captured documents. The first was a MACV study of 70 documents that produced an estimate that communist KIA in 1966 were probably 4.5 percent above the official body count. In a second effort we used the same 70 documents and estimated the communist KIA in 1966 were probably 20 percent below the official figures.[1]

In the third analysis we examined 84 documents in Washington and concluded that total communist KIA for 1965 through 1968 were probably 30 percent lower than the official estimates, but that total losses were probably higher than the official figures if losses due to disease were taken into account.[2]

In the fourth attempt we used 136 documents and further refinements in the method of analysis to conclude that both communist KIA and their total losses probably amounted to about half of the official estimates.[3] This result fits the practice of one seasoned operations analyst with experience in World War II and Korea. He cut the counts of enemy KIA by 50 percent as a rule of thumb. The attempts to analyse stopped at this point. Meanwhile, in an interview with Oriana Fallaci in 1968, General Giap reportedly acknowledged the loss of about 500,000 men in the war, which is more than the official KIA count of 435,000 at the end of 1968. It is unlikely that the actual figures will ever be known.

Table 10.1 shows the balance sheet approach to estimating communist casualties. Losses were subtracted from estimated manpower inputs and the results compared with changes in communist force levels which were estimated separately in the order of battle process. The table shows inputs and losses roughly in balance for the 1965-1972 period as a whole, but communist force levels increased by 95,000. The result is a discrepancy of about 110,000 in the balance

TABLE 10.1
The Balance Sheet Approach Showed A
Discrepancy of 110,000 Between Communist
Force Changes and Communist Deaths

	1965	1966	1967	1968	(In Thousands) 1969	1970	1971	1972	Total
Personnel recruitment and infiltration	116	172	143	305	156	115	119	158	1,284
Personnel losses[a]	59	92	141	262	244	161	147	192	1,298
Inputs minus losses	7	80	2	43	-88	-46	-28	-34	-14
Communist force level changes[b]	6	64	-28	53	-50	-20	-25	55	+95

[a]Losses include combat deaths, deaths from wounds (based on intelligence community factor of .35 times KIA), prisoners and military defectors.
[b]Based on Table 4.2.

which averages out to about 14,000 per year. In all but two years (1967 and 1972) the actual figures moved in the same direction, although some yearly discrepancies were fairly large. All factors considered, the balance isn't too bad. It suggests that the various estimates of forces, losses and inputs have some coherence, although each was estimated by different people with different tools and techniques.

The balance is probably helped by two factors. The intelligence community periodically assessed some losses against the estimated communist force levels and the U.S. command actually used the balance sheet approach to help estimate communist force levels for a while. However, the yearly discrepancies are large enough to indicate that these two efforts were not undertaken with the aim of producing a precise balance.

Despite the uncertainties in the communist combat death estimates, the figures are worth analyzing because they shed some light on the communists' persistence and approach to the war. Such an analysis must be confined to general trends and patterns because the numbers are not accurate enough for more than this.

Table 10.2 displays the official U.S. statistics of communist combat deaths in the Vietnam war. They are a product of intensive efforts to produce reasonably good estimates but the uncertainties are great. The table says that the communists may have lost as many as 850,000 dead during 1965-1972, an average of more than 100,000 combat deaths each year. The trend rose each year to a peak of 180,000 during 1968 then fell off to about 100,000 per year by 1970-1971. Then the communist offensive in 1972 again boosted the toll to 132,000.

TABLE 10.2
An Estimated 850,000 Communists
Died In South Vietnam

	1965	1966	1967	1968	1969	1970	1971	1972	Total
(In Thousands)									
Communist Deaths	35	56	88	181	157	104	98	132	851

Source: Table 2, **Southeast Asia Statistical Summary,** Office of the Assistant Secretary of Defense (Comptroller), August 9, 1972–April 11, 1973, pp. 1–9.

Data for 1967 through 1972 showing communist combat deaths by military region in South Vietnam indicate that 35 percent of the deaths occurred in Military Region 1, which fits the pattern of intense combat already shown there. Military Regions 3 and 4 each accounted for 20 percent, and Military Region 2 was in last place with 17 percent. Operations in Cambodia and the panhandle of Laos during 1970 and 1971 accounted for about five percent.

When the combat deaths in Table 10.2 are compared with the reported sizes of the communist forces, they are high indeed. The estimated force size averaged 245,000 for the period and communist combat deaths reportedly averaged 106,000 per year. This suggests that more than 40 percent of the communist forces were killed in action every year. The figure for 1968, the year of the Tet Offensive, was more than 60 percent. Rough as these percentages are, given the uncertainties of the data, they do suggest that the communists took extremely heavy casualties.

The rule of thumb for western armies is that a military unit ceases to function in combat if 30 percent of its troops have been killed or wounded. The communists probably exceeded this percentage every year after 1966 and still managed to keep the war going. The cohesion of their units, their infrequent commitment to combat (perhaps once every six months), and their careful rebuilding after each campaign all help to explain the communists' ability to persist in the face of these very high losses.

Allied Combat Deaths

With allied combat deaths the concerns about accuracy and reliability of the figures can be discarded. American combat deaths are the most accurate statistics from the Vietnam war. Enormous effort goes into U.S. casualty reporting in any war, with a name, rank and serial number standing behind every figure added to the toll. The intense American effort to find out what happened to the missing still continues.

TABLE 10.3
222,000 Allied Troops Died In Combat

	1965	1966	1967	1968	1969	1970	1971	1972	Total
RVNAF[ab]	11243	11953	12716	27915	21833	23346	22738	39587	171331
U.S.[a]	1369	5008	9378	14592	9414	4221	1380	300	45662
Third Nation	31	566	1105	979	866	704	526	443	5221
Total	12643	17527	23199	43846	32113	28271	24644	40330	222214

Source: Table 2, **Southeast Asia Statistical Summary,** Office of the Assistant Secretary of Defense (Comptroller), April 11, 1973, pp. 1-9.
[a]Includes combat deaths in Laos and Cambodia.
[b]Includes RVNAF and paramilitary combat deaths.

The Vietnamese casualty data are much less reliable than the data for American casualties. The detailed statistics show considerable turbulence in the reporting system. Still, they are good enough for the limited analysis done here. The accuracy of the third-nation casualty data probably lies somewhere between the American and Vietnamese data, but that is purely a guess.

Table 10.3 shows that about 222,000 allied troops were killed in South Vietnam during the eight years of 1965-1972 for an average of 28,000 per year. The South Vietnamese accounted for 77 percent of the total. The U.S. share was 21 percent and the third-nation forces lost about two percent.

The toll grew each year to a peak in 1968 and then declined to the 1967 level by 1971. The offensive in 1972 raised allied combat deaths to the 1968 level but the South Vietnamese took virtually all of the losses this time.

The reduction in allied KIA rates from 1968 through 1971 was caused by a reduction in combat starting in 1969, and by the withdrawal of U.S. troops from mid-1969 on. South Vietnamese combat deaths were about the same in 1969, 1970 and 1971, while U.S. deaths declined sharply, accounting for most of the reductions in the totals.

Chapter 2 showed that allied combat deaths were not evenly distributed throughout South Vietnam but were heavily concentrated in five provinces. Eleven percent of the provinces accounted for 33 percent of the allied combat deaths. The communist pattern is similar with 35 percent of the deaths occurring in the same five provinces.

South Vietnamese Combat Deaths

Problems of reliability and consistency plagued the tabulation and analysis of South Vietnamese combat deaths and they provide a

TABLE 10.4
170,000 South Vietnamese Troops
Were Killed In Combat By The End of 1972

RVNAF:	1965	1966	1967	1968	1969	1970	1971	1972	Total
Regular forces	5044	4418	6110	12930	8652	9647	8864	19735[a]	75360
RF/PF	6239	7535	6606	11393	10286	11738	13118	18962[a]	85877
Total	11243	11953	12716	24323	18938	21385	21982	38697	161237
Para-military	N/A	N/A	N/A	3592	2895	1961	756	890	10094
Total	11243	11953	12716	27915	21833	23346	22738	39587	171331

Sources: Based on calculations and assumptions using Tables 2 and 53, **Southeast Asia Statistical Summary,** Office of the Assistant Secretary of Defense (Comptroller), Table 2, April 11, 1973, pp. 1-8, Table 53, February 16, 1972, pp. 1-5.
[a]Official figures showing Regular and RF/PF deaths separately are not available for 1972. These estimates are based on a sample of OPREP-5 messages which indicate that 49 percent of the 1972 deaths were RF/PF and 51 percent were Regular. These factors were applied against the total of 38,697 to develop the figures shown.

dramatic illustration of the critical importance of good reporting. During one period of the war American combat deaths always appeared to be higher than South Vietnamese deaths. This led one Secretary of Defense to believe that the Vietnamese weren't carrying their share of the load and he criticized them harshly.

Our Investigation of the South Vietnamese reports found that the Vietnamese statistics being sent to Washington were preliminary field reports which were about 40 to 50 percent below the final, verified reports. After these data were furnished Vietnamese deaths were seen to be consistently higher than U.S. combat deaths by a wide margin.

The Vietnamese statistics are presented in Table 10.4 and they are considered reliable enough for comparisons and trend analysis. The table indicates that the South Vietnamese lost about 160,000 military KIA and about 10,000 paramilitary KIA during 1965-1972. The regular forces accounted for about 45 percent of the South Vietnamese KIA, with Regional and Popular Forces accounting for the remaining 55 percent. As to trends, the South Vietnamese deaths were steady at about 12,000 per year for 1965-1967, jumped sharply to 28,000 in 1968, then declined to a level of 23,000 during 1969-1971. They rose to 40,000 in 1972 when the South Vietnamese forces alone suffered almost as many combat deaths (39,600) as all allied forces did (43,500) in 1968.

TABLE 10.5
46,000 U.S. Troops Died in Combat By The End of 1972

Military Service	Prior to 1965	1965	1966	1967	1968	1969	1970	1971	1972	Total
Army	185	898	3073	5443	9333	6710	3508	1269	172	30,591
Marine Corps	11	335	1681	3452	4618	2254	533	41	11	12,936
Navy & Coast Guard	4	75	120	311	464*	295**	88	21	47*	1,425
Air Force	67	61	134	172	177	155	92	49	70	977
Total	267	1369	5008	9378	14592	9414	4221	1380	300	45,929

Source: "Casualties incurred by U.S. Military Personnel in Connection with the Conflict in Vietnam - Deaths Resulting from Actions by Hostile Forces," CAS 21.7, Office of the Asistant Secretary of Defense (Comptroller), Directorate for Information Services.
*Includes one Coast Guard
**Includes three Coast Guard.

As with desertions the South Vietnamese combat deaths were a constant percentage of the force, 2.1 percent each year except for 1968 (3.2 percent) and 1972 (3.4 percent). The stability of the percentages is surprising. It suggests a steady state of South Vietnamese combat effort which grew as the forces grew. Apparently they fought 50 percent harder than normal when faced with the large communist offensives of 1968 and 1972.

American Combat Deaths

The general levels and trends of American combat deaths are presented here for comparison with the other allied forces, but the detailed analysis of their causes, compositions and locations follows in the next chapter.

Table 10.5 shows that the U.S. Army and Marine Corps accounted for 95 percent of the 45,929 U.S. combat deaths through the end of 1972. Our deaths peaked in 1968 and then declined each year as U.S. troops withdrew. In 1972 the toll had declined to 300, down from 14,600 in 1968.

The Koreans accounted for about 85 percent of the 5,221 combat deaths of third-nation forces.

NOTES

1. MACV Study quoted in "Estimates of VC/NVA Combat Deaths," **Analysis Report,** (November 1967), p. 2.

2. "VC/NVA Personnel Losses: A New Estimate From Captured Documents," **Analysis Report,** (January 1968), p. 16.

3. "VC/NVA Personnel Losses Estimated From Captured Documents," **Analysis Report,** (October 1968), p. 31.

11
American Casualties Analyzed

Every war has tremendous human costs. For the United States the human costs of the Vietnam conflict are usually expressed in terms of American combat deaths which exceeded 47,000 (including the missing) by the end of 1972. But the costs went beyond that. American forces suffered more than 10,000 additional deaths from non-hostile causes in Vietnam. 150,000 troops were hospitalized for wounds received in action, many of them permanently disabled. Thousands more were hospitalized for disease and nonbattle injuries.

This chapter analyzes American military casualties in Vietnam with particular emphasis on deaths from combat and non-hostile causes. The analysis focuses on who died, where and how. It also addresses the key factors that influenced the American death rate, factors that influenced it so much that we actually predicted the rate successfully for six months ahead during one period late in the war.

Table 11.1 portrays the total number of U.S. casualties through March 31, 1973. In addition to the losses described above, 150,000 more troops were wounded but did not require hospital care.

Who Died In Combat?

Table 11.2 shows that 88 percent of all American combat deaths in Vietnam were army and marine troops fighting on the ground. An analysis in 1968 showed that 80 percent of all army and marine combat deaths were suffered by troops in maneuver units.[1] Thus about 70 percent of all American combat deaths in Vietnam were inflicted on army and marine troops serving in maneuver units.

Almost 90 percent of the combat deaths were enlisted men, mostly in grades E3 and E4, these two grades accounting for 60 percent of all U.S. battle deaths. The figures are shown in Table 11.3 which also shows that the bulk of the marine corps enlisted men killed in combat were one grade lower than those of the army and navy. Only in the air force did officers account for a significant portion (68 percent) of the combat deaths. Later, Table 11.11 indicates that 85 percent of the air force deaths came from aircraft losses in which the pilots and most of the flight crews were officers, so the pattern is not surprising.

TABLE 11.1
58,000 U.S. Troops Died and
More Than 300,000 Were Wounded

Combat Casualties	Army	Navy	Marine Corps	Air Force	Total
Killed	25,373	1,092	11,477	502	38,444
Wounded or injured					
Died of wounds	3,518	146	1,451	48	5,163
Nonfatal wounds					
Hospital care required	96,810	4,178	51,392	932	153,312
Hospital care not req.	104,723	5,898	37,202	2,518	150,341
Missing					
Died while missing	1,689	187	5	449	2,330
Returned to control	54	5	2	35	96
Missing – declared dead	246	138	91	·691	1,166
Captured or interned					
Died while captured					
or interned	38	36	10	18	102
Returned to control	133	145	37	333	648
Total Combat Deaths	30,864	1,599	13,034	1,708	47,205
Total Non-Combat Deaths	7,250	882	1,695	593	10,420
TOTAL DEATHS:	March 1973 Records				57,625
	May 1985				58,022

Source: Office of the Assistant Secretary of Defense (Comptroller),
Directorate for Information Operations, April 4, 1973. Cumulative from
January 1, 1961 through March 31, 1973, plus changes for missing
subsequently declared dead.

More than 85 percent of those who died in combat were 25 years
old or younger, with army and marine troops between the ages of 19
and 21 accounting for about 60 percent of the overall total.   Table
11.4 also shows that the marines died at younger ages than their army
counterparts, about 80 percent of them dying at the age of 21 or
below, compared to 60 percent for the army.

Table 11.5 indicates that two-thirds (65 percent) of the dead
had been in uniform for less than two years, and half of these had
served less than one year.   The marines who were killed in combat
generally had served less time than had the army dead.   However, the
length of service for many of the army dead is not shown in the data
and this may have influenced the result.   However the findings fit
the pattern of youth already seen for the marine corps in the previous
tables so they are probably about right.

TABLE 11.2
Soldiers And Marines Fighting On The Ground
Suffered 88 Percent Of The U.S. Combat Deaths

	Army	Marines	Navy	Air Force	Total
Air	2,508	575	244	851	4,178
Ground	28,087	12,361	1,126	150	41,724
Sea	0	0	56	0	56
Total	30,595	12,936	1,426	1,001	45,958

All U.S. combat deaths through March 1973, missing not included.
Source: Office of the Assistant Secretary of Defense (Comptroller),
Directorate for Information Operations, April 4, 1973.

TABLE 11.3
Ninety Percent Of The Combat
Deaths Were Enlisted Men

Rank	Army	Marines	Navy	Air Force	Total
Officers & Warrant Officers	3,324	718	226	687	4,955
Enlisted					
E6-9	2,480	359	128	59	3,026
E5	4,116	598	202	97	5,013
E4	9,252	2,030	434	103	11,819
E3	11,040	3,841	414	52	15,347
E2	296	5,079	21	3	5,399
E1	87	311	1	0	399
Total Enlisted	27,271	12,218	1,200	314	41,003
Total Killed	30,595	12,936	1,426	1,001	45,958

All U.S. combat deaths through March, 1973, (missing not included).
Source: Office of the Assistant Secretary of Defense (Comptroller),
Directorate for Information Operations, April 4, 1973.

TABLE 11.4
Eighty-five Percent Died At
25 Years of Age Or Younger

Age at Death	Army	Marines	Navy	Air Force	Total
17-18	1,039	1,557	13	0	2,609
19	3,492	3,393	113	9	7,007
20	8,200	3,486	269	26	11,981
21	5,858	1,787	262	36	7,943
Subtotal 19-21	17,550	8,666	644	71	26,931
22-25	7,869	1,902	436	214	10,421
26-30	2,230	433	171	285	3,119
31-35	1,067	231	86	229	1,613
Over 35	840	147	76	202	1,265
Total	30,595	12,936	1,426	1,001	45,958

All U.S. combat deaths through March 1973 (missing not included).
Source: Office of the Assistant Secretary of Defense (Comptroller),
Directorate for Information Operations, April 4, 1973

TABLE 11.5
Sixty-five Percent of The Dead
Had Served Less Than Two Years

Length of Service	Army	Marines	Navy	Air Force	Total
Less than 1 year	10,232	4,728	33	2	14,995
1 to 2 years	9,762	4,750	306	35	14,853
More than 2 years	7,174	3,453	1,068	765	12,460
Unknown	3,427	5	19	199	3,650
Totals	30,595	12,936	1,421	1,001	45,958

All U.S. combat deaths through March 1973 (missing not included).
Source: Office of the Assistant Secretary of Defense (Comptroller),
Directorate for Information Operations, April 4, 1973

TABLE 11.6
Twice As Many Troops Died During The First
Half of Their Tour As In The Second Half

Months in Country	Army	Marines	Navy	Air Force	Total
First three months	11,502	3,692	367	237	15,798
Second three months	7,489	2,013	225	172	9,899
Third three months	5,045	1,349	113	138	6,645
Fourth three months	1,714	569	52	70	2,405
Over 12 months	653	176	47	15	893
Unknown–Not reported	32	3,110	422	81	3,645
Total	26,435	10,909	1,226	715	39,285

U.S. combat deaths January 1967 – December 1972.
Source: Office of the Assistant Secretary of Defense (Comptroller),
Directorate for Information.

TABLE 11.7
Blacks Accounted for 12 Percent
Of The Combat Deaths

Race	Army	Marines	Navy	Air Force	Total
White	26,280	11,209	1,375	963	39,827
Black	3,994	1,600	38	30	5,662
Other	321	127	13	8	469
Total	30,595	12,936	1,426	1,001	45,958

U.S. combat deaths through March 1973 (missing not included).
Source: Office of the Assistant Secretary of Defense (Comptroller),
Directorate for Information Operations.

The one year tour for all American troops had the effect of raising the number of American combat deaths. Forty percent of the combat dead were killed during the first three months of their tour. Only six percent were killed during the last three months.

Overall, twice as many troops died during the first six months of their tour as in the second six months (Table 11.6). After the first month the number of deaths declined each month as the tour progressed. The longer one stayed alive after arriving in Vietnam, the better one's chances for survival, presumably as the result of a learning curve which each new arrival had to repeat. Longer tours would have cut the toll.

The practice of a six month tour for battalion commanders probably also had the effect of increasing American combat deaths. In South Vietnam during 1965 and 1966 U.S. maneuver battalions under experienced commanders suffered battle deaths in sizable fire fights at only two-thirds the rate of units under battalion commanders with less than six months' experience in command.[2] The short battalion commander tour apparently was not unique to the Vietnam war, because World War II records suggest that many battalion commanders served six months or less in that conflict.[3] Vietnam data and comments from some commanders suggest that the short tours generated additional U.S. casualties.

Table 11.7 shows that whites accounted for 87 percent of the American combat deaths. Blacks accounted for 12 percent. By comparison, the national population of males of military age in 1973 was 13.5 percent black.[4] About 14 percent of the enlisted deaths and two percent of the officers killed were blacks. The percentages of blacks in the U.S. armed forces at the end of 1972 were: enlisted, 13.5 percent; officers, 2.3 percent.[5] Blacks did not bear an unfair burden in the Vietnam war in terms of combat deaths despite allegations to the contrary.

Table 11.8 indicates that one-third of the Americans killed in action were draftees, almost all (96 percent) serving in the army. About half of the army combat deaths were draftees, but only five percent of the marine deaths were, although many were probably draft induced troops. The regulars, many draft induced, accounted for about 60 percent of all the American combat deaths and the reserves for only nine percent. The National Guard accounted for only 76 U.S. combat deaths, well below one percent of the total.

The information presented here indicates that the typical American killed in combat was a white, regular, enlisted man serving in an army or marine corps maneuver unit. He was 21 years old or younger. He had served in Vietnam for less than six months and was in the military service for less than two years.

Where Did They Die In Combat?

Tables 11.9 and 11.10 show where the Americans died in combat. Table 11.9 indicates that more than half (53 percent) were killed in Military Region 1 and most of the rest died in Military Region 3. Three provinces (seven percent of the total) accounted for 40 percent of the American combat deaths. They were Quang Tri, Quang Nam, and Thua Thien, all three in Military Region 1. Other provinces in

TABLE 11.8
Draftees Accounted For One-Third
Of The U.S. Combat Deaths

Category of Service	Army	Marines	Navy	Air Force	Total
Regular	13,037	11,507	1,261	716	26,521
Reserve	2,695	816	165	281	3,957
National Guard	72	0	0	4	76
Selective Service (Draftees)	14,791	613	0	0	15,404
Total	30,595	12,936	1,426	1,001	45,958

All U.S. combat deaths through March 1973 (missing not included).
Source: Office of the Assistant Secretary of Defense
(Comptroller), Directorate for Information.

Military Region 1 also had high U.S. casualty rates and appear among
the ten highest provinces shown in Table 11.10.

The ten highest provinces accounted for 77 percent of the
American combat deaths. The remaining 34 provinces accounted for
the rest. The pattern suggests that American forces were present in
largest numbers and fought hardest in Military Region 1 (where the
Marines were), in Kontum and Binh Dinh provinces of Military Region
2 and in Tay Ninh, Binh Duong, and Hau Nghia provinces of Military
Region 3. American combat deaths were concentrated in some of the
areas introduced in Chapter 2 as trouble spots since at least 1946.

What Killed Them?

Table 11.11 shows that nine percent of the American combat
dead were killed in aircraft losses, 40 percent died of gunshot wounds
and 45 percent were killed by some form of indirect fire. More than
two-thirds of the deaths from aircraft losses were army and marine
troops killed in helicopters. About 85 percent of the gunshot and
indirect fire deaths were also suffered by solders and marines.

The causes of death were distributed about the same in the army
and marine corps, except for deaths in the air. The army lost eight
percent of its deaths in the air, compared to four percent for the
marine corps. The other main differences were in the reporting of
deaths from indirect fire. The army reported that about 25 percent
of it deaths were from multiple fragmentation wounds, while the
marines reported that the same percentage were killed by other
explosives. This was probably not more than a difference in
reporting style. The marine corps also reported a higher percentage
of deaths (16 percent) from artillery or rocket fire than did the army
(eight percent). This may be a difference in reporting but it also
reflect the intensity of rocket attacks on the marine corps bases in
Military Region 1.

TABLE 11.9
More Than Half Of The U.S. Combat
Deaths Occurred In Military Region 1

Military Region	Deaths	Percentage
MR 1	20,184	53%
MR 2	5,099	13%
MR 3	10,846	28%
MR 4	1,990	5%
MR unknown	412	1%
Total	38,531	100%

All U.S. combat deaths January 1967 - December 1972.
Source: Office of the Assistant Secretary of Defense, (Comptroller),
Directorate for Information Operations.

TABLE 11.10
Ten Provinces Accounted For 77 Percent
Of The American Combat Deaths

Province	American Combat Deaths	Percentage
Quang Tri (MR 1)	6,352	16%
Quang Nam (MR 1)	5,725	15%
Thua Thien (MR 1)	3,382	9%
Subtotal	15,459	40%
Quang Ngai (MR 1)	2,444	6%
Tay Ninh (MR 3)	2,438	6%
Binh Duong (MR 3)	2,413	6%
Quang Tin (MR 1)	2,245	6%
Binh Dinh (MR 2)	1,734	5%
Kontum (MR 2)	1,526	4%
Hau Nghia (MR 3)	1,303	4%
Subtotal	14,103	37%
TOTAL - Ten Provinces	29,562	77%
The Other 34 Provinces	8,969	23%
TOTAL	38,531	100%

All American combat deaths January 1967 - December 1972.
Source: Office of the Assistant Secretary of Defense (Comptroller),
Directorate for Information Operations.

TABLE 11.11
Causes Of American Combat Deaths

	Army	Marines	Navy	Air Force	Total
Aircraft Loss:					
Fixed wing	84	132	172	775	1,163
Helicopter	2,424	443	72	76	3,015
Subtotal	2,508	575	244	851	4,178
Gunshot or Small Arms Fire	12327	5638	398	22	18,385
Indirect Fire					
Artillery/Rocket	2,334	2,117	319	109	4,879
Other explosion[a]	4,133	3,064	259	15	7,471
Multiple fragmentation wounds	7,385	1,004	75	1	8,465
Subtotal	13,852	6,185	653	125	20,815
Other causes	1,799	517	113	3	2,432
Unknown or not reported	109	21	18	0	148
Total	30,595	12,936	1,426	1,001	45,958

All American deaths through March 1973 (missing not included).
[a]Grenades, Mines and bombs.
Source: Office of the Assistant Secretary of Defense (Comptroller),
Directorate for Information Operations.

In conclusion, the analysis of American combat deaths shows that most of the Americans killed were young, white enlisted men serving in army and marine corps maneuver units. Most of them died in Military Region 1, in Kontum and Binh Dinh provinces of Military Region 2, and in Tay Ninh, Binh Duong, and Hau Nghia in Military Region 3. They died on the ground of gunshot wounds or fragments from indirect fire or mines. Longer tours of duty probably would have led to fewer American combat deaths.

Accidental and Other American Deaths

We now turn to the U.S. deaths that resulted from accidents, illness and other causes not directly related to combat.

Table 11.12 indicates that 82 percent of the 10,300 American deaths not resulting from combat action occurred in accidents. Illness and other causes accounted for nine percent each. The largest single cause of noncombat deaths was helicopter accidents which accounted for 22 percent of the total. Aircraft accidents of all types accounted for 30 percent of the deaths. Such accidents accounted for half of the air force noncombat deaths, 30 percent of the army and marine corps deaths and 17 percent of the navy deaths.

118

TABLE 11.12
Eighty-Two Percent of the Non-Hostile
American Deaths Occurred In Accidents

Accidents	Army	Marines	Navy	Air Force	Total
Aircraft losses					
Fixed wing	284	47	200	284	815
Helicopter	1,920	246	60	19	2,245
Subtotal	2,204	293	260	303	3,060
Vehicle loss/crash	826	148	37	54	1,075
Drowned/suffocated	633	168	190	24	1,015
Burns	96	31	13	7	147
Accidental self-					
distruction	632	131	5	25	793
Accidental homicide	581	312	59	21	973
Other accidents	867	402	97	54	1,420
Total accidents	5,849	1,485	661	488	8,483
Illness					
Malaria/hepatitis	451	98	29	41	619
Heart attack/stroke	208	28	24	50	310
Total illness	659	126	53	91	929
Intentional Homicide	159	22	4	5	190
Suicide	353	22	4	0	379
Other causes	96	22	154	5	277
Unknown or not reported	31	4	10	0	45
Total	7,147	1,681	882	593	10,303

Through March 1973 (Missing not included).
Source: Office of the Assistant Secretary of Defense (Comptroller), Directorate for Information Operations, April 1983.

Other significant losses occurred from vehicle accidents, drownings, accidental homicides and self-destruction and illness.

The profile of troops dying from noncombat causes is similar to those who died in combat but the patterns are not as clear. Enlisted troops accounted for 83 percent of the noncombat deaths compared to 89 percent of the combat deaths. Seventy-six percent of the noncombat dead were 25 year old or younger. The figure for combat deaths was 85 percent. Forty-two percent of the noncombat dead had been in the military service for less than two years compared to 65 percent for combat deaths.

The pattern of noncombat deaths as a function of length of service in Vietnam was much the same as for combat deaths. As time elapsed in a 12 month tour of duty the chance of suffering a noncombat death declined. The first three months of the tour generated 31 percent of combat deaths (compared to 40 percent of the

TABLE 11.13
American Combat and Non-Hostile Deaths

Deaths	1966	1967	1968	1969	1970	1971	1972
Combat	5,008	9,368	14,592	9,414	4,221	1,380	300
Non-hostile	1,045	1,680	1,919	2,113	1,844	968	261
Total	6,053	11,058	16,511	11,527	6,065	2,348	561
Non-hostile U.S. deaths as % of U.S. total	17	15	12	18	30	41	47
Deaths per 1000 Troops							
Combat	18	21	28	20	11	6	5
Non-hostile	3.8	3.8	3.7	4.4	4.9	4.3	4.7

Sources: "Non Hostile U.S. Deaths in RVN," **Southeast Asia Analysis Report,** January-February 1971, p. 30. Table 2, **Southeast Asia Statistical Summary** and **CAS 23.7** (through Jan. 1973), Office of the Assistant Secretary of Defense (Comptroller), Directorate for Information Operations.

combat deaths), and the percentage declined as the year progressed. In the final three months only ten percent of the noncombat deaths occurred.

In terms of race the combat and noncombat death patterns were about the same. Eighty-four percent of the noncombat deaths were white compared to 87 percent of the combat deaths. About 15 percent of the noncombat deaths were among blacks, compared to 12 percent of the combat deaths.

The troops killed in noncombat incidents represented much the same profile as those who died in combat, although the noncombat deaths were more evenly distributed throughout the forces. The most striking factor about the noncombat deaths was the large number resulting from helicopter crashes. A total of 5,260 Americans died in helicopters during the Vietnam war, 43 percent of them in accidents.

What Factors Influenced The Number Of American Deaths?

Two basic factors had to be present for American deaths to occur. One was American troops and the other was the action that killed them. This suggests that U.S. force levels could be an important influence on the levels of combat deaths and noncombat deaths. Table 11.13 shows the relationship expressed as deaths per 1,000 American troops. It suggests that combat deaths are heavily influenced by something besides troops strengths because the deaths per thousand troops did not remain constant but, until 1972, followed the intensity of combat in South Vietnam, building to a peak in 1968 and declining every year thereafter. By 1972 there were so few American troops left in Vietnam that the 1972 offensive had little effect on the American death rates.

So, the troop strength was an important factor in the number of American combat deaths but cannot explain all of the fluctuations in those rates. The other factors are discussed below following a discussion of the noncombat deaths.

Noncombat deaths, as could be expected, were directly rated to American troop strength. The relatively consistent behavior of the number of noncombat deaths per 1,000 troops from 1966 through 1972 is a clear indication of this. The increase during 1969-1972 (Table 11.13) was probably related to the following factors. After U.S. withdrawals began in 1969, troops previously in combat were engaged more and more in noncombat related duties (i.e., maintaining equipment, training, construction). Accidents related to these activities would contribute to noncombat death rates and these rates could be expected to rise slightly. With fewer combat operations more free time was available to the troops, possibly resulting in more mishaps during off duty hours. The lowering of morale, the drug and race problems in South Vietnam, and easy access to alcoholic beverages and opportunities to use them, could have contributed to a rise in noncombat deaths.

The mix of American forces changed as combat troops were withdrawn faster than support forces. Combat troups accounted for 28 percent of the total American force in July 1969 when withdrawals started. Two years later only 21 percent were combat troops. By then American combat forces in South Vietnam had been reduced by 65 percent, compared to a 54 percent reduction of total U.S. forces. After mid-1969 a higher percentage of our forces were located in cities and in densely populated American bases. These are the places where deaths from noncombat causes were more likely to occur.

The stability of the noncombat death and troop strength relationship is supported by a detailed examination of the noncombat deaths per 10,000 troops each month for the five years from 1966 through 1970. The analysis showed that the ratio remained within a narrow range. At its widest extremes it never went below 2.1 deaths per 10,000 troops per month or above 5.4.[6] Thus it seems safe to conclude that the level of noncombat American deaths in South Vietnam was fundmentally determined by the numbers and types of U.S. forces stationed there.

As already mentioned, troop strength alone does not explain the fluctuations in American combat death rates. An analysis of them in South Vietnam from 1965 through 1970 suggested that two factors influenced the levels of American combat deaths. The first was the yearly cycle of combat, which peaked during the spring and ebbed in early summer and fall. The Second was the level and type of U.S. troop strength which, during periods of low activity, seemed to establish a floor, or minimum level, of American combat deaths.

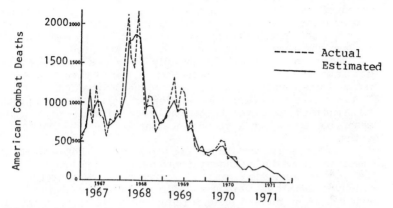

Figure 11.1   American Combat Deaths in South Vietnam

Using these two observations as a starting point, in December 1970 we attempted to establish the probable number of U.S. combat deaths for each of the next six months (January through June, 1971).[7] The forecast began with the previous year's data averaged around a given month and then adjusted for current trends and magnitudes. The results of this exercise are portrayed in Figure 11.1 which shows actual combat deaths and estimated combat deaths over four years. The techniques appeared to work well for the past but the uncertainty of the forecast was still great.   The chances were estimated as one in three that the actual number of combat deaths in any given month would be outside the range predicted.

As it turned out the forecast of future combat deaths was remarkably accurate on two counts and less satisfactory on a third. The prediction called for an average of 42 U.S. combat deaths per week for the six-month period.   The actual figure was 43.   In addition, the forecast traced the month to month patterns fairly well. The three months predicted to be highest were highest and the three months predicted to be lowest were lowest.   On the third count   the average monthly error was 22 percent.   The forecast picked the average level of combat deaths correctly and predicted which months would be high and which would be low, but did less well on estimating each monthly figure.

Encouraged by the results, we attempted to predict American combat deaths for the next six months (June through December 1971). This time an average of 20 combat deaths per week was estimated for the period.   Fortunately the actual figure was 11.   Only one month fell within the predicted range.[8]

What went wrong?   The answer lies in the tempo of communist activity and in the redeployment of American maneuver battalions from South Vietnam during the period.

Part of the answer is that the communist attack rate, a good sign of their willingness to fight and which correlated well with American combat deaths, dropped 50 percent in the second half of 1971, the period of the second forecast. In the previous year attacks had dropped only 30 percent in the second half. The same had been true in 1969. So the attacks and the communist willingness or ability to increase the tempo of combat were overestimated.

The second factor not taken fully into account was the effect of withdrawing U.S. maneuver battalions. Recall that U.S. Army and Marine Corps maneuver battalions accounted for about 70 percent of all American combat deaths in the Vietnam war. If a large portion of the American maneuver battalions were withdrawn, it would be reasonable to expect a proportional decrease in American combat deaths.

The forecast was based on a planned withdrawal of 71,000 American troops during the six month period, a decline of 28 percent. The actual reduction was 34 percent. More important, U.S. maneuver battalions were reduced from 33 at the beginning of the period to 16 at the end of it, a reduction of 52 percent, the largest percentage reduction up to that time. Symbolic of the change, on July 1, 1971, the start of the forecast period, the U.S. command announced the "biggest single cutback of American troops in Vietnam" up to that time. Forty Army units with an authorized strength of 6,095 men were pulled out of combat that month. The strong role of the maneuver battalions in setting American combat death rates is suggested by Table 11.14. It shows that the percentage reductions of American combat deaths and U.S. maneuver battalions for 1970 through 1972 are quite similar.

It seems reasonably clear that the low communist combat levels, the high percentage of maneuver battalions withdrawn, and the small number of maneuver battalions left in the country resulted in American combat death rates below the estimates.

TABLE 11.14
The Percentage of American KIA and
U.S. Maneuver Battalions Moved Together

	1970	1971	1972
Percentage reduction of U.S. KIA[a]	-55%	-67%	-78%
Reduction of U.S. Maneuver Battalions	-43%	-70%	-100%

[a]Reduction from the previous year.

Conclusion

Given the commitment of American troops to war in Vietnam, it is likely that fewer Americans would have been killed if the tours of duty had been longer and the communist control over a portion of the American combat deaths had been acknowledged and acted upon sooner. Tragically, most Americans died in the same places and the same cycles of time as the French troops had died in South Vietnam twenty years before.

NOTES

1. "Army and Marine KIA," **Analysis Report,** (November 1968), pp.20-21.
2. "Experience in Command and Battle Deaths," **Analysis Report,** (January 1968), pp. 24-30.
3. "Computer vs. Battalion CO," **Army Times,** (December 4, 1968), p. 71.
4. "Volunteer Army - Is It Working?" U.S. **News and World Report,** (August 6, 1973).
5. Table 306 "U.S. Military Personnel on Active Duty by Service, Pay-Grade, and Race," As of December 31, 1974, Department of Defense, OASD (Comptroller), Directorate for Information Operations, April 24, 1973.
6. "Non-Hostile U.S. Deaths in RVN," **Analysis Report,** (January-February 1971), pp.30-31.
7. "U.S. Death Rates in RVN: A Forecast," **Analysis Report,** (November-December 1970), p. 47.
8. "U.S. Death Rates in RVN," **Analysis Report,** (May 1971), p. 3, as updated for this analysis.

12
More than a Million
Civilian Casualties

In Laos they have a saying, "When elephants fight the grass suffers." When the allies and communists fought in Vietnam the civilians suffered. By the time the Americans departed more than one million South Vietnamese civilians had been war casualties, with approximately 200,000 of them killed and 500,000 seriously wounded by either allied or communist action. During the cease fire period when American troops were no longer present, many thousand more undoubtedly were killed or hurt but the author has not seen any data for this period on which to base an estimate. The analysis here is confined to the period of 1965-1972 when the Americans operated in South Vietnam.

"Statistics are not available which would permit an estimate to be made of civilian casualties in Vietnam caused by U.S./ARVN/FWMAF/VC/NVA in the course of military operations," according to the State Department early in 1979.[1] What the Department should have said is that no official U.S. estimate of civilian casualties exists for the Vietnam war, because statistics are available which permit estimates of the toll. Indeed, an estimate is developed here and compared with another made by the U.S. Senate Subcommittee on Refugees but both estimates are unofficial guesses.

Civilian casualties are found in records of civilian war casualties admitted to American military or South Vietnamese hospitals and in computer records of combat actions. The combat actions data are incomplete and obviously fragmentary because none of the civilian casualties resulting from American or third nation combat actions are recorded. The focus here is on the hospital admissions data which appear to be more nearly complete and are the best statistics to use as the point of departure for an estimate of civilian casualties. The data are shown in Table 12.1

The table suggests that the average monthly rate of civilian war casualties admitted to hospitals ranged from about 3,000 per month in 1971 to about 7,000 per month in 1968, but actual civilian casualties surely were much higher. The most obvious omissions from the hospital data were the civilian casualties who were never admitted to a South Vietnamese or American hospital. This included civilians killed outright, those treated as outpatients at a hospital or in the field, and those treated by doctors or hospitals outside of the reporting system.

TABLE 12.1
Civilian War Casualties[a]

Year	Total	GVN Hospitals	U.S. Military Hospitals	Total Hospital Admissions From all Causes
1967	48,734	46,783	1,951	473,140
1968	84,492	76,702	7,790	456,972
1969	67,767	59,223	8,544	525,772
1970	50,882	46,247	4,635	574,814
1971	39,395	38,318	1,077	597,423

[a]From statement of Robert H. Nooter before the Senate Judiciary Subcommittee on Refugees, May 8, 1972, p. 40.

The count of hospitals includes only the government and American hospitals although these were the vast majority. It does not include the two or three hospitals run by private charitable groups such as the Catholics and American Friends.[2] Civilian war casualties treated at such hospitals are not included in the table. Chinese doctors practicing traditional Chinese medicine may have treated some casualties and the communists may have treated still others.

Hospital admissions reporting was not precise and this also must also be taken into consideration. Senate investigators in 1968 said that ten percent of the South Vietnamese hospitals were not reporting at all.[3] On the basis of spot checks in those that did report they said that the figures were ten to 50 percent below the number of civilian casualties actually present in the hospitals.[4] Finally, no data from 1972 are shown in the table because the intense combat in that year with its high patient loads washed out the remaining reliability of the statistics.

Despite all these problems the hospital admissions data are the best point of departure for estimating civilian casualties.[5] The availability of hospital treatment and its quality rose sharply in 1966–1970 because of major American efforts to improve them.

Table 12.2 shows that the hospital admissions data for civilian war casualties fluctuated with the intensity of the war as measured by allied combat deaths. The narrow range of the ratios listed in the table (1.6 to 2.1) shows that the relationship between the two figures was strong, although civilian hospital admissions fell faster than military combat deaths in 1970 and 1971. This downturn in 1970 and 1971 could be accounted for by the movement of the war out of densely populated areas as indicated by the population control figures in Chapter 13 and by the air sortie data shown later in this chapter.

Another type of downturn is suggested if the reader returns to Table 12.1. Civilian war casualties as a percentage of total hospital admissions dropped from 18 percent in 1968 to six percent in 1970. Total admissions went up every year as medical care and facilities

TABLE 12.2
Hospital Admissions Of Civilian War Casualties Moved With
Military Combat Deaths, But Fell Faster in 1970 and 1971

	(Deaths in Thousands)				
	1967	1968	1969	1970	1971
Total RVNAF/U.S./Third Nation Combat Deaths[a]	23	44	32	28	25
Hospital Admissions of Civilian War Casualties[b]	49	85	68	51	39
Ratio	2.1	1.9	2.1	1.8	1.6

[a]Source: Chapter 10.
[b]Source: Table 12.1 preceeding.

increased. This undoubtedly influenced the percentages shown but it is not enough to account for the entire change. The increase in medical care may even have led to better reporting of civilian war casualties after 1968, but in the absence of solid evidence this must remain an assumption. At any rate, the trend of civilian casualties as measured by the hospital admissions data from 1968 through 1971 was clearly down until 1972.

Estimates of Civilian Casualties

Two estimates of civilian casualties in South Vietnam for 1965–1972 are discussed here. The first is constructed here step-by-step while the second is an estimate made by the U.S. Senate Subcommittee on Refugees and Escapees.

The first estimate addresses three kinds of civilian war casualties: those admitted to hospitals, wounded who didn't need hospital care or couldn't get it, and deaths.

From the ratios between military combat deaths and hospital admissions shown in Table 12.2 it is possible to develop an estimate of hospital admissions of civilian war casualties for the missing years of 1965, 1966 and 1972. On average there were 1.9 war casualty admissions for each allied combat death from 1967 through 1971. Applying this factor to the killed in action figures for 1965, 1966 and 1972 yields a total of 135,000 assumed hospital admissions of civilian war casualties for those three years. Adding this to the Table 12.2 figures yields a grand total of 427,000 hospital admissions for the period from 1965 through 1972.

Spot checks by the Senate investigators caused them to suggest that the reported figures are too low that and some hospitals and doctors were outside the reporting system. The 427,000 is therefore increased by 20 percent, which yields a new total of 512,000 and that figure rounds off to 515,000.

In December 1967 the former assistant director of USAID's Public Health Division in Saigon estimated that hospital admissions probably represented about 50 percent of all wounded Vietnamese civilians.[6] He further suggested that the additional 50 percent consisted of 30 percent who suffered minor wounds not requiring hospital treatment and 20 percent who were killed outright or died before reaching a hospital.[7] Applying these rules of thumb to the raw hospital admissions estimate would yield a total of 854,000 casualties for the period from 1965 through 1972. This 854,000 casualties would consist of 427,000 hospital admissions, 256,000 minor wounded and 171,000 deaths. Adding the 20 percent factor would take the total to 1,025,000, which would include 205,000 deaths.

The military casualty data lend some credence to the AID official's factor. His estimate of civilian war deaths works out to one death per 2.5 seriously wounded compared to one South Vietnamese military death per 2.65 seriously wounded from 1965 through 1972. His notion that one additional casualty exists for each one admitted to a hospital gets some support from the American wounded in action figures for 1965 though 1972. Those numbers indicate one minor injury (not hospitalized) in addition to each serious wound (hospitalized). In the U.S. case the killed must be added to the entire total because they do not come out of the non-hospitalized category.

Application of the South Vietnamese factor of 2.65 seriously wounded for each combat death, plus the American pattern of doubling the wounded number and then adding the combat deaths, plus adding 20 percent to the hospital admissions figure yields a 1965-1972 civilian casualty total of 1,225,000. This includes 515,000 hospitalized, 515,000 more not hospitalized and 195,000 killed.

Some evidence suggests that most of the civilians wounded but not hospitalized probably suffered from minor wounds not requiring a trip to the hospital. American military medical officers and technicians administered more than 2.2 million outpatient treatments to the civilian population in 1969 alone as part of civic action programs in the countryside. This included 16,000 treatments of civilian war casualties.[8] In addition, a total of 102,406 Vietnamese civilians (not restricted to war casualties) were transported by U.S. medical aircraft in the 25 month period from January 1969 through February 1971.[9] This suggests that widespread medical treatment was being made available to the rural areas.

This also suggests that where allied troops or American district advisory teams were functioning civilian casualties had a reasonable chance of receiving medical care and evacuation to hospitals if required. If this is so it indicates that the civilian casualties can be reasonably stated as 195,000 killed, 515,000 seriously wounded and 515,000 not seriously wounded. This suggest a toll in serious casualties that was closer to 700,000 than to 1,225,000.

In the second estimate the U.S. Senate Subcommittee to Investigate Problems Connected with Refugees and Escapees estimated that civilian war casualties in South Vietnam were 415,000 killed and 935,000 wounded, for a total of 1,350,000 civilian casualties.[10]

The two estimates are not very far apart. The principal difference lies in the estimate of 195,000 civilians killed versus 415,000 killed. This is a significant difference and there is no way to resolve it. The higher estimate assumes that the civilian casualty pattern was markedly different from the military pattern in terms of the ratio of killed to wounded. The lower estimate assumes that the patterns were similar. It also makes a distinction between serious wounds and minor wounds.

The higher estimate suggests that civilian casualties averaged about 165,000 per year. The low estimate suggests a maximum of 150,000 per year with about 85,000 being seriously wounded or killed. In either case the casualties amounted to less than one percent of the population each year with the low estimate's seriously wounded and killed hovering at about 0.5 percent. This is not to belittle the tragic losses, but to place them in some perspective and to indicate that they (plus the military losses) were not large enough to keep the population from growing by three percent or so each year during 1965–1972.

Causes

Much of the discussion in the United States about civilian casualties seemed to imply that the American forces and their firepower were responsible for most of them. This is not true. The communists systematically attacked civilians. The South Vietnamese troops reported some civilian casualties from their operations and the Koreans allegedly inflicted high civilian casualties in their areas of operation. This is not to say that Americans did not cause civilian casualties. We must have caused many of them given the kind of war we had to fight.

As the allied forces succeeded in pushing the war out of the populated areas evidence emerges that the communists became increasingly responsible for the civilian casualties. Again, the hospital admissions data furnish the clues. The South Vietnamese Ministry of Health required that reports be submitted by ministry hospitals on the causes of wounds. No absolute conclusion can be drawn from these but they can be crudely grouped as inflicted by the communists (mines, mortars), by either side (guns, grenades), or by the allies (bombing, artillery). Table 12.3 suggests a clear increase in the percentage of communist inflicted wounds, a moderate drop in those inflicted by either side and a 50 percent drop in those caused by the allies.

The downward trend for shelling and bombing shown in Table 12.3 is supported by data from the HES and from analysis of air strikes near populated areas. The HES asked, "Were any friendly artillery or air strikes directed in or near the inhabited areas of the village this month?" Negative answers increased noticeably from December 1969 through December 1971, as shown in Table 12.4. The increased intensity of combat in 1972 shows up as fewer negative replies in 1972.

TABLE 12.3
Shelling And Bombing As A Cause Of Civil Casualties
Declined From 43 Percent To 22 Percent Of The Total

	Mine & Mortar	Gun/ Grenade	Shelling & Bombing	Total
1967	15,253	9,785	18,811	43,849
1968	31,244	15,107	28,052	74,403
1969	24,648	11,814	16,183	52,645
1970	22,049	7,650	8,607	38,306

Source: W. E. Colby, Statement to the Senate Subcommittee on Refugee and Escapees, April 21, 1972, p. 41 and Annex K.

TABLE 12.4
Were Any Friendly Artillery Or Air Strikes Directed In
Or Near The Inhabited Area Of This Village This Month?

	Percentage of Population			
	1969 Dec.	1970 Dec.	1971 Dec.	1972 Dec.
No	69.9	83.5	89.0	82.7
Yes:				
Once	3.1	4.7	2.7	4.8
Sporadically	16.2	9.4	5.8	8.2
Repeatedly	7.8	2.2	2.3	3.7
Total Yes	27.1	16.3	10.8	16.7

Source: Hamlet Evaluation System question VMC-2 for the months shown.

A much clearer picture of the downward trend in civilian casualties caused by the allies emerges from an analysis of air strikes in relation to hamlet locations. It yields a much more precise statement, one that shows a sharp decline in air strikes near populated areas between January 1969 and January 1972.

The distance of air strikes from hamlets is one measure of how close the main force war was to the population. As pacification proceeded and as allied forces gained superiority over the communist main forces, the distance ought to have increased. As a result the likelihood of civilian casualties and disruption of civilian life should decline. To measure the distance of tactical air sorties from population centers in South Vietnam the following data were used:

1. Air Strike Locations. Computerized pilot reports from JCS-J3 (Joint Chiefs of Staff - Director of Operations) (1969) and 7th Air Forces (1971 and 1972) systems. One set of geographical coordinates is available for each fighter attack mission that dropped ordinance (one mission averaged two sorties). Similar data on B-52 bombers and helicopter gunships are not available.

2. Population Locations. Data contained in computer tapes sent to Washington (see Chapter 13). American district advisors provided geographical coordinate locations for the centers of all 12,000 reported hamlets in South Vietnam containing about 16 million people. Saigon's two million people are excluded from the analysis for 1969 and 1971 because air strikes rarely occurred there and detailed coordinates were not reported for all precincts until 1972.

Clearances for air strikes in populated areas were required in advance from either the province chief or Vietnamese military commanders responsible for the area. The friendly civilian population was supposed to have advance warning that their area was in a target zone. The HES was not sensitive enough to reflect temporary population movements so the exact numbers of people actually present in their hamlets on the days and hours of the reported air strikes is not known. Therefore all inhabitants are assumed to be present. January of 1969, 1971 and 1972 were the three sample months selected for the analysis. Since they span a three year period they should reveal any meaningful trends.

Air strikes affected less of the population in 1972 than in 1969 or 1971.[11] Table 12.5 shows that in January 1969 twenty-three percent of the population had one or more air strikes within three kilometers of their hamlet. In January 1972 the figure dropped to less than four percent. The population within one kilometer of the air strikes fell from five percent in 1969 to 0.5 percent in 1972, declining by a factor of ten.

The air strike data support the downward trends shown in the hospital admissions data used for judging the proportion of civilian casualties that can be attributed to each side.

There are at least two reasons for the improvement. First, military operations and pacification separated the main force war from the population so the distance of sorties from hamlets increased. In 1969 thirty-two percent of all attack missions were flown within three km of hamlets. By 1971 the figure was down to 16 percent.[12] Second, the number of tactical air strikes flown in South Vietnam declined from 17,500 in January 1969 to 3,620 in January 1972.[13]

Movement of the war away from the population was the more important of the two reasons. As noted earlier, 23 percent of the population of South Vietnam lived within 3 km of air strikes during January 1969 when 17,500 attack sorties were flown. In April 1972 the same level of air activity (17,200 attack sorties) affected 14 percent of the population.[14]

TABLE 12.5
Air Strikes Moved Away From The Population

Population (In Thousands)	1969[a] Jan.	1971[b] Jan.	1972[b] Jan.
Within 1 km of air strikes	700	150	100
From 1-2 km	1,240	330	230
From 2-3 km	1,330	420	310
Outside 3 km	10,900	15,100	17,910
No Geographical Coordinates reported	(2,600)[c]	(1,900)[c]	(250)
RVN Total	14,170	16,000	18,500

Cumulative Percent of Population
With Reported Geographical
Coodinate Locations

Within 1 km of air strikes	4.9	0.9	0.5
Within 2 km	13.7	3.0	1.8
Within 3 km	23.1	5.6	3.5

[a]Source: "Air Strikes Near RVN Population," **Southeast Asia Analysis Report,** March-April 1971, p. 29.
[b]Source: "Air Strikes Near RVN Population," unpublished paper by Office of the Assistant Secretary of Defense (Systems Analysis), October 17, 1972, p. 3.
[c]Includes Saigon's 1.7 million population.

    Table 12.6 provides further support for the pacification explanation by showing that the more secure the hamlet, the less the chance of an air strike near it. For the secure (A-B) and relatively secure (C) hamlets the chances of an air strike nearby declined as time passed. Add to this the increase in secure population during the period and it is clear that the main reason for fewer air strikes near hamlets was the movement of the war away from populated areas, not the reduction in air sorties. This probably also contributed to the decline in civilian casualties reflected in the hospital admissions figures.

Conclusion

    The evidence suggests that the communists were responsible for an increasingly larger portion of the civilian casualties in South Vietnam as the war droned on.

TABLE 12.6
The More Secure The Hamlet The Less
Chance Of An Airstrike Near It

	Population In Millions		
Population Within 3 Kilometers Of Air Strikes	1969 Jan.	1971 Jan.	1972 Jan.
A-B Hamlets			
Pop. near air strikes	.9 (17%)	.5 (4%)	.3 (2%)
Pop. not near	4.5	10.9	15.2
C Hamlets			
Pop. near air strikes	1.0 (19%)	.3 (9%)	.2 (8%)
Pop. not near	4.3	3.4	2.2
D-E VC Hamlets			
Pop. near air strikes	1.4 (41%)	.1 (11%)	.1 (17%)
Pop. not near	2.0	.8	.5
All Hamlets			
Pop. near air strikes	3.3 (23%)	.9	.6 (3%)
Pop. not near	14.2	16.0	18.55

Source: "Air Srikes Near RVN Population," **Southeast Asia Analysis Report,** March-April 1971, p. 30.

NOTES

1. "Vietnam: Policy and Prospects, 1970," **Hearings before the Committee on Foreign Relations, United States Senate, Ninety-First Congress, Second Session, on Civil Operations and Rural Development Support Program,** (February and March 1970), p. 40.

2. "Civilian Casualty and Refugee Problems in South Vietnam," **Findings and Recommendations of the Subcommittee to Investigate Problems Connected with Refugees and Escapees, of the Committee on the Judiciary,** United States Senate, (May 9, 1968), p. 17.

3. **Ibid.,** p. 16.

4. **Ibid.,** p. 17.

5. **Statement of Robert H. Nooter, Deputy Coordinator, Bureau of Supporting Assistance, AID,** before the Judiciary Subcommittee on Refugees, U.S. Senate, (May 8, 1972), p. 32.

134

6. "General Accounting Office, Supplemental Inquiry Concerning the Civilian Health and War-Related Casualty Program in Vietnam (B 133001)," p. 40 of Senate Subcommittee Report cited in Footnote 2 above.

7. Ibid.

8. Statement of Ambassador William E. Colby, Deputy to Commander, U.S. Military Assistance Command, Viet-Nam (COMUSMACV) for Civil Operations and Rural Development Support, April 21, 1971, p. 37 and Annex I. For an account of U.S. Army medical aid to civilians see Viet-Nam Studies: Medical Support of the U.S. Army in Viet-Nam, 1965-70, Department of the Army, Washington, D. C., 1973.

9. Ibid.

10. "Vietnam War Casualties," New York Times, (January 24, 1973).

11. For a description of the change between January 1969 and January 1971 see: "Pentagon Defends Air War," Washington Star, (April 25, 1971), p. 4.

12. "Air Strikes Near RVN Population," Analysis Report, (March-April 1971), p. 28.

13. Table 2, Southeast Asia Statistical Summary, Office of the Assistant Secretary of Defense, (Comptroller), pp. 1 and 4, (April 11, 1973 and July 26, 1972 respectively).

14. "Air Strikes Near RVN Population," Unpublished paper by the Office of the Assistant Secretary of Defense (Systems Analysis), (October 17, 1972), p. 2.

15. "Air Strikes," Analysis Report, (March-April 1971), pp. 32-34.

Part Four

Pacification: "The Other War"

13
How Secure Was
the Countryside?

The most important objective of both sides in a war without fronts is control of the population. Influence over the population and support from it is what such a war is all about. Mao Tse Tung, Ho Chi Minh, Vo Nguyen Giap and others understood this principle very well. So did the British in Malaya and Magsaysay in the Philippines.

The Americans and French gave it lip service in Vietnam, but a really significant effort was never directed to this objective. In the American case the attrition strategy dominated, as shown by the pattern of resource allocation described in Chapter 3. Nonetheless, after 1967 the pacification program made significant strides in gaining population support for the Government of Vietnam when resources and leadership began to flow into it.

Security for the South Vietnamese population from Viet Cong and North Vietnamese harassment and exploitation always had to be an essential part of pacification in South Vietnam and a key objective of the allied war effort. Security of the populace is used here as a key criterion for evaluating the progress of pacification, although the pacification effort encompassed much more. Efforts to measure the level of security began at least as early as 1963 and they continued throughout the war amidst publicity and controversy. This chapter describes those efforts, presents the trends they showed, and discusses their validity.

The Measurement System

Vietnamese attempts to measure the security of the population began at least as early as 1963 and featured a wide variety of systematic reports about the situation in the countryside.[1] However, the reporting was oversimplified and of poor quality and exaggerated the amount of security that actually existed in the countryside. For example, after the death of President Ngo Dinh Diem in November 1963, the number of "secure" hamlets in Long An Province was revised downward from over 200 to about ten. The discussion here begins with the joint South Vietnamese–U.S. reporting system that was adopted in May 1964 and

continued in use until June 1967, when the American Hamlet
Evaluation System (HES) became the only official system.

The joint system[2] attempted to portray military security
with little emphasis on administrative control and economic
development. Reports on each hamlet in the South Vietnamese
pacification plan were developed by both the American district
advisor and the Vietnamese district chief and sent separately to
their respective headquarters at the province level and in Saigon.
The U.S. advisor was supposed to make an independent assessment,
but this was often impossible because he seldom knew the history
of his district very well and he had to rely on Vietnamese
interpreters to obtain information in the hamlets. The system is
best described as a joint one.

An optimistic bias probably exists in the 1964-1967
statistics because the reporting tended to concentrate on
changes resulting from ongoing work. As a result, backsliding in
areas previously pacified probably didn't show up as well as
progress in active areas. The data support the notion of an
optimistic bias.

A major new departure occurred in January 1967 when U.S.
advisors began reporting their evaluations of hamlet status
through the HES. Shortcomings in the previous joint reporting of
population and hamlet control in South Vietnam led the Secretary
of Defense to request a better system for measuring pacification
progress in October 1966. HES was the result. The HES was
designed to to yield comprehensive, quantifiable data on the
security and development of every hamlet in South Vietnam under
some degree of government control and to identify hamlets that
were under communist control. Data collation at the Saigon level
was completely automated for computer processing and duplicates
of the computer tapes were sent to Washington.

The basic evaluation of each hamlet's status came from the
lowest possible level of the American advisory chain, the district
advisors who filled out the work sheets. Each hamlet was
evaluated on six factors, with three indicators in each factor and
each indicator graded from A (=best) to E (=bad) for a total of 18
grades per hamlet. Three of the factors related to the security
status of the hamlet: communist military activities, Viet Cong
political and subversive activities, and allied capabilities. The
other three measured development status: administrative and
political activities, economic development and health, education
and welfare. The letter grade assigned to each factor depended
on the numerical scores given to each indicator, and the average of
the six factor grades determined the single composite grade for
the hamlet. The reporter also stated the level of confidence he
placed on his evaluation. In addition, information regarding
progress areas in each hamlet was reported, and this was also sent
to Washington.

The system was an American reporting system although
advisors had to work closely with their Vietnamese counterparts
in implementing parts of it. This turned out to be a critically
important difference from the old system, because it gave the U.S.
advisor complete control of the final scores and enabled him to

make an independent report on the pacification performance of his Vietnamese counterpart. The new system also represented the view from the cutting edge, since higher echelons were not allowed to change the ratings.

Top Vietnamese officials in Saigon came to rely on the HES as an independent report card on their provincial and district leaders, and this gave American advisors in the field a good deal of leverage on them. While pacification always remained a Vietnamese program, in contrast to the military effort, it was graded by the Americans and even the President and Prime Minister of South Vietnam acted on the reports.

The district HES reports were collated by the American interagency province team before being sent to Saigon for countrywide collation. The results were displayed in computer printouts and monthly summaries.

In setting up the system, the U.S. command ran into problems but made rapid progress. For example, a complete and accurate inventory of the hamlets in South Vietnam was not available. No census had been taken for years. In compiling a new inventory and checking the location and characteristics of each hamlet in the system, officials found that many hamlets no longer existed or had little population. These were dropped from the list.

In addition to the ratings, basic elements of information reported in the HES included the name of the hamlet, its coordinate location, its village, district, province and military region, and its population. The system also provided information regarding the control status of people living in provinces, towns and other locations outside the officially recognized hamlets. It therefore yielded information about the control status of everyone in South Vietnam.

Because all 18 indicators entered into a hamlet's overall rating, it is difficult to give a concise interpretation of what constituted an "A" or a "B" hamlet. There is not a clear relationship between the previous joint categories and the HES classification. This makes it difficult to link the two systems for an analysis of trends.

The composite HES scores were weighted more toward social and economic development than the criteria for the 1964-1967 joint reports and they gave a better measure of permanent pacification progress as opposed to increased security protection. The latter can be examined separately in the HES as can many other questions. For example, the August 1967 HES score on the nine security indicators alone included two percent more of the South vietnamese population in the A-B-C hamlet grouping than did the overall HES scores. Security ratings were slightly higher that development scores in this case.[3]

The first version of HES remained in use until January 1970 when a complete revision was adopted. Seeing shortcomings in the HES, pacification advisors undertook a two year reassessment of it and implemented a carefully revised system called HES/70. HES/70 attempted to overcome the known biases that had developed in three years of HES reporting. It asked district senior advisors to supply facts, not subjective judgments, and it applied

TABLE 13.1
The Old HES Was More Subjective Than HES/70

HES January 1967–December 1969	HES/70 Began January 1970
Summary: Subjective A-E A-E ratings by District Senior Advisors (DSAs).	Summary: Objective Reports by DSAs; conversion to experts' A-E ratings.
37 multiple-choice questions per month per hamlet (18 indicators, 19 problem areas).	21 monthly hamlet questions. 4 monthly village questions. 56 quarterly hamlet questions. 58 quarterly village questions.
Training required to make ratings.	Asks detailed questions about verifiable facts.
Different DSAs used different criteria at different times.	Standard countrywide rating criteria did not change over time.
Gaps in coverage (e.g., economics information, education, land reform).	Covered all aspects of pacification (security, political, socio-economic).
DSAs disliked unclear rating criteria.	DSAs preferred providing facts even though more detailed.
Three-year data base.	One-time discontinuity in trend lines; but new data base rested on more realistic foundation.

expert weighting criteria uniformly throughout the country to develop the composite hamlet and village scores. Table 13.1 shows the differences between HES and HES/70.

To obtain A, B, C, D, E or VC ratings comparable to the earlier ones in HES, HES/70 used a uniform but complex weighting scheme built upon expert judgments of 18 different aspects of pacification. The experts' judgments were converted to A, B, C, D, E and VC scores by a standard mathematical technique called Bayesian probability analysis. The HES/70 reports for the testing period of July-December 1969 showed about one percent less A-B population and four to six percent less A-B-C population than the old HES showed for the same period, and they registered less sensitivity to changes in government pacification goals. The difference suggests that HES/70 was more conservative than the previous HES.

In January 1971 the scoring system was changed and called HES/71 to give greater weight to political factors (communist infrastructure, terrorism, etc.) in describing security. The HES/71 was still in use at the end of 1972 and the system was gradually turned over to the Vietnamese before the American forces completed their withdrawal. By the end of 1972 eighty percent of all HES/71 reporting was being done by the South Vietnamese personnel themselves and they took it over completely after the Americans departed.

The detailed questions and observations contained in the HES can be used to analyze many dimensions of the situation in South Vietnam. HES/70 contained data about the communist infrastructure, land reform, economics, politics, health care and communist forces and actions. In the diversity of its components, the HES was similar to the Pacification Attitude Analysis System (PAAS) and the HES data are used in other chapters in the same manner as the PAAS data are used. For example, the land reform analysis contains data from the HES and PAAS as well as from the Land-to-the-Tiller Program.

The HES data are also useful because they constitute the only record in South Vietnam of where the population was located. The locations are marked by UTM map coordinates which can be compared with similar location data in other computer files to judge the relationship of a given activity to the population. This technique was used to match air strikes to civilian population in the analysis of civilian casualties and to match the spraying operations to the population in the herbicides analysis.

Finally, the HES data base may be the most complete and systematic record that exists anywhere of rural security and development in a less-developed country, despite problems with the reporting of the development indicators.

The Trends

The trends portrayed by the joint South Vietnamese-American system appear in Table 13.2. The raw data are adjusted retrospectively to compensate for changes to the system during 1964-1966. Tests of the assumptions that went into the adjustments indicate that the trends shown in the table constitute an accurate portrayal of the results from the system, although the accuracy of each figure is not precise.[4]

The retrospective estimate suggests an increase of 4.2 million people in the "secure" category between December 1964 and June 1967 and a reduction of about 900,000 in the number of people under VC control. In terms of percentages, the secure population increased from 42 percent to 64 percent of the total.

The gains appear to be significant ones for the government but Table 13.2 suggests that much of the increase resulted from the movement of people into secure areas instead of expansion of territory protected by allied military forces. Take the period from December 1965 to June 1967 when the secure population increased by two million. There were about 1.2 million officially recorded refugees during the period, which may account for 60

TABLE 13.2
Population Security Increased 1964-1967

4.2 Million People Entered the Secure Category

Population in Millions

Degree of Military Security	1964 Dec.	1965 June	1965 Dec.	1966 June	1966 Dec.	1967[a] June	1964-67 Change
Secure	6.8	7.7	9.0	9.5	10.3	11.0	4.2
Contested	6.0	4.9	4.0	3.8	3.9	3.8	-2.2
Communist Control	3.3	3.7	3.5	3.4	2.8	2.4	- .9
Total Population	16.1	16.3	16.5	16.7	17.0	17.2	1.1

But Gains In Territory Did Not Explain The Increase

Hamlets in Thousands

Secure		3.5	4.2	4.2	4.7	4.7	1.2
Contested		4.5	3.6	3.6	3.7	4.1	- .8
Communist Control		3.9	4.1	4.1	3.5	3.1	- .4
Total Hamlets		11.9	11.9	11.9	11.9	11.9	0

Source:"Population Security Statistics", **Southeast Asia Analysis Report,** October, 1967, p. 22.
[a]The GVN/US system continued during the first six months of HES reporting (January-June 1967).

percent of the increase. Natural population growth of at least 2.5 percent per year would account for another 0.3 million (15 percent) of the increase.[5]

Other factors could account for the remainder: extension of allied protection, job seekers moving to the cities, unofficial refugees and optimistic evaluation of programs. The hamlet data suggest that the extension of allied protection is probably the main factor. About 500 hamlets were added to the secure category and the average population per hamlet was about 1,000 at that time so this would yield the 500,000 people needed to complete the two million gain.[6] This is not to say that the gain occurred precisely this way, but simply to indicate the kind of factors at work which suggest that the gain may be reasonably valid.

Intelligence reports and captured communist documents lent some credence to the trend in the Viet Cong's loss of control shown in Table 13.2, but they also suggest that the VC-control figures

were too low. A captured document of early 1966 stated that five
million people lived in liberated (Viet Cong) areas and nine million
resided in government-held areas.[7] The retrospective estimate
for December 1965 showed the same nine million in the government-
secure category, but only 3.6 million in the VC-controlled
category, a shortfall of 1.4 million.

The method of reporting also suggests that the population in
communist controlled areas was understated because the pre-1967
joint system counted only the hamlets planned for pacification.
It ignored the ones not in the pacifications plan, most of which
were probably communist hamlets. Table 13.2 shows 11,900
hamlets, but the HES counted about 12,600 of them and the South
Vietnamese counted more than 13,000 for administrative purposes
other than planning.[8]

The same 1966 captured documents lamented the communist
loss of a million people from the countryside into government-
controlled urban areas as a result of the presence of American
troops. The estimates in Table 13.2 show a loss of only 200,000 in
Viet Cong control between June and December 1965. But 900,000 of
the contested category moved up to secure during the same period,
and this may account for the rest of the million to which the
document referred.

A captured document of October 20, 1966 indicated that
allied operations and programs produced "some relatively
significant results" in the form of 400 additional government
hamlets built and 400,000 people brought under government
control. Other documents referred to a loss of communist
influence and control over the rural population and described the
declines in communist food production, tax revenues and manpower
as a result of shrinkage in its population base.[9]

The trends shown in Table 13.2 are also consistent with
results of the September 1967 presidential election in South
Vietnam. About 5.9 million voters registered for that election,
more than one-half of the secure population of June 1967. This
was a gain of 600,000 over the estimate of registered voters a year
earlier.[10] The estimates in Table 13.2 show an increase in the
secure population of 1.5 million over the comparable period (June
1966 to June 1967), of whom approximately one-half would be
eligible to vote. Details are not available to verify that both
gains occurred in the same group of population, but at least the
trends moved in the same direction.

The figures in Table 13.2, captured communist documents and
the voter registration statistics all show the same trends.
While the evidence is by no means conclusive, it does suggest that
the portrayal of the situation in Table 13.2 is probably not too far
wrong, except that the truly secure population is probably
overstated and more people and hamlets were almost certainly
under communist control than the table shows. But the
fundamental trends appear to be sound and they support the notion
of a gain of four million people in the secure category between
December 1964 and June 1967.

TABLE 13.3
Population Security Increased 1967-1972

8.2 Million People Became Secure Between 1967 and 1972[a]

Countrywide Population	Population in Millions - End of Year						1967-72 Change
	1967	1968	1969	1970	1971	1972	
Secure (A&B)	7.2	8.2	12.5	13.4	15.8	15.4	8.2
Relatively Secure (C)	4.3	5.2	3.8	3.5	2.3	2.6	-1.7
Contested (D&E)	2.7	1.9	.8	.9	.6	1.0	-1.7
Communist control	2.9	2.2	.4	-	-	.2	-2.7
SVN Total[b]	17.2	17.5	17.6	17.9	18.7	19.3	2.1

Which Raised the Percentage "Secure" From 42% to 80%

	Percentage of Population						
Secure (A&B)	42	47	71	75	84	80	38
Relatively Secure (C)	25	30	21	20	13	14	-11
Contested (D&E)	16	11	5	5	3	5	-11
Communist control	17	12	2	0	0	1	-16

Source: Hamlet Evaluation System Computer Tapes 1967-1972.
[a]All figures are based on **total** HES scores which include the security political and socio-economic dimensions. The table includes the urban population. The C-D-E-Communist population is mostly concentrated in the rural areas.
[b]Total includes population in unevaluated hamlets which are not shown in the table so some of the columns do not add up precisely.

Trends From The HES

The major trends from the Hamlet Evaluation System appear in Table 13.3 which suggests that:

1. 8.2 million people were made secure during the five years between December 1967 and December 1972. This raised the proportion in this category to 80 percent of the total population in South Vietnam.
2. Losses in the Tet Offensive were recovered by the end of 1968. Indeed, gains were made, with one million people added to the secure category by year's end.
3. The pacification effort really produced results in 1969, when 4.3 million people were added to the secure category. The contested and communist controlled populations fell below all previous levels.
4. The communist offensive in 1972 eroded the gains but not in any major way for the country as a whole.

TABLE 13.4
The South Vietnamese Gained Some
Control Over 11 Million People

	Population in Millions		
	1964	1967	1972
Secure Population[a]	6.8	11.5	18.0
Total Population	16.1	17.2	19.3
Percent of total secure	42%	67%	93%

[a] Secure category from GVN/U.S. system for 1964; A+B+C HES population (total scores) for 1967 and 1972.

Table 13.4 shows what happens when a time series is constructed joining the old joint system and the results of the HES. The linkage is crude, and it simply assumes that the HES A-B-C total was roughly equivalent to the joint secure population, which was the case in January 1967 when the systems were operating side by side. The results are not precise but they do suggest significant allied progress between December 1964 and December 1972.

The table indicates that the GVN gained some sort of control over more than 11 million people. In percentage terms, the gain is from 42 percent of the total population in 1964 to 93 percent in 1972. The qualitative improvement doesn't show in the table, but from table 13.3 it can be determined that 15.4 million of the 1972 figure represented population in the A-B categories, as opposed to only 7.2 million of the 1967 figure.

Validity of the HES Trends

A key question at this point is whether the HES results are valid. It has already been suggested that the early joint system results were not too bad. The analysis of HES validity proceeds in three stages and examines (1) some formal studies conducted to check the validity of the HES, particularly in its first stages from 1967 through 1969, (2) what rigorous analyses of the HES details revealed, and (3) what streams of evidence from other reporting systems, independent of HES, implied about the validity of HES trends.

Formal Studies

When the HES was adopted, considerable concern was expressed about the validity of the system, particularly in its early stages of development, and several studies to identify problems in the HES and check its validity were undertaken. Their main results are summarized below.

In December 1967, we noted the factors that combined to make HES reporting difficult.[11] Only a few of the 18 indicators could be rated on the basis of direct observation of a clear-cut condition. HES/70 solved much of this problem. Much of the HES information could be obtained only from the Vietnamese and surveys indicated that American advisors relied on their Vietnamese counterparts for at least half of the raw data they were using to answer the HES questions. Finally, most advisors could not visit all of the hamlets during any one month.

Despite these difficulties we found that the HES results correlated well with non-HES data such as communist initiated incidents. For example, anti-aircraft fire tended to occur over communist-controlled hamlets and incidents around secure hamlets tended to be characterized by terror. We also found by statistical analysis of the April 1967 HES reports that the raters were not mechanically grading all of the indicators according to a single criterion. the wide variety of hamlet characteristics was reflected in the range of grades for each hamlet.

Another early study was performed in Washington by the Institute for Defense Analysis.[12] This developed a three-part methodology to check the HES results. One part compared map plots of HES data with map plots of communist military actions, while the second part showed combinations of various levels of security and development factors. The third step assigned communist military incidents to the closest hamlet by matching the geographical coordinates of the incident and the hamlet.

The methodology was applied to three sample districts with use of the HES data for January 1967 through May 1967, the earliest stage of the HES operation. Most of the conclusions dealt with methodological problems but one of them stated: "Application of the methodology to the development of HES data gave many indications that the HES will provide meaningful data when the system is fully in operation. ...The sample data studied were found to be very compatible within themselves and with other data."[13]

The next study was a major effort conducted in Vietnam by the Simulmatics Corporation for the U.S. Army Concept Team in Vietnam.[14] The U.S.-Vietnamese study team conducted interviews, researched records, and went into the field to develop its conclusions. Basically the team compared the advisor's input to the HES with the opinions of other observers, such as the people in the hamlets, the hamlet chief, and the team members themselves, after direct observation of the hamlet being studied. The major conclusions were:

> The results of this study indicate that the Hamlet Evaluation System (HES) as a total system is basically sound as a reporting device for the entire country and for political divisions down to the district level, and should be continued. A distinction is made, however, between security and development factors.... HES is a reasonably reliable method of estimating security trends. The interjudge reliability of the development factors is less clear.

Aggregate data on a hamlet appear to be sufficiently reliable for evaluation of the progress of pacification within districts. Ratings of some specific indicators in a hamlet, however, appear questionable if used to evaluate individual hamlets.

Our data suggest that there is a relationship between an advisor's knowledge of Vietnamese and the reliability of his overall ratings.

The evidence indicates that advisors are not inflating their ratings. There is no evidence that indicates an upward bias to advisors' ratings over the length of their tours. There is evidence that advisors tend to make the largest number of rating changes at the beginning and the middle of their tours.[15]

A third study in the form of an informal working paper in November 1969, attempted to establish the statistical characteristics of the HES data. It found that the average hamlet security scores represented a normal distribution of data, which meant that approximately 68 percent of the time the reported score would be within 0.2 point of the real score (five point scoring scale), and 95 percent of the time it would be within 0.4 of the real score. For example, if the composite hamlet score was reported as 3.7 then the actual score would be between 3.3 and 4.1 ninety-five percent of the time.

From these types of studies and working with the data from the system, the following consensus developed among HES analysts:

1. Changes in the HES security scores were sensitive enough to identify progress or regression in areas over time.
2. HES measurements were not precise enough to make point estimates--that is, to measure precisely the position along a scale between least secure and most secure. The precision, naturally, increased for higher levels of aggregation. At lower levels (village, district, province) it was generally agreed to be on the order of plus-or-minus one letter grade.
3. Comparisons among different geographic areas in South Vietnam at a single point in time may be of questionable reliability because of wide differences in the characteristics of various areas.

Analysis of HES Details

Considerable insight into the reliability and meaning of the HES trends can be gained from analyzing the details reported in the HES. Several examples of such analysis are presented here. The first describes the development of an indicator of rural security and its trends. The rest present trends resulting from some of the detailed questions asked by the HES about each hamlet or village.

Of course the HES trends presented above include people living in cities in the secure population. They were reasonably secure to begin with and with few exceptions, they remained so throughout the period. The emphasis of the pacification effort was on the rural countryside and the situation there was masked by the presence of the urban population in the estimates. American pacification advisors used rural HES data alone for their own management analyses. Moreover, the HES data shown so far included many items besides security factors because many of the HES questions related to the socio-economic and political situations.

To overcome these problems an indicator of rural control was developed out of HES data. It used ten carefully selected HES questions and began with the assumption that a primary objective of both sides in the Vietnam was was to achieve control of the people and resources of the countryside. The rural control indicator assigned a hamlet to the side which had enough military and political strength to administer the hamlet effectively, while preventing the other side from doing so. Doubtful cases were assigned to a neither side controls category. The indicator made the following assumptions.

1.   The South Vietnamese Government required both military strength (local security forces) and political and administrative organization (hamlet chief, village council, administrative personnel) to achieve control over a hamlet. However, a single indicator of significant communist presence such as armed enemy forces, regular covert VCI activity or significant access at night could veto government control.

2.   The communists, on the other hand, could achieve control with a strong political organization alone (the communist infrastructure). The government could veto communist control with a strong military or political/administrative presence.

3.   The government could achieve control only when full local security was provided. When a hamlet had to rely primarily on external forces for defense, a key element of lasting control--local participation--was considered lost. External forces could not serve as a proxy for government military strength in the hamlet.

Table 13.5 shows the results for 1969 through 1972. Comparing them with the results in Table 13.3 shows that the rural control indicator portrays a somewhat different rural picture than the HES total scores for the entire country:

1.   In December 1969 the total HES scores suggest that 71 percent of the total population was secure. However, only 48 percent of the rural population was under South Vietnamese control. In 1972 the figures were 80 percent and 68 percent. The HES A-B security scores for rural population alone indicated that 55 percent of

TABLE 13.5
GVN Control Showed Large Gains In
The Rural Areas During 1970

	Rural Control Indicator			
	1969 Dec.	1970 Dec.	1971 Dec.	1972 Dec.
GVN Control	48%	67%	76%	68%
Contested	46%	31%	23%	29%
Communist Control	6%	2%	1%	3%
Rural Population In Millions	10.5	11.1	11.8	11.6

the rural population had A-B security ratings in December 1969, as opposed to a reading of 48 percent for rural control. The rural A-B ratings for HES showed the same trends as the rural security indicators, but usually they were eight to ten percentage points higher.

2. The total HES scores indicate that pacification progress was slow in 1970 (gain of four percentage points) after large gains in 1969, but the rural control indicator suggests that pacification really began to show results in the countryside during 1970 (gain of 19 percentage points).

3. The impact of the 1972 offensive shows more clearly in the rural control indicator. Government control slipped eight percentage points as opposed to four percent for total HES scores, and control by the communists rose to three percent (as opposed to 0.2 percent).

After all the calculations, assumptions and effort that went into constructing the rural security indicator, it is interesting to see that both ways of measuring pacification progress show the same result between 1969 and 1972. The HES total scores indicate that 2.9 million people were made secure during the period, while the rural control indicator suggests that 2.8 million people were brought under control in the rural areas.

At the minimum the data suggest that after 1969 government security for the population was really reaching out into the countryside, in contrast to earlier years when much of the increase consisted of people moving from the countryside into the secure areas. The statistics also suggest that one can gain almost as much insight as U.S. pacification advisors did into the rural situation by using the HES A-B scores for the rural population only. However, this analysis continues to use the

TABLE 13.6
What Do Detailed Questions From HES/70
Say About Communist Control?

	Population in Thousands			
Population Under Communist Control	1969 Dec.	1970 Dec.	1971 Dec.	1972 Dec.
HES/70 (Total Scores)	412	38	7	220
Rural Control Indicator	590	233	153	370
Population in Hamlets Where:[a]				
1. Communist forces physically control	412	38	7	220
2. Communist military forces regularly present	537	191	106	384
3. Communist infrastructure is primary authority[b]	594	219	133	339
4. The GVN Hamlet Chief not regularly present	975	796	284	316

[a]The four factors are based on the following HES/70 questions: (1) HMB-1; (2) HMB-4; (3) HQB-1; (4) HQE-2. An attempt to add the figures shown will result in an unknown degree of double counting.
[b]This judgement is highly subjective and may be of questionable validity.

control indicator to view results in the rural areas because the rural control indicator statistics happen to be readily available and rural HES scores are not.

Table 13.6 compares answers to some of the individual HES/70 questions with the communist control data from the total scores and from the rural control indicator. The table gives some insight into what the indicators really mean. For example, the total HES scores define a communist controlled hamlet simply as one in which the communist forces physically control the hamlet. As it turns out the communists could be present in the hamlet regularly, or the communist infrastructure could reportedly be the primary authority in the hamlet but the HES/70 total score would not place that hamlet in the communist control category. This indicates what the D and E categories must have been like.

Do Trends Reported From Other
Sources Agree With HES Trends?

Another way to add perspective to the validity of HES results is to examine the security situation as reported independently of HES. Casualty data, public attitude surveys and reports of the security conditions of roads and waterways furnish data for crude comparison.

Allied casualty levels and favorable HES results tended to move in opposite directions. During 1969-1971 the allied casualties declined each year and HES security ratings rose. In 1972 the casualties rose with the communist offensive and HES showed a loss of security for the population. This is a crude comparison but it does suggest that HES results moved with the intensity of the war.

The public attitude surveys suggest that on average the hamlet residents felt less secure than the HES ratings showed. In one comparison 44 percent of the hamlet residents described their hamlets as being less secure than the HES ratings indicated, 54 percent of the respondents generally agreed with the HES description of their hamlet, and two percent said security was better. The Simulmatics Corporation study of HES validity, employing U.S. researchers in the field, found the same phenomenon. Hamlet residents were more conservative in their assessments than were the independent researchers and the latter implied that the results were as much in the eyes of hamlet residents as in the facts of the situation. Perhaps the results of the attitude survey have the same characteristics.

The data reporting the security status of essential roads and waterways support the HES population security trends in general. There are problems with the time series, but in December 1971 eighty percent of the essential roads and 75 percent of the essential waterways were considered safe. In addition polls in the summer of 1972 suggested that 75 percent of the rural population had no difficulty getting themselves or their produce to market. In this case the polls were more optimistic than the HES data which indicated that 70 percent of the rural population was free of communist taxation on produce moving to and from their hamlets. The progress in making roads and waterways safe for travel was significant. All three sets of data support the assertion that conditions were reasonably good by the end of 1971 and held fairly well in 1972.

Comments of American advisors and other American personnel returning to the United States in 1971 and 1972 consistently supported the notion that considerable progress had been made in making roads safe. Often the returning person whose experience in Vietnam was normally limited to one year, was unaware of the significance of his remarks until another person who had served in the same area a few years before expressed astonishment at the conditions being described. The surprise was usually expressed in response to a casual comment from the new arrival that he had taken a jeep and driven from point A to point B by himself. The old timer would sputter, "It used to take a battalion to travel on that road." Such exchanges were frequent.

The data all combine to suggest that it is possible to gain some notion of how secure or how well under control the population is, but it all depends upon how security and control are defined and on what population is being measured, urban or rural. In the absence of an absolute criterion of truth, the data can be interpreted in many ways and at various levels of aggregation. Indeed, this chapter has done so and has shown the futility of assuming that the data represent a completely accurate statement at any point in time.

The question of validity remains. Were the HES reports reasonably valid? Did they reflect reliably the changing situation in South Vietnam and particularly in the rural areas? The answer to both questions is yes. The trends seem reasonable. Detailed analysis of the HES data confirm them and so do independent reporting systems outside the HES.

Obviously, great progress was made in gaining influence and control of the South Vietnamese countryside. It is apparent that the process of providing government security for the population, as measured by the HES results and the other data presented here, took hold gradually and made great strides in 1969 and 1970. Most of those gains held through the intense fighting of 1972 although significant regressions were clearly evident in the areas of most intense combat.

Most of the credit for this probably belongs to the pacification program. It undoubtedly benefited from South Vietnamese regular forces, who furnished a critical shield for the program, but it seems clear that without a pacification program the gains would not have been anywhere near as great. After years of criticism of the HES results, it was interesting to read in 1974 accounts of the situation in South Vietnam which cited the strong government influence and control of the countryside.

The security improvement in the countryside permitted other important developments. Food production rose dramatically, reducing South Vietnam's reliance on rice imports and bringing new prosperity to the farmers. The improved security also permitted the massive 1970-1973 land reform effort which distributed 2.5 million acres of land to 800,000 tenant farmer families. As a result the farm tenancy rate dropped from 60 percent of all cropland to ten percent of it.

All of these results, achieved for less than six percent of the total resources expended, were lost in 1975 when the communist offensive employed regular troops to defeat the South Vietnamese army in battles similar to conventional warfare. The shield collapsed and control was lost.

NOTES

1. Annex D, **Report of the MACV Information and Reports Working Group,** (January 1963).

2. A detailed description of the GVN-U.S. system and its shortcomings appear in "Population Security Statistics," **Analysis Report,** (October 1967), pp. 21-35.

3. **Ibid.,** p. 30.

4. For a full account of the changes and assumptions made see **Ibid.,** p. 26-27.

5. **Ibid.,** p. 27.

6. **Ibid.**

7. **Ibid.,** (Five million in rural areas and four million in cities and towns).

8. **Ibid.,** p. 24.

9. **Ibid.,** p. 29.

1Ø. **Ibid.,** p. 28.

11. "Statistical Trends From the Hamlet Evaluation System," **Analysis Report,** (December 1967), p. 33.

12. C.W. Marshall, **Proposed Research Paper: Preliminary Examination of the Hamlet Evaluation System (A Methodological Study),** (February 1, 5968) IDA Log No. HQ 67-6959/3.

13. **Ibid.,** p. 6.

14. Army Concept Team in Vietnam. **Hamlet Evaluation System Study (HES) ACG6ØF,** A report prepared by the Simulmatics Corporation, Cambridge, Mass., (1 May 1968).

15. **Ibid.,** pp. 1 and 2.

14
The Territorial Forces:
Unsung Heroes

Chapter 7 discusses the improvement of South Vietnamese military effectiveness and suggests that forces from outside the country seldom win a war without fronts. Indigenous forces are critical to the outcome. It deals mostly with the regular South Vietnamese forces. This chapter deals with the South Vietnamese territorial forces who were badly neglected until 1967 when the pacification advisors took over the American advisory effort and their support.

The territorial forces were extremely important to the allied war effort in Vietnam. A principal objective this war without fronts was to gain the support of the rural population in Vietnam so the insurgent forces couldn't hide among them. The territorial forces were the troops closest to that population and had the mission of protecting the people from communist attacks and terrorism. Action could occur throughout the country with forces of both sides operating in the same areas for years at a time. The permanent forces residing in the contested areas of South Vietnam were the territorial forces on each side: the communist guerrillas, local forces, and cadre versus the government's territorial forces and cadre. The outcome of the struggle to gain the support of the rural population depended heavily on the effectiveness of these opposing forces.

The GVN forces were under the command of pacification authorities somewhat separated from the formal chain of command for the GVN regular forces. Their mission was to defend the people and to bring them over to the government behind the security shield furnished by the regular forces.

Five types of forces are considered:

1. Regional Forces (RF) who operated as infantry companies within a district or province.
2. Popular Forces (PF) who were local platoons usually assigned to a specific village or other local security task.
3. National Police who operated in the cities and towns and later in most of the villages.

4. Revolutionary Development (RD) and Truong Son Cadre who went into villages and hamlets after a modicum of security had been established to bring government programs to the people and organize support for the government. The RD Cadre operated in Vietnamese hamlets and the Truong Son Cadre in Montagnard villages.

5. People's Self Defense Forces (PSDF) who were village and hamlet militia, lightly armed and trained to resist small communist incursions into their hamlets.

Table 14.1 displays their personnel strengths. The total grew from 320,000 in 1965 to a high of 680,000 in 1971. The PSDF are not included in the total because they were not full-time troops paid by the government and because the meaning of the data is in considerable doubt.

The Regional (RF) and Popular (PF) Forces furnished most of the full time South Vietnamese territorial forces. The RF and police grew throughout the period, while the PF and RD Cadre grew to a peak and then declined during the later years of the war.

The basic mission of the territorial forces was to provide hamlet and village security. A series of questions in the Hamlet Evaluation System shed some light on which forces were primarily responsible for security, and on the tempo of activity in and around the hamlets.

PF were considered to be the primary security forces for about 45 percent of the South Vietnamese population, and the PSDF covered another 30 percent as shown in Table 14.2. The trends show increasing security roles for the police and PSDF as the RF-PF roles in hamlet security declined late in the war.

The increasing security roles of the police and PSDF fit well with the results of Table 14.3 which show a growing percentage of the South Vietnamese population living in areas where government security operations were no longer necessary. The pattern reflects progress in establishing security in the countryside, which allowed the police and PSDF to take over much of the security function, freeing the RF and PF for additional missions.

Table 14.4 further supports the notion of growing self-reliance and movement of the war away from populated areas. It suggests that government forces from the outside operated in the populated areas less and less and made fewer and fewer contacts there until the communist offensive reversed the trend in 1972. Local forces had assumed the security role.

Table 14.5 suggests that few of the local security forces made contact with the communists during the month. It also shows a slight declining trend in the population living where contacts occurred until 1972.

Regional and Popular Forces

The RF and PF were the main territorial troops operating for the government in the countryside but they received a small share of the resources devoted to the war. Both relied heavily on local

TABLE 14.1
South Vietnamese Pacification Forces

End of Year Strength in Thousands

	1965	1966	1967	1968	1969	1970	1971	1972
Regional Forces	132	150	151	220	261	283	284	301
Popular Forces	136	150	149	172	214	251	248	219
Subtotal:	268	300	300	392	475	534	532	520
National Police	52	58	74	79	85	88	114	121
Revolutionary De-velopment Cadre	—	27[e]	37	46	44	37	28	21
Truong Son Cadre	—	6[e]	7	7	7	7	5	2
Total GVN Forces	320	391	418	524	611	666	679	664
People's Self Defense Forces[a]				1481[b]	3219	3489[c]	4429	3829[d]

Source: Table 3, **Southeast Asia Statistical Summary,** Department of Defense, Office of the Assistant Secretary (Comptroller), February 14, 1973
[a]Source: Army Activities Report: Southeast Asia (U), Final Issue (CSDCS-74), December 20, 1972, pp. 45 and 50.
[b]June 1969 figure. No data for 1968.
[c]November 30, 1970 figure.
[d]September 30, 1972 figure.
[e]Source: "Revolutionary Development (RD) Personnel," **Southeast Asia Analysis Report,** July 1967, p. 32.

TABLE 14.2
Which Force is Primarily Responsible
For The Security of This Hamlet?

	Percentage of SVN Population			
	1969 Dec.	1970 Dec.	1971 Dec.	1972 Dec.
Regional Forces	16	12	8	7
Popular Forces	47	48	44	39
National Police	5	9	14	17
People's Self Defense Forces	24	29	33	35

Source: Hamlet Evaluation System (HES) Quarterly Question HQC1.

158

TABLE 14.3
Do GVN Local Security Forces
Conduct Security Operations?

| During the Day? | Percentage of SVN Population | | | |
	1969 Dec.	1970 Dec.	1971 Dec.	1972 Dec.
No	3	1	2	1
Yes	82	79	62	58
Not Needed (No Threat)	13	20	36	40
At Night?				
No	3	1	2	2
Yes	93	93	83	78
Not Needed	2	6	15	19

Source: HES Quarterly Questions HQC-2 and HQC-3. From unpublished computer printouts.

TABLE 14.4
Have GVN Forces From Outside Operated
In This Village During the Month?

| | Percentage of SVN Population | | | |
	1969 Dec.	1970 Dec.	1971 Dec.	1972 Dec.
No	38	62	73	59
Yes	35	24	19	29
Yes - Contact with Communist Forces	24	14	8	11

Source: HES Monthly Question VMC-1.

TABLE 14.5
Have Local Security Force Operations Resulted In
Contact With Communist Forces During the Month?

	Percentage of SVN Population			
	1969 Dec.	1970 Dec.	1971 Dec.	1972 Dec.
No	88	92	94	91
Yes, Once	6	5	4	5
Yes, More than once	4	3	2	3

Source: HES Monthly Question HMC-3, as stated above. From computer printout.

TABLE 14.6
Regional And Popular Forces Increased by 73 Percent

	Troop Strength in Thousands						
Military Region	1966	1967	1968	1969	1970	1971	1972
MR 1	45	46	58	74	82	80	78
MR 2	72	74	95	110	119	121	116
MR 3	68	65	91	109	122	115	118
MR 4	115	115	148	182	211	216	208
SVN Total	300	300	392	475	534	532	520

Source: Table 106, **Southeast Asia Statistical Summary,** Office of the Assistant Secretary of Defense (Comptroller), pp. 1, 3, and 5.

recruiting and normally did not operate outside their own provinces or districts. Some RF troops did fight outside their provinces in 1972, particularly in Military Region 4.

Table 14.6 displays the combined RF and PF strength by military region in South Vietnam. The forces grew by 73 percent between 1966 and 1972. The increase was fairly uniform among the four military regions where gains ranged from 60 to 80 percent.

Regional Forces operated in 100 man companies. The number of RF companies doubled, from 895 to 1823, between January 1968 and December 1972 as shown in Table 14.7. Some of the companies were organized into battalions late in the period but the company remained the basic operating unit and the discussion here focuses on companies.

The RF buildup shows up primarily as more units assigned to hamlet and village security until December 1969, although companies on offensive missions increased too. After 1969 the RF shifted to local offensive operations as the need to use RF and PF for hamlet and village security missions declined.

In December 1969 forty-three percent of the companies were on hamlet or village security missions. This dropped to 24 percent two and one-half years later as the percentage of units on active missions increased from 27 to 50 percent (see Table 14.8). The RF patterns in the four military regions were similar to the countrywide pattern. The period began with 755 RF companies on security missions, compared to 140 on active missions, and ended with approximately 830 companies assigned to each mission.

The PF platoons were 30 man units that operated in specific villages or hamlets. They were doubled between January 1968 and December 1971 and then declined by 606 platoons for a net growth of 80 percent (Table 14.9).

As expected the PF buildup focused on security missions although the platoons on active missions also increased. Platoons on hamlet or village security missions increased from 2,714 in January 1968 to 5,181 in December 1971 and then declined. In December 1969 72 percent of the platoons were on hamlet or village security missions. By June 1972 this had declined to 60 percent. In the same period platoons on active missions increased from seven to 18 percent. Table 14.10 displays the data. The military regions reflect similar movement throughout South Vietnam.

The RF and PF buildups and their gradual shift to more active missions accord well with the HES results, which show the police and the PSDF taking more of the responsibility for hamlet security as time passes. The HES data also reflect the sharp decline in RF responsibility for hamlet security and the much slower decline in the PF role.

Combat Role of the RF and PF

The RF and PF took the brunt of the war more than any other South Vietnamese armed force. They had a higher proportion of combat deaths than the regulars and were the prime targets of communist attacks until 1972.

Their share of combat deaths was higher than their share of the South Vietnamese forces. In 1971 they accounted for 51 percent of the total forces but at least 60 percent of the combat deaths and 60 percent may be too low. The Territorial Forces Effectiveness System (TFES) reports more RF/PF combat deaths than does the Southeast Asia Statistical Summary data used here. The TFES figures raise the RF/PF share of 1972 RVNAF combat deaths to 68 percent.

TABLE 14.7
Regional Force Companies
Doubled in Five Years

	Regional Force Companies					
	1968 Jan.	1968 Dec.	1969 Dec.	1970 Dec.	1971 Dec.	1972 Dec.
MR 1	122	155	212	227	235	252
MR 2	242	293	359	411	412	427
MR 3	219	272	371	407	413	429
MR 4	312	399	529	627	616	715
SVN Total	895	1119	1471	1672	1676	1823

Source: MACV CORDS, Territorial Forces Evaluation System (TFES).
Computer Printouts.

TABLE 14.8
The Regional Forces Buildup Focused
On Hamlet-Village Security First,
And Then Shifted to Active Operations

	Regional Force Companies					
	1968 Jan.	1968 Dec.	1969 Dec.	1970 Dec.	1971 Dec.	1972 June
Missions						
Security:						
Hamlet-Village	319	348	626	560	513	395
Roads & Waterways	127	159	191	167	185	170
Other	309	283	257	252	266	273
Subtotal	755	790	1074	979	964	838
Active:						
Offensive Operations	55	182	280	206	374	448
Reaction Forces	28	57	62	70	130	206
Other	57	90	55	417	208	177
Subtotal	140	329	397	693	712	831
TOTAL	895	1119	1471	1672	1676	1669

Source: MACV-CORDS, TFES Computer printouts.

TABLE 14.9
Popular Force Platoons Doubled
By 1971 and Then Declined

Popular Forces Platoons

	1968 Jan.	1968 Dec.	1969 Dec.	1970 Dec.	1971 Dec.	1972 Dec.
MR 1	708	755	920	1,115	1,218	1,209
MR 2	1,055	1,177	1,311	1,586	1,843	1,752
MR 3	739	851	1,028	1,194	1,266	1,304
MR 4	1,669	1,948	2,413	3,327	3,752	3,208
SVN Total:	4,171	4,31	5,672	7,222	8,079	7,473

Source: MACV-CORDS, TFES computer printouts.

TABLE 14.10
The Popular Force Buildup Focused
On Hamlet and Village Security

Popular Force Platoons

Missions:	1968 Jan.	1968 Dec.	1969 Dec.	1970 Dec.	1971 Dec.	1972 June
Security:						
Hamlet-Village	2,714	3,114	4,079	3,887	5,181	4,695
Roads-Waterways	517	579	548	674	945	1,005
Other	693	684	621	631	786	776
Subtotal	3,924	4,377	5,248	5,192	6,912	6,476
Active:						
Offensive Operations	86	108	141	168	240	366
Reaction Forces	32	43	58	78	134	338
Other	129	203	225	1,784	793	692
Subtotal	247	354	424	2,030	1,167	1,396
TOTAL	4,171	4,731	5,672	7,222	8,079	7,872

Source: MACV-CORDS, TFES computer printouts.

TABLE 14.11
It Was More Dangerous to Serve With The
RF/PF Than with the Regular Forces

Regional and Popular Forces:	1967	1968	1969	1970	1971
As a % of RVNAF Forces[a]	47	48	49	51	51
As a % of RVNAF Combat Deaths[b]	52	47	54	59	60
RF/PF Combat Deaths per 1000 RF/PF Personel Strength[c]	22	29	22	22	25
Regular Force Combat Deaths per 1000 Regular Personnel Strength[c]	18	30	17	16	17

[a]Source: Derived from Table 3, **Southeast Asia Statistical Summary,**
Office of the Assistant Secretary of Defense (Comptroller), February
14, 1973.
[b]Source: Derived from Table 53, **Southeast Asia Statistical Summary,**
Office of the Assistant Secretary of Defense (Comptroller), March 18,
1971, and February 16, 1972, p. 1-5.
[c]Source: Derived from Tables 3 and 53 noted in [a] and [b] above.

TABLE 14.12
RF/PF Took the Brunt of
Communist Initiated Action

	1967	1968	1969	1970	1971	1972
RF/PF % of RVNAF Killed by VC/NVA initiatied actions	60%	55%	55%	66%	65%	45%

Source: Computer File Printout.

The intensity figures of combat deaths per 1,000 troops
show the same relationship. In every year except 1968 the
chances of getting killed in the RF/PF were higher than in the
regular forces (Table 14.11). The gap widened each year from 1969
through 1971. Service in the RF/PF got more dangerous each year
compared to service in the regular forces. One reason for the
widening gap between the regular and territorial forces was that
the territorial forces accounted for an increasing proportion of
the South Vietnamese military personnel killed in communist
attacks. They suffered 55 to 65 percent of all such deaths in
every year except 1972 (Table 14.12).

TABLE 14.13
RF/PF Accounted for About 3Ø Percent
of The Communists Killed By RVNAF

	1967	1968	1969	197Ø	1971	1972
Percent of Communist Combat Deaths Inflicted by RF/PF	N/A	23%[a]	3Ø%	3Ø%	33%	28%

Source: **MACV Measurements of Progress Report,** April 1968 through December 1972.
[a]April through December.

The other question is how well did they inflict casualties on the communist forces. Table 14.13 has the answer. The data suggest that the RF/PF accounted for about 3Ø percent of the communist deaths inflicted by South Vietnamese forces although this figure is probably conservative too. Other figures from TFES imply that a higher percentage of communist combat deaths were inflicted by the RF and PF. In any case, it is clear that the RF and PF forces inflicted a lower percentage of communist casualties than they took, 33 percent inflicted versus 68 percent taken in 1971.

Several factors help to explain the discrepancy. First, the territorial forces operated in rural areas where the communist forces found them more readily available, softer targets than the regular forces. They bore the brunt of communist offensive actions, and the communists enjoyed exceptionally favorable kill ratios in such actions. At one point actions initiated by the communists inflicted 28 percent of the total allied combat deaths, while costing them only five percent of theirs.[1] The RF and PF forces suffered accordingly.

Second, their fights with the communists tended to occur at night, often unexpectedly and far from combat support. Data from Military Region 3 from October 1966 to March 1967 suggest that the RF and PF received outside support in only 45 percent of the attacks and ground reinforcements arrived only 11 percent of the time. When RF/PF offensive operations engaged the communists they received outside help in only 17 percent of the Military Region 3 actions and ground reinforcements in only three percent of them.[2]

With Vietnamization the situation undoubtedly improved, but even as late as 1969 the territorial units were receiving only 3Ø percent of the Vietnamese-fired artillery support and half of that consisted not of support during a contact but of small barrages at suspected communist locations, or preplanned fires against likely communist routes of attack.[3]

Finally, the RF and PF simply had poorer leadership, training and arms than their communist counterparts for much of the war. They could not hold their own without outside support.

The Vietnamization program improved the situation by furnishing M-16 rifles, mortars, radios, training, etc. to every Rf and Pf unit but even this did not redress the imbalance between casualties inflicted and casualties absorbed.

The territorial forces performed well in helping to counter the communist Easter Offensive in 1972. The shift to large scale, main force combat put them in the position of supporting main force units in battle and in many cases they fought communist regular units by themselves. A review of RF and PF operations during April-July 1972 suggests that they made a major contribution to the war effort. The data indicate that they even temporarily redressed the imbalance between casualties taken and casualties inflicted which may mean that they were not surprised as often by the communists and received more combat reinforcement and support. However, this is conjecture. Whatever the case they suffered 28 percent of the South Vietnamese combat deaths and claimed 37 percent of the communist combat deaths.[4] Their kill ratio (communist to South Vietnamese) was two to one, the same as for the regulars. This all suggests that the Vietnamization effort paid off handsomely in the 1972 offensive when the RF and PF apparently fought about as well as the regulars in terms of casualty exchanges.

Adding cost data to the assessment of effectiveness suggests that the RF and PF, dollar for dollar, were the most effective large force in killing communist troops in South Vietnam. The figures indicate that they accounted for 30 percent of the communist combat deaths inflicted by South Vietnamese forces but received less than 20 percent of the South Vietnamese program budget costs. More startling, the territorial forces accounted for 12 to 30 percent of all communist combat deaths, depending on the year, but for only two to four percent of the total program budget costs of the war as shown in Table 14.14.

These are macabre calculations because they purport to equate dollars and deaths which is nonsense. They do, however, point out the incredibly unbalanced allocation of resources within the allied war effort. The attrition objective alone would seem to have called for more resources and emphasis to the territorial forces. If 30 percent of the communist casualties can be attained for only four percent of the resources, what might have happened if the allies had allocated ten percent of the resources to the territorial forces? The potential effects might have been significant. And their role in establishing territorial security has not even been put into the calculations yet.

As stated above, the primary mission of the territorial forces was to protect and secure the population, particularly in the rural areas. The HES data suggest that about half of the population relied on the RF and PF for the security of their hamlets (Table 14.2). Chapter 17 indicates that these forces killed or captured more of the communist clandestine infrastructure than any other force.

TABLE 14.14
RF/PF Account For Up To 30 Percent of the Communist
Combat Deaths For Four Percent of the Total War Costs

RF AND PF	1969	1970	1971
Percentage of Total Communist Combat Deaths[a]	12	20	30
Percentage of Total Program Budget Cost[b]	2	3	4

[a]Source: **MACV Measurements of Progress Reports,** January 1969-December 1971.
[b]Source: "Where The Money Went," **Southeast Asia Analysis Report,** August-October 1971, pp. 32-34.

There is no doubt that the RF and PF contributed to the increasing security of the countryside discussed in Chapter 13. It is tempting to give them all of the credit for the gains but that is probably not the case because the situation is more complex than that. Many other forces and programs participated in the pacification effort and surely had some effect. Nonetheless, it is interesting to note that the RF and PF increased 58 percent during 1968-1969 while the secure population (A and B) increased 74 percent. Most of the gain in security came in 1969 and 1970 after most of the force buildup was complete.

Comparing the growth of the territorial forces with progress of the HES Rural Control Indicator in 1970-71 yields the interesting statistic that about 60 rural inhabitants came under government control for each territorial soldier added during the period.[5] From mid-1969 to mid-1970 the increase of 807 new units in Military Region 4 closely parallels the pacification gain of 801 hamlets in the A and B security range.[6]

However, relying on the foregoing data to make the case for RF and PF can be misleading because the analysis of the period from April to September 1968 yields the dismaying findings (for territorial force boosters) that the security ratings of the population not protected by these forces improved about as often as the population they protected (11 percent of the unprotected population increased, compared to 12 percent of the protected).[7] This clearly suggests that other factors were also working to improve population security ratings.

The same analysis indicated that RF and PF working together had the best effect on HES scores, followed by PF operating alone. The RF alone tended to be associated with security regressions except in Military Region 4 where the territorials were the primary South Vietnamese combat forces.[8] The findings are reasonable. The Regional Forces were considered to be a flexible, mobile force which could take part in large unit operations with regular forces, replace army battalions in providing territorial security and provide a security umbrella for PF, RD Cadre, PSDF and other government personnel tied down to hamlets.

The territorial forces working together provided mobile and static defense and they could be expected to have a favorable impact on HES scores. About 80 percent of the PF units were recruited primarily from their own or adjacent villages so they could not appear on the scene until the RF and regulars had established enough security in the area to allow the government to recruit the PF. Logically then, one could expect to find improving security where they appear. On the other hand, RF units were the mobile units that were supposed to show up in trouble spots to counter communist actions which dragged down the HES scores.

The results of public opinion surveys in South Vietnam suggest the people were more impressed with RF performance than with PF performance and equated it with the regular army performance. Forty percent thought the PF were effective and 70 percent thought the RF were effective. Seventy percent of another sample thought the regular army was effective.[9] The Regional Forces seemed to rate as well with the rural population as the regular army.

It seems clear that the territorial forces by their combat performance and their permanent presence in the countryside had a profound and perhaps decisive effect on improving the security of the rural population. Yet they consumed less than five percent of the total costs of the war. There can be little question that the RF and PF were the most cost-effective military forces employed on the allied side. However they were consistently neglected by both South Vietnam and the United States until the big pacification effort began in 1967-1968.

The Paramilitary Forces

The paramilitary forces discussed here are the National Police, the RD Cadre, Truong Son Cadre and the People's Self Defense Forces (PSDF). These forces were not expected to seek combat with the communist forces but they took a significant number of casualties while inflicting some on the communists. From 1968 through 1972 about 10,000 paramilitary personnel were killed in action.[10] They were credited with about 2,500 communist combat deaths which indicates the disadvantage they suffered in fights with those forces.[11]

The National Police

The National Police of South Vietnam performed normal police functions throughout the country, particularly in the cities and towns. In addition, the Field Police and Special Police (an intelligence collection branch) had special roles to play in

the South Vietnamese war effort. Their primary mission was
supposed to be the anti-VC Infrastructure (VCI) campaign.[12]
Their performance in this task is discussed later in Chapter 17.
It was not very good but they did manage to account for 20 percent
of the VCI neutralized in 1970.[13] Table 14.1 shows that the
strength of the National Police increased from 52,000 in 1965 to
121,000 in December 1972, a gain of 130 percent. The National
Police had three components, Regular Police, Field Police, and
Special Police. The Field and Special Police made up about 30
percent of the police strength from 1969 onward.

Until 1969 the National Police were most active in the secure
areas where the population density was highest and they
concentrated on providing the services of a civil police body.
Below the provincial level, police operations were centered in
district towns. As security increased in the rural areas during
1969 the police expanded their operations from coverage of the
district towns downward into villages, and at the end of 1969 more
than 6,000 uniformed police were assigned to 1,621 villages.[14]
From then on much of the police expansion went into the rural
areas.

The HES data support the notion of the police moving into the
countryside. In December 1969 about 65 percent of the population
lived in villages that had police substations within the village.
Three years later the figure was 95 percent.[15] As already seen in
Table 14.2, the National Police were the force primarily
responsible for the security of 17 percent of South Vietnam's
population by December 1972.

In the villages the police were charged with registering the
village population (issuing identification cards, establishing
family books, census of village residents, etc.). In December 1969
the HES reported that these measures were complete and up to date
for 40 percent of the total South Vietnamese population. Three
years later the figure was 89 percent.[16]

The villagers were not impressed with the performance of
the police. Only 30 percent thought they were effective in
maintaining order.[17] Only 19 percent through they were effective
in upholding the law.[18] On the other hand, 71 percent of the
villagers thought that the National Police acted fairly and justly
with the people of the community all or most of the time. Twenty
percent thought they didn't.[19] This runs counter to the
stereotype of the South Vietnamese police held in the United
States. But the sample was large (7,201 people) and the question
was asked in eight different months so the stereotype may be
overdrawn. The data suggest that the police were considered to
be inept but tolerably fair.

Most observers would probably agree that the police weren't
as effective as they needed to be. They didn't receive much in the
way of government attention or resources until late in the war
partly because military mobilization absorbed all of the available
manpower. As security spread into the countryside the
government finally turned its attention to the police,
transferring army personnel to the force and initiating other
measures to improve its capability.

Revolutionary Development Cadre

The 59-man Revolotionary Development Cadre (RD Cadre) teams began in 1965 in Binh Dinh Province. RD Cadre teams became the cutting edge of the Ministry of Revolutionary Development which was created in 1965. The structure of the 59 man team was a defense platoon of 34 men, with the rest in small civic action teams. A team would go into a rural village and spend some time working with the people attempting to gain their support for the government through a variety of civic action projects and then move on to another village. Later, beginning with the Accelerated Pacification Campaign of late 1968 when army battalions and the territorial forces were providing more security for pacification, each team was split into two 30 man civic-action teams which were assigned to villages on a semi-permanent basis.

The effectiveness of the RD Cadre and Truong Son Cadre is implied by the extent of communist efforts against them. The cadres were designed to help the people and to counter the operations of the communist cadres operating in the hamlets and villages. The communists immediately recognized the significance of the new group. Intelligence reports signified their intent to attack RD Cadre teams which began taking casualties soon after they started operating in 1966 when they lost almost 700 killed and captured.[20] By 1967-1968 the cadre were being killed and were deserting at higher rates than the South Vietnamese military forces. Losses of the RD Cadre for the first half of 1968 were at an annual rate of 26 percent.[21]

As pacification succeeded and fewer new hamlets needed the cadre treatment they were phased down from a peak of 53,000 in 1968 to 23,000 by the end of 1972.

The People's Self Defense Forces

The People's Self Defense Forces (PSDF) were created in 1968 as civilian forces organized into combat and support forces ostensibly for local defense and as a supplement to the territorial forces. Major purposes were to commit as many people as possible to the government and to soak up manpower so as to deny it to the communist recruiters. Membership in the support forces was voluntary and all citizens seven years of age or older could join. Support forces consisted of three groups: youth, women and elders. Although support members were theoretically trained in first aid, medical evacuation, etc., a key purpose was to commit a large bloc of the population to the government.[22]

The combat forces consisted of male citizens of ages 16 and 17 and those between 38 and 50 who were required by the National Mobilization Law to serve in the Combat PSDF. This encompassed all the non-draft age men up to the age of 50. Able-bodied women and elders over 50 could volunteer to serve in the combat forces.[23] Included in the combat forces were key interteam members who were organized into 35 man teams with each man being armed.

TABLE 14.15
The People's Self Defense Forces

	Personnel Strength in Thousands			
COMBAT	1969	1970	1971	1972
Inter Team Members				
Organized		447	498	460
Trained		372	486	435
Other Combat				
Organized		731	895	543
Trained		671	837	324
Armed		380	593	558
Support				
Organized		2,311	3,036	2,826
Trained		1,597	2,508·	N/A
TOTAL				
Organized	3,219	3,489	4,429	3,829
Trained	1,898	2,640	3,831	N/A
Armed	400	380	593	558

Source: **Army Activities Report: Southeast Asia** – Final Issue
(SDCS-74, December 20, 1972, p. 51.

Combat PSDF in general were supposed to receive about one weapon
for each five persons. The key interteams were called KIT's.
Their leaders and members were supposed to receive training over
and above that given to general Combat PSDF and several members
from each KIT attended a 4-week leader course.[24]

Table 14.15 shows the size and status of the various
segments of the force. The figures are notoriously unreliable,
but they do serve to indicate the magnitude of the program which
claimed to have armed more than 500,000 people with M-1 rifles,
Browning Automatic Rifles, M-1 and M-2 carbines and a few
shotguns.[25]

It seems clear from Table 14.15 that the PSDF KIT's did
replace some PF units as the force primarily responsible for the
security of certain hamlets with high security ratings.[26]
Coverage of the population by the PF dropped from 47 percent to 39
percent. By December 1972 more than 90 percent of the population
reportedly lived in hamlets where the PSDF were standing armed
guard (20 percent) or were conducting armed patrols within the
hamlets (73 percent).[27]

When asked if they took part in PSDF activities, 66 percent of the rural PAAS respondents said no.[28] When asked why, they gave sex and age as the reason for not participating which suggests they may not have been aware of the requirements for joining the PSDF.[29] However, 22 percent of the respondents said they had been issued weapons and stood guard in the hamlet. Asked about the performance of the PSDF 49 percent of the respondents rated them effective.[30] This was a better rating than the PF received.

The territorial forces were the unsung heroes of the war. If they and the paramilitary forces had received sufficient support from the beginning the results probably would have been quite interesting and helpful to the South Vietnamese cause. If the government had designed and implemented a program of rotating regular soldiers out of the army after a fixed tour of duty (they served forever) and letting them serve in territorial units near their homes, the development of a fully effective territorial army might have been possible, particularly if the appointment of territorial force leaders could have remained independent of politics and adequate training and combat support were provided.

NOTES

1. "Enemy Initiated Activity Against Vietnamese Armed Forces," **Analysis Report,** (July 1968) p. 3.
2. "The Plight of the Vietnamese Popular Forces," **Analysis Report,** (July 1968), p. 21.
3. Artillery Support for RVNAF," **Analysis Report,** (May-April 1970), p. 20.
4. "Territorials and the Offensive," Paper by the Office of the Assistant Secretary of Defense (Systems Analysis) Regional Programs, December 8, 1972, p. 1.
5. Calculated on the basis of present-for-duty strength in territorial forces combat units, not the authorized strengths shown elsewhere in this chapter.
6. "Military Region IV," **Analysis Report,** (November-December 1970), p. 38.
7. "RF/PF and Territorial Security in Viet-Nam," **Analysis Report,** (February 1969), p. 1.
8. **Ibid.**
9. PAAS Rural Question 54 asked of a total of 1969 respondents during July and August 1972.
10. Table 2, **Southeast Asia Statistical Summary,** Office of the Assistant Secretary of Defense (Comptroller), (April 11, 1973), pp. 1-5.
11. **MACV Measurements of Progress Reports,** Monthly (April 1968 through December 1972).
12. "National Police," **Analysis Report,** (March 1970), p. 4.
13. "Phoenix," **Analysis Report,** (June-July 1971), p. 5.

172

14. "National Police," **Analysis Report,** (March 1970), p. 4.

15. HES Question VQD-1.

16. HES Question VQD-4.

17. PAAS Rural Question 65, asked in January, June and July 1972. Cumulative sample was 2766 respondents.

18. PAAS Rural Question 66 asked in January 1972 of 926 correspondents.

19. PAAS Rural Question 35, asked in March, April, May, June and July 1971, and in January, June and July 1972. Cumulative sample was 7201 respondents.

20. "Revolutionary Development Highlights - From RD Report," **Analysis Report,** (April 1967), p. 37.

21. "RD Cadre Attrition: A Correction," **Analysis Report,** (October 1968), p. 39.

22. **Army Activities Report: Southeast Asia** - Final Issue, December 20, 1972, p. 50.

23. **Ibid.**

24. **Ibid.,** p.51

25. **Ibid.**

26. "The Situation in MR4," **Analysis Report,** (June-July 1971), p. 33.

27. HES Question HQC-7.

28. PAAS Rural Question 58 asked in January, March, June and July 1972. Cumulative sample was 3429 repondents.

29. PAAS Rural Question 59 asked in January, March, June and July 1972. Cumulative sample was 2376 respondents.

30. PAAS Rural Question 61 asked in January, March, June and July 1972. Cumulative sample was 3441 respondents.

15
Vietnamese Popular Attitudes

> The Vietnamese peasant was not an idiot.
> He knew exactly what the war was about.[1]

Sir Robert Thompson

Extensive efforts were made to discern popular attitudes in a war that was regarded as being fought for the people's support. Again, it was the American pacification advisors who took the lead with monthly opinion polls from late 1969 onward.

Three sets of Vietnamese public opinion surveys are analyzed here. The first set consists of two surveys by the Joint U.S. Public Affairs Office (JUSPAO) in South Vietnam from October through December 1965. The second survey was done for CBS by the Opinion Research Corporation a year later (November 1966 to February 1967). The third and most important set of surveys is the Pacification Attitude Analysis System (PAAS), a monthly survey started during the fourth quarter of 1969. The JUSPAO and CBS polls are summarized briefly below. Some general findings from the PAAS are also discussed but specific results dealing with security, land reform, economics, etc., appear where those topics are discussed.

The JUSPAO surveys were not taken as carefully as the CBS survey.[2] Interviewers could select their respondents at will in many cases. Age, sex and religious distributions were distorted and the lower economic classes were over-represented. Similar problems appear in the PAAS but in both cases the results are interesting and useful.

The JUSPAO surveys suggest that the average Vietnamese in 1965 considered personal economic problems to be his primary concern. Forty-two percent of a Saigon sample of 410 people cited the high cost of living or personal finances as the most important problem they faced. In a combined urban-rural sample (1,141 people), 41 percent were dissatisfied with life. Most of them cited the cost of living and family finances as the source of dissatisfaction.

The one wish for life cited most often by 35 percent of all respondents was for better working conditions and a lower cost of living. A desire for greater government responsiveness to their

173

needs was the next most frequent with (29 percent), followed by a wish for peace and unity (20 percent). The Vietnamese in late 1965 were engrossed in their personal economic problems. Only six percent considered the war to be of primary concern.

The CBS survey covered 436 Saigon residents, 132 residents of smaller cities and 745 people in 11 provinces, all in secure areas.[3] The survey under-represented males of military age and farmers, but had the virtue of being conducted without the knowledge of American or South Vietnamese officials. It used rigid statistical sampling techniques to ensure a representative sample of all age categories and social strata.

The CBS survey confirms that economic goals ranked very high in Vietnamese personal aspirations. A majority (64 percent) of the 1,413 respondents chose better employment, income or cost of living conditions as their first wish for self or family. They cited economic factors (cost of living, unemployment, income opportunities, family finances) most frequently as the main causes for improvement or deterioration in their lives during the past year.

For their country the Vietnamese ·respondents overwhelmingly desired peace and security as their first wish (84 percent). Victory, independence and freedom drew a response of only nine percent. In answer to the question "What should the American forces do in the South?" the Vietnamese responded as shown in Table 15.1. When asked whether the Americans should devote more attention to negotiating with North Vietnam or fighting, 63 percent opted for more negotiations. Only 15 percent chose more military action and 22 percent had no opinion.

The Pacification Attitude Analysis System (PAAS)

The PAAS attempted to portray urban and rural South Vietnamese attitudes toward security, politics and economic development. It was developed by the U.S. Pacification Studies Group in Saigon and by the Central Pacification and Development Council of the GVN with the help of U.S. contract survey experts. Monthly PAAS results began with October 1969 for the rural population and with March 1971 for the urban population. The surveys portrayed trends or shifts in opinion and reactions to specific events. To indicate trends the same questions were asked at reasonable intervals. Special questions were asked to elicit reactions to specific events. As the system matured special questions became the rule and the trends are difficult to follow.

The surveys were based on semi-structured interviews conducted by trained Vietnamese interviewers who worked for American pacification advisors not the GVN. A typical rural survey covered 30 to 35 provinces. Three-man teams (three teams per province) were assigned to a specific hamlet for interviews. The cadre memorized the survey questions before entering the hamlet and selected their respondents according to pre-established criteria. The questions were asked indirectly in the course of a conversation and the replies were coded in

TABLE 15.1
What Should The American Forces Do In The South?

Go On Fighting	39%
Stop Fighting, stay as advisors	21%
Stop fighting, go home	10%
No Opinion	30%

Source: CBS Survey (November 1966-February 1967).

predetermined categories immediately afterward. The same procedure was followed in the urban interviews which concentrated on the 13 autonomous cities.

Any systematic effort to portray attitudes and beliefs is subject to error and conditions in South Vietnam further limited the accuracy. The limitations of PAAS outlined below need to be kept in mind when reviewing the PAAS data presented here and elsewhere but it was the only regular polling done in South Vietnam other than elections and was quite useful in providing indications of Vietnamese public opinion. In August 1970 for example, answers to the question "What tickets will win in the Senate election?" called the first three winning tickets in exact order.[4]

Two limitations of the PAAS should be kept in mind when viewing the results. They stem from the way in which the data were collected and from deficiencies in the sampling techniques used.

Semi-structured interviews which sought opinions indirectly during conversation instead of posing direct, precise questions were probably the only realistic means to obtain a frank response from the Vietnamese at any time, let alone in the middle of a war. Unfortunately the technique could not avoid introducing the bias of the questioner into the results because PAAS actually presents what the interviewer thought the respondent meant in response to a line of conversation developed by the interviewer. The PAAS did not record a respondent's clear-cut answer to a direct, precisely stated question. It therefore differs from some public opinion polls conducted in the United States and the results must be viewed as being much less precise.

Interview training can minimize interview bias and the training was careful and rigorous but could not completely eliminate the interviewer's tendency to interject his own beliefs and opinions into the way he phrased the question and interpreted the response. Additionally, most respondents were probably reluctant to be completely candid on all subjects surveyed (the results on payment of taxes bear this out). The questioners were not formally identified as South Vietnamese agents and they employed a wide range of covers designed to allay suspicion. But they could not help being viewed as strangers by respondents who probably often associated the questioner with the government because of his conversational interests. Respondents undoubtedly considered these factors in responding. This limited the accuracy of the survey.

Quota rather than probability sampling techniques were used to select the hamlets and the individual respondents, so the sample from which interviews were drawn was not necessarily an accurate representation of the South Vietnamese population. The rural PAAS tended to over-represent the attitudes of C hamlet populations in 1970. In October 1970 C hamlets accounted for only 18 percent of the rural population but for 37 percent of the rural respondents to PAAS. Women represented only 30 to 40 percent of the respondents and no civilian authorities or paid members of a military organization were interviewed.

The second difficulty with the sample was its size. As many at 3,000 respondents were interviewed in a given month, but in most cases each respondent was asked only one-third of the questions involved in the three-part interview. In effect only about 30 people in a given province answered a given question in the monthly rural PAAS. A different sample was supposed to be used each month but even so the limitations were probably significant.

Despite its limitations the PAAS was a useful system and provided considerable insight into the situation in South Vietnam. Insight that probably could not have been gained in any other way.

PAAS Results

A few themes from the PAAS 1970-1972 are explored here.[5] These include surveys of the people's views about their problems and aspirations, security, the media, government performance, the war and the Americans. Other themes such as inflation, land reform, performance of allied forces, the Chieu Hoi Program, etc., are addressed in the chapters devoted to those subjects.

During every month in 1970 and in February 1971, the PAAS teams asked rural respondents, "What are your aspirations for the future?" Altogether about 15,000 people responded as shown in Table 15.2. About 75 percent of the respondents expressed a desire for peace or security as their first aspiration, with the monthly percentages ranging from 73 to 85 percent. These results agree well with those of the CBS poll taken four years earlier, when 84 percent expressed an aspiration for peace and security.

The proportion aspiring to peace jumped to about 60 percent after the allied peace initiative in October 1970 with most of the gain coming out of the aspiration for security. Awareness of the peace initiative was high. In the November 1970 survey 79 percent of the rural respondents said they were aware that a new proposal had been made. A special survey conducted in provincial capitals, areas of greater exposure to national news media, indicated that 97 percent knew about the initiative. The high

TABLE 15.2
What Are Your Aspirations For the Future?

Peace for Vietnam	49%
Security in the Countryside	27%
Stabilization and normalization of social standards	12%
Better economic life	11%
Number of respondents	15,000

Source: PAAS Rural Question 55 from PAAS Published Reports for 1970 and February 1971.

rates of awareness reflect the extensive publicity that accompanied the proposal in South Vietnam and the strong desire for peace.

An urban survey in October 1971 suggested that aspirations of the city dwellers were less concerned about security than those of the rural respondents, and were more concerned about social standards and a better economic life.[6] The pattern reflects the insulation of city dwellers from the security problems of the war and it seems reasonable.

In 1971 and 1972 rural and urban respondents were asked "What do you consider the most important problem facing the country at this time?" Table 15.3 again shows a difference between the rural and urban attitudes. Sixty-eight percent of the rural respondents considered peace and security the most important problem, while 59 percent of the urban dwellers agreed. Only 13 percent of the rural respondents considered economic problems the most important in comparison to 20 percent of the urban dwellers. But the similarity regarding the war was perhaps most significant. Few urban (11 percent) and rural (13 percent) respondents thought fighting harder against the communists was the main problem. This was comparable to the CBS response of only nine percent who aspired to victory, independence and freedom rather than peace and security.

Throughout 1970 PAAS rural surveys asked "What is the most severe problem facing you?" The cumulative answer is shown in Table 15.4. Increased prices and financial problems were considered the worst problems by more than half of the respondents. The trend during the year was upward from 48 percent in the second quarter of 1970 to 64 percent in the fourth quarter of 1970.

The percentage who considered security their worst problem stayed fairly constant at about 24 percent throughout 1970. This percentage is about the same as the 27 percent who aspired to security for Vietnam during the same period. Taken together they suggest that at least 25 percent of the South Vietnamese

TABLE 15.3
What Do You Consider the Most Important
Problem Facing The Country at This Time?

	Rural[a]	Urban[b]
Peace--End the war as soon as possible	52%	45%
Security	16%	14%
Fight the VC harder	13%	11%
Economic	13%	20%
Number of respondents	3,781	3,183

[a]Source: PAAS Rural Question Number 135 asked in June 1971 and June, July and August 1972.
[b]PAAS Urban Question Number 5038 asked in March, June, July 1971 and June, July and August 1972.

TABLE 15.4
What Is the Most Severe Problem Facing You?

Increased prices and financial problems	56%
Security	24%
Other	20%
Number of Respondents	27,483

Source: PAAS published reports for 1970.

population in the rural areas lived under insecure conditions during 1970.   According to HES 75 percent of the population were rated secure (A and B) in December 1970 so there is some convergence of PAAS and HES here.   In January 1972 when 922 rural respondents were asked "What is the most severe rural problem?" 25 percent answered "security."   The urban form of insecurity seemed to be theft.   When asked "what is the most severe urban problem?" twenty-nine percent of the urban respondents answered "theft."   The range of responses is shown in Table 15.5
From the beginning of PAAS in late 1969 respondents were frequently asked to compare the state of security this month with security last month.   The results at the end and middle of each year are shown in Table 15.6.   The only pronounced trend seems to

TABLE 15.5
Rural and Urban Problems

What is The Most Severe Rural Problem?[a]

None	18%
Security	25%
Lack of Means (12%) or money (5%) to grow crops	17%
Lack of essential goods or their very high prices	17%
Number of Respondents	922

What is The Most Severe Urban Problem?[b]

Theft	29%
Crowded conditions, lack of housing	14%
Inadequate garbage collection, water and electricity	14%
Flooding in slum areas	13%
Traffic	10%
Poor social environment for raising children	9%
Number of respondents	3,054

---

[a]Source: PAAS Rural Question 467 asked in January 1972.
[b]PAAS Urban Question 5101 asked in March, April, May, June, July and October 1971, and in September 1972.

TABLE 15.6
How Does Security Compare With Last Month?

	Percentage of Respondents						
	1969 Dec.	1970 June	1970 Dec.	1971 June	1971 Jan.	1972 June	1972 Dec.
Better	35	33	45	22	30	14	25
Worse	15	20	6	11	9	16	9
Same	48	47	48	67	59	69	63
Number of Rural Respondents	N/A	N/A	104	936	930	898	1,343

Source: PAAS Rural Question 32.

be a one time shift of opinion from the "security is better" category to the "security is the same" category in June 1971. This can be interpreted to suggest that the security situation had stabilized by then in the eyes of most of the rural population. The urban surveys tended to support this because the respondents in the cities were more secure to begin with and 85 percent of them indicated security was the same this month as last month.[7]

The other pattern of interest suggests that the rural Vietnamese clearly felt the war cycle described in Chapter 2. The "better" ratings were always higher in December and January than in June. Each year the "worse" ratings were highest in June, the month when the communist winter-spring offensive was finally coming to an end. The same pattern held for the urban respondents.[8]

Radio, newspapers for city dwellers, and local officials were the predominant sources of news and information about international, national and local affairs according to PAAS.

Three rural surveys asked 2,846 respondents whether they owned a radio and one survey (895 respondents) also asked if they had access to one.[9] Fifty-one percent of the rural respondents said they owned a radio, seven percent said they had regular access to one and 20 percent had infrequent access. Only 22 percent had no radio or no access to one.

In the urban areas 76 percent of the respondents said they owned a radio in each of the two surveys taken.[10] The question of access was posed to 687 respondents in the second urban survey. Ten percent had regular access to a radio, five percent had infrequent access and nine percent had no access to a radio. Thus, 86 percent of the urban respondents either owned or had regular access to a radio.

Urban respondents also read newspapers. A survey of 269 respondents in March 1972 revealed that 40 percent read newspapers frequently, 31 percent read them, but seldom, and 29 percent did not read them at all.[11] The sample was small but the results probably were roughly correct because newspapers remained a contentious issue in Vietnam and were for sale everywhere in Saigon.

The South Vietnamese people were being reached by modern methods of communication. Table 15.7 shows that 49 percent of the rural respondents received their national and international news from radio. The city dwellers got their national and international news from radio (28 percent) and the newspapers (31 percent). The prime source of local news was local officials (rural, 34 percent; urban, 43 percent).

More Vietnamese in the rural areas than in the cities seemed to expect the government to assume more responsibility for their well-being. When asked if the people had the responsibility of helping the government keep the communists out of their hamlet, 24 percent of the rural and 11 percent of the urban respondents answered "no." (Table 15.8)

The same tendency showed up in response to the question "Whose responsibility is it to improve community life?" More

TABLE 15.7
How Do You Get Information About
National, International and Local Affairs?

	Percentage of Respondents			
	National/International		Local/Provincial	
Source	Rural	Urban	Rural	Urban
Radio	49	28	19	18
Television	3	13	a	7
Newspapers	6	31	5	4
Local Officials	16	3	34	43
Friends and Neighbors	12	8	21	13
Don't know or				
Don't care	13	18	11	10
Number of respondents	4,904	599	4,904	599

Sources: PAAS rural surveys taken in March, July, October, December 1970; and February 1971 (Questions 46 and 47). PAAS Urban survey January 1972; Questions 5269 and 5270.
[a]TV was not a response for local/provincial affairs in the rural surveys.

TABLE 15.8
Do The People Have the Responsibility of Helping the
Government Keep the VC Out of Their Hamlet?

	Rural[a]	Urban[b]
No	24%	11%
Yes	71%	83%
Number of respondents	11,190	1,989

[a]"What the Vietnamese Peasant Thinks," **Southeast Asia Analysis Report,** January–February 1971, p. 21. Includes data for all of 1970.
[b]PAAS Urban Question 5065, March, June and July 1972.

rural people expected the government to shoulder the responsibility (see Table 15.9).

Country and city respondents felt about the same when asked about the performance of the national government although a higher percentage of urban respondents thought government performance was inadequate (15 percent urban to eight percent rural) as shown in Table 15.10. The differences between the two stem largely from the fewer urban responses in the "don't know" category (nine percent urban versus 20 percent rural).

In both the country and cities the number of people who thought the government was performing fairly well outnumbered those who though it was only adequate or inadequate. This could stem from a reluctance to criticize the national government. Nonetheless, a significant number of people did not hesitate to label the government as inadequate. The respondents did not hesitate to express their dissatisfaction with the performance of their local provincial or city council although the number of "don't know" responses was large (see Table 15.11).

The War

Four PAAS questions were designed to solicit the Vietnamese people's view of the war. They asked how and when the war would end, why the communists continued to fight, and if the respondent wanted a cease fire. The "how, when and why" questions drew many "don't know" responses, people only seemed to have clear opinions on a cease fire.

Rural responses about how the war would end are shown in Table 15.12. Urban responses are not available. The big shift of views came in 1972 when the percentage expecting South Vietnamese victory dropped sharply with most of the drop showing up in the "don't know" category and some going into "Paris talks." The 1972 surveys were taken in June and July and the results suggest that the communist offensive had taken its toll of hopes for a South Vietnamese victory.

The communist victory choice drew little or no response, but this notion may have entered into some of the "don't know" responses. There is no way to tell if this was the case. The trends may be more reliable than some others from the PAAS because it is possible to compare two sets of identical months with similar sample sizes and the "don't know" responses did not change much over time. Rural and urban data are available for both samples. The data suggest that in 1971 few people expected the war to end within a year (eight percent rural and 11 percent urban), but many changed to a more optimistic view in 1972 (rural 29 percent, urban 40 percent) as shown in Table 15.13. The shift came from those who had expected the war to last longer because the "don't knows" changed little.

When asked why the communists continued to fight, the most frequent response (37 and 53 percent) cited the influence of North Vietnam and other foreign powers. A few mentioned the communist inability to accomplish their goal. Table 15.14 displays the data.

Did the South Vietnamese people want a cease fire? The PAAS data answered with a resounding "yes." The "don't knows" all disappeared as the people answered with some variation of "yes."

TABLE 15.9
Whose Responsibility Is It To Improve Community Life?

	Rural	Urban
The Government	36%	24%
The People	7%	6%
Both	52%	61%
Number of respondents	898	700

Source: PAAS Rural Question 129 and Urban Question 5129, both asked in June 1972.

TABLE 15.10
How Well Does the Government Perform?

	Rural	Urban
As well as can be expected under the circumstances	41%	45%
Adequate	30%	29%
Inadequate	8%	15%
Number of respondents	4,209	2,865

Source: PAAS Rural Question 243 and Urban Question 5243, both asked in June, July, August and December 1972.

TABLE 15.11
How Well Does Your Provincial (City) Council Perform?

	Rural	Urban
As well as can be expected under the circumstances	6%	4%
Adequate	17%	16%
Inadequate or Incapable	36%	46%
Does not know	40%	30%
Number of respondents	4,414	2,063

Sources: PAAS Rural Question 201 and PAAS Urban Question 5202; both asked in March, April, May and June 1971 and in May 1972.

TABLE 15.12
How Will the War End?

	Percentage of Respondents		
Rural	1970	1971	1972
GVN Victory	28	32	12
Paris Talks	16	15	21
Don't Know	18	23	48
Number of rural respondents	11,149	1,968	1,744

Source: 1970 data are from "What the Vietnamese Peasant thinks," **Southeast Asia Analysis Report,** January-February 1971, p. 18. 1971-1972 data are from PAAS Rural Question 266 asked in February and May 1971 and in June and July 1972.

TABLE 15.13
When Will The War End?

	Percentage of Respondents			
	Rural		Urban	
	1971	1972	1971	1972
Within 6 months	1	13	5	18
Within One year	7	16	6	22
Subtotal	8	29	11	40
Within 1-2 years	16	7	11	9
Will go on indefinitely[a]	22	9	39	14
Don't know	53	55	35	37
Number of respondents	2,736	2,693	1,192	1,895

Source: PAAS Urban Question 5214 and PAAS Rural Question 213 for May, June and July in 1971 and in 1972.
[a]Includes within 2-4 years and within 4-8 years responses.

Table 15.15 shows the results. The cease fire pattern fits well with the answers to questions about the people's aspirations over the years in which peace and security consistently accounted for 75 to 85 percent of the responses.

TABLE 15.14
Why Do The VC/NVA Continue to Fight?

	Percentage of Respondents		
	Rural		Urban
	1970	1972	1972
Influence of North Vietnam	38	24	30
Influence of other foreign			
powers	6	13	23
Subtotal	44	37	53
Believe their cause is just	6	10	7
Haven't accomplished their			
goal	11	18	18
Don't know or won't respond	34	31	22
Number of respondents	1,806	1,852	1,384

Source: PAAS Rural Question 56 in June and July 1970, plus Question 244 in June and July 1972. PAAS Urban Question 5244 in June and July 1972.

TABLE 15.15
Do You Want A Ceasefire?

	Rural	Urban
Yes, under any circumstances	16%	14%
Yes, if no GVN Territory is lost	72%	74%
Yes, if I don't have to live		
under VC/NVA control	1%	1%
Number of respondents	1,843	2,182

Source: PAAS Rural Question 26 asked in June and July 1972, and PAAS Urban Question 5263 asked in June, July and October 1972.

The Americans

During the first half of 1971 the urban and rural surveys asked questions about the Vietnamese attitudes toward Americans and relations with them. One finding that emerged from all of the questions was that the rural population held Americans in higher regard than did the urban population. This may be partly due to American backed pacification programs that were focused primarily in rural areas with U.S. pacification advisory teams in every district and province.

Table 15.16 indicates that 18 percent of the rural population thought anti-American feeling existed in their communities and most of that feeling was thought to be limited to a very few people. The urban response was 33 percent. In both cases, though, more than half of the respondents thought there was no perceptible anti-American feeling in their communities.

In March and May 1971 the PAAS conducted a special survey asking about the Vietnamese view of Americans and the relations between the two. Again, the rural respondents had a more favorable view of the Americans. Table 15.17 indicates that 60 percent of the rural respondents felt the American presence had been beneficial to the people of South Vietnam. Forty-six percent of the urban respondents thought so, too. These percentages agree well with those who felt that no anti-American feeling existed in their communities (62 percent and 51 percent in Table 15.16)

TABLE 15.16
Is There Anti-American Feeling In Your Community?

	Rural	Urban
Yes	5%	10%
Yes, but only among a very few people	13%	23%
Subtotal – Yes	18%	33%
No	62%	51%
Does not know	18%	16%
Number of respondents	4,463	1,975

Sources: PAAS Rural Question 219 and PAAS Urban Question 520, both asked in March, April, May, June and July 1971.

TABLE 15.17
Has The Presence of the Americans Been
Beneficial To The People of Vietnam?

	Rural	Urban
Greatly	36%	13%
To some extent	24%	33%
Subtotal-Beneficial	60%	46%
Scarcely	19%	30%
No benefit, No harm	11%	11%
Bad Effect	2%	5%
Number of respondents	1,732	774

Source: PAAS Rural Question 214 and PAAS Urban Question 5215 asked in March and April 1971.

In Table 15.18 thirty-seven percent of the rural respondents said they liked Americans but only 12 percent of the urban respondents said they did. More than half of all respondents said they did not like Americans but they didn't hate them either. A few hated them. The size of the two groups who like Americans corresponds closely to those who thought that the American presence was greatly beneficial and the other categories match fairly well also.

TABLE 15.18
Whether Or Not you Think The Americans Have Helped
Vietnam, Do You Like Them Personally?

	Rural	Urban
Like	37%	12%
Don't Like, but don't hate	52%	78%
Hate	3%	6%
Number of respondents	1,729	772

Source: PAAS Rural Question 215 and PAAS Urban Question 5216, both asked in March and April 1971.

The next question asked about the harmony between the American and Vietnamese characters. Very few thought good harmony existed between the two. Most thought there was little harmony or disharmony. Table 15.19 shows the results.

In another variation on the theme, the surveys asked if dislike or hostility existed between Americans and Vietnamese.[12] The patterns are similar to those regarding the anti-American feelings in Table 15.16. When the respondents who said hostility existed were asked on which side the hostility lay, the rural and urban respondents agreed for the first time (Table 15.20). More than half felt the dislike was on both sides. Thirty-five percent felt it was on the American side because "Americans do not like Vietnamese."

TABLE 15.19
How Do You Think The American Character
Harmonizes With The Vietnamese Character?

	Rural	Urban
Good harmony	4%	0%
Fair harmony	26%	13%
Little harmony	34%	34%
Disharmony	13%	32%
Don't know	22%	19%
Number of respondents	1,732	774

Source: PAAS Rural Question 216 and Urban Question 5217, asked in March and April 1971.

TABLE 15.20
On Which Side Does Most Of The
Dislike or Hostility Lie?

	Rural	Urban
On the Vietnamese side	9%	3%
Equally on both sides	54%	53%
On the American side	35%	37%
Number of respondents	368	274

Source: PAAS Rural Question 218 and PAAS Urban Question 5219, asked in March and April 1971.

American Troop Withdrawals

The PAAS rural surveys asked people what they thought of the American troop withdrawals in 1970, 1971 and 1972. Some of the same months were used in all of the years so trends can be addressed. Table 15.21 shows the results. In the second quarter of 1970 forty-two percent of the rural respondents didn't know about the withdrawals although they had started in the summer of 1969. By May 1972 only 16 percent were aware of them. Vietnamese opinion remained fairly stable during the periods shown and no trends are apparent.

TABLE 15.21
What Do You Think Of the U.S. Troop Withdrawal?

	Percentage of Respondents				
	April–May–July[a]		May[b]		
	1970	1971	1970	1971	1972
GVN Troops should replace U.S. forces as soon as possible	2[c]	7	2[c]	7	6
Withdrawal necessary but do it only when GVN forces can replace	12	19	15	18	18
GVN can replace but need some U.S. until war is over	19	23	21	24	23
Withdrawal will make it harder for GVN to win	11	9	15	11	17
Not aware of withdrawal	42	31	34	31	16
Don't know	12	7	11	5	17
Number of respondents	2,621	2,695	856	927	848

[a]Sources for 1970 are published PAAS reports for April, May and July 1970. Source for 1971 is computer printout displaying PAAS Rural Question 67 for April, May and July 1971.
[b]Sources are published PAAS report for May 1970 and computer printouts displaying Rural Question 67 for May 1971 and May 1972.
[c]In 1970 this statement said that GVN troops can and should replace U.S. forces as soon as possible.

If the respondent was aware of the troop withdrawals he or she was asked why the troops were withdrawing. Data for several months in 1970 and 1971 indicate that the largest percentage of the rural respondents (37 percent) said that the withdrawals were caused by pressure from the American people. The results are shown in Table 15.22.

TABLE 15.22
Why Are the American Troops Being Withdrawn?

	Rural
They have defeated the VC/NVA so are no longer required	9%
They can't defeat the VC/NVA so are withdrawing	4%
GVN has asked the U.S. to withdraw because they are strong enough to defeat the VC/NVA	20%
The U.S. is negotiating with North Vietnam so that U.S. and NVA forces will leave Vietnam	13%
Pressure from the American people has forced the withdrawal of U.S. forces	37%
Number of respondents	3,500

Source: Published PAAS reports for April, May and July 1970. PAAS Rural Question 68, asked in April, May, June and July 1971.

Respondents aware of the withdrawals were also asked whether the decision was wise. The data indicate that 64 percent thought it was wise in 1970 but in May 1972, when the communist offensive peaked, people were having second thoughts and the percentage was down to 44 percent. Table 15.23 shows the results for three comparable periods in 1970, 1971 and 1972.

TABLE 15.23
Is It Wise for the U.S. Troops to Withdraw?

	Percentage of respondents		
	May–June 1970	May–June 1971	May 1972
Wise	64	59	44
Unwise	15	17	18
Don't know	20	23	38
Number of respondents	2,650 (est)	1,212	804

Source: PAAS published reports for May and June, 1970. PAAS Rural Question 69 for 1971 and 1972.

TABLE 15.24
Why Do You Think the Decision To
Withdraw U.S. Troops Is a Wise One?

	Percentage of Respondents		
	May–June 1970	May–June 1971	May 1972
Neutralizes an important VC/NVA propaganda weapon	33	23	32
Promotes nationalism and self sufficiency	17	18	28
Will help promote results at the Paris peace talks	16	13	19
Will help reduce disruption of the Vietnamese economy	11	3	7
Will help silence anti-war sentiment in the U.S.	8	31	10
Withdrawal will reduce fighting and killing in Vietnam	14	8	4
Number of respondents	1,700 (est)	715	354

Sources: Published PAAS reports for May and June 1970. Rural Question 70 from computer printout for 1971 and 1972.

Respondents who thought it was wise for American troops to withdraw were asked why they thought so and the results are shown in Table 15.24. A major emphasis on neutralizing communist propaganda is apparent in all years, particularly 1970 and 1972. Silencing American antiwar sentiment was given as a major reason (31 percent) in 1971 and the promotion of nationalism and self-sufficiency was a major reason given in 1972 (28 percent).

In 1971 and 1972 rural surveys asked 4,450 respondents what would happen to the war if all American troops left Vietnam. The results are shown in Table 15.25. Fifty-five to 60 percent of the respondents consistently thought there would be some problems or danger if all U.S. forces left Vietnam. May 1972 is the most pessimistic month, as it often is in other data, but the differences are not great.

Sir Robert Thompson was right. The Vietnamese people were aware of what was going on and they were willing to disclose some of their views about the events.

TABLE 15.25
If All U.S. Troops Leave Vietnam
What Will Happen to The War?

	Percentage of Respondents		
	Total 1971	May 1971	May 1972
No problem	13	14	8
Some problems	36	40	30
Very dangerous	22	20	25
Total: problems/danger	58	60	55
Coalition Government, cede some areas to the VC/NVA	2	2	4
Communists will win	2	1	2
Don't know	24	21	26
Don't want to respond	2	1	5
Number of respondents	4,450	928	848

Source: PAAS Rural Question 71, asked in April, May, June and July 1971, and in May 1972.

NOTES

1. Thompson, **No Exit,** p. 128.
2. "Aspirations of the Vietnamese People," **Analysis Report,** (August 1967), pp. 47 and 50.
3. **Ibid.,** pp. 47-49.
4. "What the Vietnamese Peasant Thinks," **Analysis Report,** (January-February, 1971), p. 14.
5. Most of the figures used here and in the following chapters were derived from the U.S. pacification advisors' computer tapes. They sometimes differ slightly from those published in the PAAS monthly hard copy report because they have been adjusted to reflect the actual geographical distribution of the rural South Vietnamese population. The adjustment compensates for the tendency of the quota interview system used by the PAAS to over-represent the opinions collected from less populated areas of the country.
6. PAAS Urban Question 5053 which had 339 respondents.
7. PAAS Urban Question 5055. Data for May, June, July 1971 and January, March, May, June, July and August 1972.
8. **Ibid.**

9. PAAS Rural Question 191 in December 1971 and March 1972 with a cumulative total of 1951 respondents. PAAS Rural Question 134 in June 1972 with 895 respondents.

10. PAAS Urban Question 5160 in December 1971 and PAAS Urban Question 5278 in June 1972. Cumulative total of 1292 respondents.

11. PAAS Urban Question 5530 with 269 respondents.

12. PAAS Rural Question 217 and Urban Question 5218.

16
Chieu Hoi:
Defections from the Communist Side

Through its Chieu Hoi ("Open Arms") Program the GVN offered the communists operating in the south an opportunity to defect, gain a political pardon and even take vocational training to help them find jobs after they left the Chieu Hoi Center. The defectors were called hoi chanh or ralliers.

The government established the Chieu Hoi Program in 1963 at the urging of advisors who were familiar with the successful amnesty and resettlement programs in the Philippines and Malaya.[1] Despite misgivings about amnesty for the communists, President Diem approved the program and almost 5,000 ralliers came in during the first three months. The South Vietnamese were not enthusiastic about the program and 18 months later it remained a modest under-funded effort.

By 1965 the U.S. Government had endorsed the program but did not pour any resources into it. Only one American was formally associated with the program in Vietnam. The South Vietnamese noted this and continued to give the program a low priority, downgrading it to the point where a Vietnamese Army captain was the top Chieu Hoi official.[2]

By 1966 the low cost and high benefits of the program were evident to all and it began to gain momentum. American officials, fortified by the program's success, gave it more attention and by December 1967 it was being run by a South Vietnamese Cabinet Minister. But the GVN was still not completely convinced.

Meanwhile in April 1967 the South Vietnamese adopted the policy of "national reconciliation." Its intent was not only to give the rallier amnesty and return his political and civil rights, but to add training and aid in finding new careers tailored to the hoi chanh's experience, ability and loyalty. The policy was designed to induce high level communists to rally, but few did and the program was never widely implemented. The government remained reluctant to give the hoi chanh good jobs.

The Tet Offensive in 1968 marked a watershed in the program. At first it lost momentum but its assets and people survived intact. More important, the South Vietnamese attitude changed for the better because with few exceptions the ralliers remained loyal during the offensive.[3] As 1968 drew to a close the hoi chanh began to pour in and the Chieu Hoi Program hit its peak in 1969 as factors contributing to a large flow of ralliers came into full play. A well-organized and well-funded Chieu Hoi Program was in operation and more potential ralliers were tapped as the government expanded its presence into the countryside.[4]

The rural South Vietnamese said that the Chieu Hoi Program was a good idea but they shared the government's reluctance to trust the hoi chanh who came in. In August 1969 a PAAS rural survey asked 1,025 respondents "Do you feel that it is wise for the government to give the VC an opportunity to rally?"[5] Eighty percent said yes, two percent said no and the other 18 percent didn't know. In October 1971 and August 1972 the PAAS asked a total of 1,943 rural respondents "Do you feel that the existence of a Chieu Hoi policy will help end the war more quickly?"[6] This time only 65 percent of the respondents said yes (72 percent said yes in the August sample).

Both results are highly favorable to the program but the respondents were less enthusiastic about the ralliers themselves. In the October 1971 and August 1972 polls, 1956 rural respondents were asked "Do you trust hoi chanh?"[7] This time only 17 percent replied with an unqualified yes while an additional 23 percent would "only trust those hoi chanh who showed their good will." Thirty-four percent would "trust, but their actions should be watched," and eight percent wouldn't trust them at all.

Key Elements of the Chieu Hoi Program[8]

The key elements of the Chieu Hoi Program were the inducements to rally and the rallier's reception, vocational training, resettlement and follow-up. The latter three turned out to be the weakest parts of the program.

Inducements took the form of psychological operations and rewards to persuade the communists to rally to the government. The psychological warfare material focused on the potential rallier's grievances, emotions and aspirations, not--except for hard-core Viet Cong Infrastructure or North Vietnamese--on ideological commitment. Information about the program reached potential ralliers through a variety of channels: leaflets dropped from aircraft or distributed by hand, newspapers, aerial loudspeaker broadcasts, radio, TV, movies, family influence and contact with ralliers.

The leaflet proved to be an effective Chieu Hoi appeal and a multilingual "Safe Conduct Pass" blanketed South Vietnam. Ralliers described it as the best known appeal and the one most conducive to rallying. After one engagement 90 percent of the communists searched afterward were carrying it despite the risk of punishment if their leaders caught them with the passes.

Two kinds of cash rewards were employed to lure ralliers. The first rewarded hoi chanh who came in with a weapon or led government forces to weapons or weapon caches. The other rewarded people who induced communists to surrender and this was called the third-party inducement program. The weapons reward program was established in September 1964 and reaffirmed in 1967. By March 1970 the rewards ranged from VN$1,200 ($10. U.S.) for a hand weapon up to VN$1 million for leading allied troops to large communist weapons caches. Many large caches were found in this manner.

The third-party inducement program began in the summer of 1967 in Military Region 4. The program paid rewards to any Vietnamese citizen or rallier who could get a communist to rally. It proved quite successful in raising the rallier counts but corruption killed it off two years later. Before it ended there were all kinds of schemes created to collect the reward money. Too many ralliers turned out to have an "inducer" who had little or nothing to do with their decision to rally and the government seemed to be getting little for its money.

The rallier's reception at the Chieu Hoi Center was important. The inducement promises had to be fulfilled if the program was to be effective. On arrival at the reception center the rallier was screened to determine his legitimacy as a defector. An interrogation to gain tactical intelligence followed, and then the rallier had to attend political lectures, usually mediocre at best, and then he could receive vocational training if he desired (few did). After 45 to 60 days the rallier left the center as a free person with a military deferment for six months.

Resettlement and employment of the hoi chanh after leaving the center were also important. Many ralliers volunteered for the government's military and paramilitary forces and some found jobs in government agencies, particularly the Chieu Hoi ministry. After 1969 hoi chanh were used increasingly as interrogators in the Phung Hoang Program to neutralize the communist infrastructure. Resettlement of the ralliers who did not join the military or the government was a problem since employers were reluctant to hire hoi chanh because they didn't trust them.

Follow-up of ralliers after they left the Chieu Hoi Center was not effective and there was no system to do this until late 1971 when an automated tracking system under the National Police was established. An assessment of the ralliers' economic, political and social activities is not possible.

How Many Defected?

The communists rallied for personal not ideological reasons. With few exceptions the growing pressure of allied military efforts, hardship, war-weariness, uncertainty about the future, doubts about their ability to take over South Vietnam, disillusionment with communist policies and promises and family concern all went into decisions to rally.[9] The Chieu Hoi Program was their escape hatch.

Table 16.1 shows that in the ten years from 1963 through 1972 more than 200,000 communists surrendered to the government through the Chieu Hoi Program. The table indicates a buildup to a peak in 1969 when 47,000 ralliers came in, followed by a steady decline to 1972 when 11,000 came in, matching the 1965 level.

TABLE 16.1
More Than 200,000 VC/NVA Rally to
The South Vietnam Government

Communist Ralliers in Thousands

1963	1964	1965	1966	1967	1968	1969	1970	1971	1972
11	5	11	20	27	18	47	33	20	11

Total Ralliers   203,000

Source: Table 2, **Southeast Asia Statistical Summary,** Office of the Assistant Secretary of Defense (Comptroller) March 25, 1971 – January 17, 1973, pp. 1 through 7.

Military Region 4 was far and away the leader in ralliers, accounting for more than half of them from 1968 on. The Chieu Hoi Program in Military Region 4 took off in 1968 when the region accounted for 57 percent of all hoi chanh that year and it never fell below 60 percent after that. Two reasons for its success were that few North Vietnamese troops were present and the program there was well managed.

However, a more important reason was the increased allied pressure after the 1968 Tet Offensive. Hoi chanh in Vinh Long province began to complain during 1968 about the effectiveness of allied military operations which reportedly destroyed 20 percent of the guerrilla forces in Vinh Long and caused five percent of them to defect.[10] In 1969 allied pressure intensified and the percentage of secure population in Military Region 4 jumped from 38 percent in 1968 to 64 percent in 1969. Progress continued until the 1972 offensive. The rallier rate in Kien Hoa province rose sharply in 4th quarter 1970 accounting for 62 percent of the region's ralliers. This was the result of South Vietnamese forces opening up Viet Cong strongholds and erecting permanent outposts there.[11]

Another reason for the large numbers of ralliers reported in Military Region 4 was the third-party inducement program which began in Vinh Binh and Vinh Long provinces during the summer of 1967. During the first six months of 1969 seventy percent of the Military Region 4 ralliers were attributed to this program. Some of these ralliers were later reclassified as refugees or impressed laborers and some turned out to be party to false inducement practices, but even allowing for inflation of the figures the flow was large.

The defector rate remained fairly stable throughout the year. The lowest month was June (about 1,600) and the highest March (about 2,400). January and February were the months in which the Vietnamese Lunar New Year (Tet) usually occurred and every year intensive efforts were made to induce communists to rally at Tet. January and February never attracted high numbers although March is the top month. The high March defector rate may be due to some spillover from the Tet campaign. Another possible explanation is that the tempo of combat usually picked up in February and the potential ralliers may have known that the heavier fighting would continue until June so they simply decided not to endure it and rally. Also, as they emerged from the isolation of their base areas to enter combat this may have given them their first opportunity to defect in a long time.

The combat cycle had some impact on the flow of defectors. The high periods of the war cycle had lower Chieu Hoi rates. The low periods had higher rates although the variance between high and low rates were not great.

Who Rallied?

A detailed study of 20,000 returnees from July 1965 through June 1967 gave a fairly complete profile of the hoi chanh for that period.[12] About two-thirds of the ralliers were military but the civilian proportion tended to increase when the rate increased. About 40 percent of the defectors were village and hamlet guerrillas, 20 percent were civilians from party organizations, ten to 20 percent were regular military personnel and the remaining 25 percent defected from militia, liberations associations, labor groups, etc. The proportion of cadre in the group ranged from 15 to 19 percent indicating little difference between cadre and rank-and-file defection trends during the two years. Senior cadre accounted for only five to eight percent of the ralliers.

A majority of the defectors were 16 to 30 years old. Generally the higher the rallier's unit the lower his average age. Guerrillas were usually older than main force troops. Military returnees from Military Region 3 and 4 were older and had longer services than those from Military Regions 1 and 2. Cadre were generally older than their followers and a majority of the ralliers had 12 or more months of communist service. Less than 15 percent were South Vietnamese deserters or had served the government before joining the communists.

The defectors may have represented only a partial manpower loss to the communists because most of them came from Viet Cong villages and wanted to return home. A few (0.5 percent) were defecting for the second time. A much higher percentage probably faced further service with the Viet Cong if they went home and, later in the war, they might have been executed if they returned to communist areas.

The study indicated that it was tougher to defect from regular force units than from other communist organizations. The proportion of defectors from regular forces in the sample was about half of the proportion of regular forces in the total communist strength. The percentage of guerrilla and civilian ralliers was greater than their share of communist strength. One interpretation of the difference is that few regular force

TABLE 16.2
Sixty Percent of the Ralliers Were Military

Type of Rallier	Ralliers in Thousands							
	1965	1966	1967	1968	1969	1970	1971	Total
Military	7.9	12.9	17.7	12.6	28.4	17.1	10.9	107.5
Political	2.6	6.3	7.9	3.8	12.6	11.4	6.6	51.2
Other[a]	.6	1.0	1.6	1.8	6.0	4.1	2.8	17.9
Total	11.1	20.2	27.2	18.2	47.0	32.7	20.3	176.6

Sources: For 1965: "Chieu Hoi: VC/NVA In 1968," **Southeast Asia Analysis Report,** February 1969, p. 31. For 1966-1971, Koch, J.A., **The Chieu Hoi Program in South Vietn-Nam 1963-1971,** R-112-ARPA, The RAND Corporation, January 1973, p. 11.
[a]Includes dissidents, followers, draft dodgers, deserters, porters, etc., who actively supported the VC/NVA.

troops were able to defect while another is that the strengths of guerrilla and civilian units were under-estimated. Evidence exists to bolster either case.

Table 16.2 shows that 60 percent of the hoi chanh came from military units of one sort or another and 30 percent were from the communist political structure. Approximately 1,200 North Vietnamese troops rallied, or one percent of the military total through 1971.[13]

Many defectors decided to work with the government after their release from the Chieu Hoi Center. Some worked as interrogators in the Phung Hoang Program to neutralize the subversive infrastructure. Others volunteered to serve with South Vietnamese military or paramilitary forces. They were particularly effective in the Armed Propaganda Teams and the Kit Carson Scouts.

The Armed Propaganda Teams were lightly armed paramilitary units that became the primary action arm of the Chieu Hoi ministry for face to face inducement of potential defectors in communist areas. The teams would go into communist controlled or contested areas as former Viet Cong who had seen the light and would tell the people how to rally. The teams also assisted the National Police as interrogators and helped identify Viet Cong trying to pass through government check points. They helped train the PSDF and five-man lecture teams visited schools, business groups and military camps.

Kit Carson Scouts were defectors who volunteered to serve with American and third nation units in combat. They usually served in their home areas and were helpful because the knew how and where the communist units operated. By the end of 1968 1,500 Scouts were deployed with American and third nation units all over the country.

The communist reaction to the defector program ranged from propaganda to attacks on Chieu Hoi centers. Their activities increased as the program continued to induce defectors from the communist political and military units. At first the communists regarded defectors who had passed through the Chieu Hoi Center as misguided brothers to be given a second chance.[14] However, if the rallier had turned his weapons in, or had helped the government locate communist weapons and supplies, or furnished intelligence, he was to be killed.

By 1970 the communist leadership was disturbed enough to announce that anyone who killed a returnee would become a member of the Order of the Valiant Knights. Up to this point the honor had been reserved for communist troops who had killed at least ten Vietnamese and American soldiers.[15] A captured document assessed the program in April 1971:

> The trend of defection continued to increase.... The defections among the local force and guerrilla elements were critical.... In some districts half of the local guerrillas joined the enemy.... Mass defections were also recorded among troop units and included battalion and company political cadres.[16]

Efforts were made to prevent knowledge of the Chieu Hoi Program from reaching the communist troops, but they were not successful given the flood of leaflets, and the growing word-of-mouth news about the program. Propaganda leaflets and safe-conduct passes were quickly gathered up and burned. Attempts were made to interfere with broadcasts from aircraft and communist propaganda stressed the torture and mistreatment that awaited the person who tried to rally to the government. After the defection of a high-ranking cadre (few defected) the political cadres subjected their people to thorough reindoctrination.

The danger of infiltration is inherent in any defector program and the Chieu Hoi Program was no exception. Evidence of false ralliers appeared first in April 1967.[17] By late 1970 and early 1971 recurring evidence suggested a coordinated communist strategy for infiltration of the Chieu Hoi Centers in which the agent would rally and then join a local paramilitary force. Thirty-one territorial force outposts were overrun in the spring of 1971, compared to nine during the same period a year before, and there were strong indications of collusion between some of the false ralliers in the outposts and the communist forces outside.[18] Evidence also suggests that the communists used the Chieu Hoi Program to secure legitimacy for some of their people as the cease fire approached. However, no evidence of widespread infiltration was found despite a program of surveillance and interrogation directed at spotting such cases.

All factors considered, the communist reactions to the Chieu Hoi Program suggest that it caused them real problems.

The Chieu Hoi Program probably had the most favorable cost/benefit ratio of any allied program in South Vietnam. The cost of bringing in 27,789 ralliers from 1963 through 1965 was $14 apiece. By 1966 the cost was up to $150 per rallier, and by 1969 it had leveled off at $350. Contrast this with the $60,000 it cost to kill a communist soldier during fiscal 1969 in a main force operation.[19]

More important, the Chieu Hoi Program removed communists from their military forces at no direct cost in allied casualties at least until the communist infiltration of Chieu Hoi started. During 1963-1972 more than 200,000 defectors surrendered to the government and approximately 60 percent, or 120,000 of them, came from military units. Meanwhile 890,000 communist troops were reportedly killed. Thus, the military Chieu Hoi total is equivalent to approximately 14 percent of the communist combat deaths. During the same period the allied forces lost 235,000 killed in action, or 0.27 killed for each communist killed. By extrapolation it might have cost 32,000 allied lives to kill the 120,000 communist troops if they hadn't rallied.

This calculation shouldn't be taken seriously because many communists were driven to defect by pressure of allied military operations and because such calculations ignore the complexity of the factors at work. But it does serve to make the point that, by any standard, and by any calculation, the Chieu Hoi Program furnished a low cost escape hatch for communist defectors and thereby generated high benefits for low costs.

NOTES

1. J. A. Koch, **The Chieu Hoi Program in South Vietnam, 1963-1971.** Rand Report R-1172 ARPA, (January 1973), p. v.
2. **Ibid.,** pp. vi and 25.
3. **Ibid.,** p. vii.
4. Recall the population security data for 1969 (Chapter 13) which showed the government moving out into the countryside in a significant way for the first time ever.
5. PAAS Rural Question 272.
6. PAAS Rural Question 270.
7. PAAS Rural Question 271.
8. Except where noted this entire section draws heavily on Koch, **Chieu Hoi,** pp. viii, ix, x and 59 through 90.
9. Koch, **Chieu Hoi,** p. v.
10. "Chieu Hoi: VC/NVA in 1968," **Analysis Report,** (February 1969), p. 29.
11. Koch, **Chieu Hoi,** p. 51.
12. J. M. Carrier, **A Profile of Viet Cong Returnees: July 1965 to June 1967,** RM-5577-ISA/ARPA, The RAND Corporation, October 1968. Material here taken from a summary published in a "Profile of Chieu Hoi Returnees," **Analysis Report,** (November 1968), pp. 18-19.
13. Koch, **Chieu Hoi,** p. 11.
14. "Profile of Chieu Hoi Returnees," **Analysis Report,** (November 1968), p. 18.

15. Koch, **Chieu Hoi,** p. 5.
16. **Ibid.,** p. 18.
17. Koch, **Chieu Hoi,** pp. 49 and 57.
18. **Ibid.,** p. 49.
19. Nine billion dollars cost of U.S. and South Vietnamese main force operations in fiscal 1969 divided by the 155,727 communists reportedly killed in fiscal 1969. Cost data are from Chapter 3. The combat deaths are from Table 6, **Southeast Asia Statistical Summary,** Office of the Assistant Secretary of Defense (Comptroller).

17
Dismantling the Communists'
Subversive Apparatus

Only now can it be seen just how much of the ranks of the pro-American administrations in South Vietnam were riddled with Viet Cong.[1]

September 9, 1975

When the Viet Minh marched into Hanoi in 1954 everyone was amazed to learn how many of the agents had been working secretly within the French structure. The same thing happened again when the communists moved into Saigon in 1975. Scores of trusted employees and supporters of the GVN turned out to be working for the communists. One officer on the losing side was heard to exclaim, "There was no way we could win with penetration into our ranks like that."[2]

The communist subversive apparatus in South Vietnam was often called the Viet Cong Infrastructure (VCI). It was the clandestine organization that not only commanded most communist operations, but directed the flow of manpower, supplies, and intelligence to their local forces and conducted much of the terrorism and other actions against the populace and local South Vietnamese officials. Many members of the VCI held military commands.

This chapter discusses the official estimates of VCI strength and where it was concentrated, the Phung Hoang or Phoenix campaign against the VCI, what the Vietnamese thought of the campaign, and its probable impact on the subversive apparatus.

How Many and Where

As indicated in Chapter 4, order of battle estimating techniques didn't work very well to estimate the strength of the subversive infrastructure because it was not organized in military units but in a structure common to clandestine organizations, with many members operating on their own. The pacification advisors in the American command, cooperating with the intelligence community and the police, attempted to estimate the numbers and types of clandestine communists by adopting techniques used by police everywhere to compile lists of persons wanted for crimes.

The British in Malaya used those techniques which called for a description of the clandestine organizations and then attempted to find out who filled the positions in them. Since the techniques and the intelligence on which they were based were often ambiguous, the numbers presented here should be taken as order of magnitude, nothing more.

Table 17.1 indicates that the estimated VCI strength gradually declined by 22 percent between August 1967 and October 1971. However, the reporting system changed in November 1970 so the October figure is not strictly comparable to the earlier figures.[3] Comparable data, if available, would probably show a larger decline.

More interesting than the estimates of strength are the estimates of communist subversive presence that can be obtained from questions found in the HES and the PAAS, although these estimates are also tenuous. In July 1969 the HES reported that 74 percent of the population was subjected to covert communist activity and another five percent was under their covert control.[4] Only 18 percent of the population reportedly was free of communist influence. By June 1971 the figure had risen to 32 percent.

By comparison the PAAS data for July 1971 suggests that only 14 percent of the respondents lived in an area where no communist cadre were present. Another 14 percent said cadre were present but ineffective.[5] Adding these two figures yields fairly good agreement with the 32 percent from the HES data. HES applied to the urban as well as rural population so it can be expected to show a higher percentage free of communist influence. The PAAS in this case applied only to the rural population where the communist presence ought to be stronger and it was more conservative than the HES as a general rule. At any rate both sets of data suggest that as late as June 1971 the Viet Cong clandestine cadre were conducting some activities among about two-thirds of the South Vietnamese population.

TABLE 17.1
VCI Estimated Strength Dropped 22 Percent

In Thousands				
1967 Aug. Dec.	1968 Dec.	1969 Dec.	1970 Dec.	1971 Oct.
85 84	83	74	72	66

Sources: "Phoenix Program: 1970 Results," **Southeast Asia Analysis Report,** September–October 1970, p. 20. "Phoenix" **Analysis Report,** June–July 1971, p. 2. **MACV Measurement of Progress Report,** December 1971, p. 67.

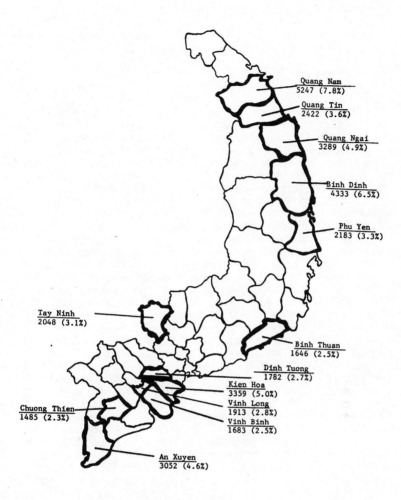

Figure 17.1 Provinces with high VCI strength

Data for March 1971 indicate that more than half of the estimated communist clandestine strength was found in 13 provinces of South Vietnam.[6] Figure 17.1 suggests that the situation in those areas was more serious than the numbers alone would indicate because 11 of the 13 provinces formed three continguous groups. The grouping suggests pockets of strength and the ability to provide mutual support and operating flexibility. The pattern of the map is not unfamiliar.

The Phung Hoang (Phoenix) Program

Defeating a flexible clandestine organization requires more than a purely military effort. Ideally it demands the type of multi-level, coordinated counter-espionage organization that the British developed so well during the Malayan emergency. By contrast the South Vietnamese counter-espionage effort was splintered, badly led, poorly financed and understaffed.

Throughout the Vietnam war the South Vietnamese tried to get at the clandestine communists but their efforts were so uncoordinated and diffused that they had little impact. In 1967 the Phung Hoang Program was established in an attempt to remedy some of the shortcomings. The basic concept was to enlist and coordinate the efforts of local leaders, police and paramilitary groups to identify and dismantle the subversive apparatus.

The Phung Hoang Program itself was not intended to be the actual instrument of neutralizing the covert threat. It was only supposed to coordinate the efforts of district and province intelligence coordination committees in identifying the local communist cadre and planning operations against them. These committees in turn were coordinating bodies. In addition to a full-time police staff, they included village council chairmen, village commissioners, hamlet chiefs and others as ex officio members. PSDF group leaders and other paramilitary personnel also participated. Phung Hoang was a Vietnamese program although this coordinating effort was pressed on them by the Americans. The U.S. role was to provide advisory support, technical advice and very limited logistical help.

Once plans were developed and subversive cadre identified, the operations were carried out by various Vietnamese forces. They included the National Police, the Field Police, Special Police, Military Security Teams, Armed Propaganda Teams, Census Grievance Cadre, RD Cadre, Provincial Reconnaissance Units (PRU) and military forces.

The Phung Hoang Program was supposed to be directed at high ranking cadre. The program was to focus its greatest efforts against executive cadre at all levels of the communist organization and to concentrate special attention on members of the National Liberation Councils and Committees, finance-economy cadre of the People's Revolutionary Party (PRP), and members of the National Alliances for Democracy and Peace. The goal suffered greatly in the application. In practice well over half of all communists neutralized were nonparty members (the party was very small so this was no surprise), and three-quarters operated at the village level or lower.

Results

The objective was to dismantle the VCI apparatus. By January 1970 this was measured as all those killed, rallied or sentenced. Persons captured but not yet sentenced did not count in the official totals. The sentencing proviso was not required before January 1970.[7] Under the previous definition VCI members taken out of action included all those captured whether sentenced or not. By this definition 15,800 and 19,500 VCI members were taken out of action in 1968 and 1969 respectively.

Since those taken into custody were not always tried or sentenced, and since prisons were known to leak captives almost as rapidly as they received them, this definition clearly led to inflated figures for those years. Under the new definition about 21,000 covert communists were reported out of action in 1970 and 18,000 in 1971, but even these numbers are not precise. About 60 percent of the 1971 figure came from the 13 provinces where the VCI were concentrated.[8]

The real problems of Phung Hoang effectiveness began to appear when the quality of the communists taken out of action was examined. The purpose of the program was to dismantle the driving force behind the communist forces, namely, the party leaders operating at the top of the structure. However, in 1970 and 1971 (through March) less than three percent of the VCI members killed, captured or rallied were full or probationary party members above the district level.[9] In 1970 the five most important VCI taken out of action were:

1. A chief, Cadre Affairs Section, Peoples Revolutionary Party (PRP), captured August 1970;

2. A deputy chief, Military Proselyting Section, PRP, rallied May 1970;

3. A chief, Documentation Subsection (Espionage/Intelligence), Security Section PRP, captured February 1970;

4. A deputy detention chief, Interrogation/Detention Subsection (POW and Detention Camps), Security Section, PRP, rallied December 1970, and,

5. A deputy chief, Rear Service Section, PRP, captured October 1970.[10]

Table 17.2 shows that three out of four people killed, captured, or defected in both 1970 and early 1971 were from the lowest levels of the organization. The majority of these were not party members. Although not shown in the table, the pattern continued throughout 1971 and may have been the norm for the program.[11] The effect at the village and hamlet level cannot be dismissed as unimportant because it did make it more difficult for the communists to operate and recruit. The impact at low levels was probably the most successful aspect of the program.

The inability of the Phung Hoang effort to go to the heart of the communist control organization can be explained by looking at which South Vietnamese forces were most effective and under what circumstances. Phung Hoang forces accounted for only 20 percent of all VCI members killed, captured or rallied. Only half of their results (nine percent of the total) were the result of specific

TABLE 17.2
VCI Neutralization By Echelon and Party Membership

| | Jan. 1970 - Mar. 1971 | |
Province, Saigon, Region and COSVN	Number	Percent
Full or probationary Party member	799	3
Other	1,030	4
Subtotal	1,799	7
District		
Full or probationary Party member	1,932	7
Other	2,318	8
Subtotal	4,250	15
City		
Full or probationary Party member	149	–
Other	279	1
Subtotal	428	1
Village and Hamlet		
Full or probationary Party member	9,070	33
Other	11,877	43
Subtotal	20,947	76
All Levels		
Full or probationary Party member	11,920	43
Other	15,504	57
Total Neutralized	27,424	100

Source: "Phoenix," **Southeast Asia Analysis Report,** June–July 1971, p. 4.

targeting. Military forces killed or captured about half of the VCI taken and the remaining 30 percent rallied through the Chieu Hoi Program. In short, only ten percent of the job was being done in an organized way by the forces chiefly tasked to do it (Table 17.3). In earlier years this percentage was even lower.

Detailed data, not shown here, indicate that the territorial forces, especially in Military Regions 1 and 4, accounted for the largest share of VCI killed or captured by a single force (1970, 50 percent; early 1971, 39 percent). Police brought in 20 percent in 1970 and 14 percent in early 1971.

The single most effective anti-VCI forces were the Provincial Reconnaissance Units (PRU). This 4,400-man force killed of captured 1,683 VCI in 1970, about 380 for every thousand men in the force. In early 1971 their annual rate was 263 per

TABLE 17.3
Vietnamese Action Forces Versus Targeting

Kills and captures:	1970 Number	Percent	1971(thru March) Number	Percent
by Phung Hoang forces:				
Specific targeting	2,806	11	648	9
General targeting	2,692	10	833	12
Subtotal	5,498	21	1,481	21
by Military forces:				
Specific targeting	2,622	10	1,179	16
General targeting	10,354	40	2,254	32
Subtotal	12,976	50	3,433	48
Rallies (Chieu Hoi)	7,562	29	2,194	31
TOTAL	26,036	100	7,108	100

Source: "Phoenix,"**Southeast Asia Analysis Report,**" June–July 1971, p. 5

thousand. No other force came close to this. The police (about 109,000 strong in 1971) killed or captured only about 40 VCI per 1,000 per year and the territorial forces about 20 per 1,000 per year. The PRU were later incorporated in the the special branch of the National Police.

Critics of the Phung Hoang Program have asserted that it was used more as a convenient way to assassinate political enemies than to dismantle the subversive apparatus. Table 17.4 shows that during the 15 months from January 1970 through March 1971 less than two percent of all VCI put out of action were specifically targeted and killed by Phung Hoang forces. Most of them were either killed or captured as a by-product of military operations or as a result of general screening operations and were later identified as VCI.

There is no way of telling from the data whether any political assassinations were taking place but they do suggest that such activity was not the primary aim of the program. Indeed, if the communists were worried about the Phung Hoang Program, and there are reports that they were, they could do worse than to lable it a political assassination program. In short, the numbers alone will not answer the allegations of political assassinations but they won't support them either.

Until January 1970 there was no system to provide follow-up on persons captured as suspected agents. It was impossible to determine systematically whether captured persons were ever processed by the Province Security Committee and sentenced or

TABLE 17.4
Only 2 Percent Of The VCI Taken Out Of Action Were
Specifically Targeted And Killed By Phung Hoang Forces.

VCI Killed	January 1970 through March 1971		
	Specific Targeting	General Targeting	Total
Force responsible			
Military	2,267	6,885	9,152
Phung Hoang	616	675	1,291
Total	2,883	7,560	10,443
VCI Captured	4,372	8,573	12,945
VCI Rallied	N/A	N/A	9,756
Grand Total	7,255	16,133 .	33,144

Source: "Phoenix," **Southeast Asia Analysis Report,** June–July 1971, p. 6.

released. To remedy this situation an information system was started in January 1970. It assigned an identification (ID) number to each detainee on the basis of his name, birthdate, and time and place of capture. Data on the individual's processing and sentence or release were entered into the system at a later date, keyed to the ID number assigned.[12]

Another difficulty the government faced in dismantling the VCI was its own cumbersome and leaky judicial machinery. Despite American pleas to upgrade the judicial system, Table 17.5 shows that after a data base was established during the first quarter of 1970 the backlog of cases consistently exceeded 2,000. During the last three quarters of the period the backlog was reduced by an increase in the number of persons released after trial, transferred out of the system, or unaccounted for. The table indicates that most sentences were for less than two years but they could be extended by administrative action of the Province Security Committee.

The South Vietnamese people clearly sensed the shortcomings of the system for trying VCI suspects. When asked about the treatment given to the suspects when they were arrested or captured, 6,298 respondents in a series of PAAS rural surveys responded as follows:[13] Usually fair and Just - 56 percent; sometimes fair and just - 17 percent; usually unfair and unjust - 10 percent; don't know - 33 percent. When asked if the judicial proceedings should be made public more than half of the 4,444 respondents to this question answered "yes" (53 percent), 17 percent said "no", and 29 percent did not know.[14]

TABLE 17.5
The Backlog of VCI Cases Exceeded 2,000

	1970				1971
	1st Qtr	2nd qtr	3rd qtr	4th qtr	1st qtr
Captured in Period	2,301	3,105	2,477	2,483	2,581
Cases Acted Upon					
Sentenced	432	1,480	1,841	1,736	1,735
Released	85	223	440	356	356
Transferred[a]	28	205	428	213	248
Unaccounted for	0	0	313	473	138
Total	545	1,908	3,022	2,778	2,477
Backlog at end					
of Quarter	1,756	2,953	2,408	2,113	2,217

Most VCI Sentences (70%) Were For Less
Than Two Years But Could Be Extended

Length of Sentence[b]

0 - 6 months	54	109	178	131	107
6 - 12 months	86	198	234	203	148
12 - 24 months	168	702	841	882	933
Over 24 months	124	471	588	520	547
Total	432	1,480	1,841	1,736	1,735

Source: "Phoenix," **Analysis Report,** June–July 1971, p. 7.
[a]To military or civil court, to another province, drafted, classified
as "POW" or listed as "other".
[b]Initial sentence only. Sentence could subsequently be extended by
administrative action of the Province Security Committee.

What Did The Vietnamese Think of The Program

Vietnamese awareness of the Phung Hoang Program increased
steadily from January 1970 through August 1972, the period for
which data are available.[15] Even though efforts were made to
publicize the program, 67 percent of the respondents to a PAAS
rural survey in January 1970 said they did not know what the words
Phung Hoang meant. By August 1972 only 26 percent said they were
not aware of the program. This question was changed in March
1971 and this may have affected the figures, but the trend seems
clear; more people became aware of the program as time passed.

The level of awareness was not high. The PAAS rural surveys asked 6,431 people during 1971 and 1972 whether they were aware of the Phung Hoang Program. Only eight percent said they clearly understood the program. Thirty-two percent said they had a general idea of it, and another 32 percent said they had heard the name.[16]

Some clues to the attitude of the Vietnamese rural population toward the Phung Hoang Program are furnished by answers to questions about how much effort the National Police should devote to the VCI problem and whether rewards should be offered to the populace for information leading to the capture of communist cadre. In 1971 and 1972 5,556 respondents were asked: "How much effort should the National Police devote to dealing with the elimination of VCI?" Sixty-seven percent thought the police should spend at least half of their time on it.[17] When asked: "Should the government pay for information that leads to the capture of communist cadre?" 73 percent of the 945 respondents answered yes, five percent said no, and 22 percent didn't know.[18] But when asked if people would approve of those who provide information about communist activities for money, 49 percent of the same sample said yes, 15 percent said no, and 31 percent didn't know.[19]

Taken as a whole, the data seem to suggest that a hard core of about 40 percent of the rural population knew something about the program, thought the police should really concentrate on it more than half of their time, and would approve of rewards to people who furnished information about communist activities.

When 2,170 respondents were asked about the performance of Phung Hoang in eliminating the VCI only 30 percent thought the program was effective. Twenty-eight percent thought its performance was fairly effective because it helped force the communists to modify, but not necessarily cease, their activities. Nine percent thought performance was poor, and 20 percent didn't know.[20] When 8,219 rural respondents were asked about the performance of the National Police in dealing with the VCI, only 28 percent thought the police were effective.[21] When asked: "Do Village and district officials place emphasis on eliminating VC/VCI?" 55 percent of a sample of 5,464 replied "yes, considerable."[22] A sample of 5,470 was then asked: "What do the majority of people think of the village/district officials' efforts to eliminate the VC/VCI?" Fifty-seven percent said that their efforts were appreciated and had community support.[23]

The preceding data suggest that about 55 percent of the respondents to the question thought that the program's performance was at least fairly effective and that local officials were emphasizing Phung Hoang with the support of the community.

What Happened to The VCI?

The HES and PAAS data give some clues to the status and effectiveness of the VCI by 1972 and are probably better indicators of the state of affairs than the police approach presented at the beginning of this analysis, although they must also be viewed with caution.

The HES regularly asked a question each quarter about the state of the VCI in every hamlet. The results suggest that the population living free of the communist infrastructure tripled between 1969 and 1972 with most of the progress made in 1971, and that by December 1972 fifty-five percent had reached this condition. After 1969 the population subjected to the most intense VCI activity (regular covert activity or primary authority) leveled off at eight to ten percent of the total. Still, at the end of 1972 forty-five percent of the population was reportedly subject to at least sporadic covert activity by the Viet Cong Infrastructure.[24]

The PAAS data, one again, were more conservative than the HES data, partly because they did not include the urban population. Only 23 percent of the respondents in 1972 said that there were no communist cadre in the area or, if present, that they were ineffective.[25] The changes from 1971 to 1972 in the PAAS data show a pattern not unlike the HES, in that the "no VCI" category stayed about the same. However, 15 percent of the respondents rated the VCI more effective in 1972 compared to four percent in 1971, and only 34 percent rated the VCI as less effective in 1972, compared to 52 percent in 1971. The PAAS respondents clearly felt that the clandestine communists recovered some lost ground in 1972.

To be effective the VCI had to be able to recruit new members. The HES didn't ask a specific question about the ability to recruit but it did ask whether any people in the hamlet lived where communist recruiters, tax collectors, and other cadre could move freely at night.[26] Shown below is the growing percentage of the population which did not live in such areas:

TABLE 17.6
Percentage of Population Who Lived
Where VCI Could Not Move Freely

Dec. 1969	Dec. 1970	Dec. 1971	Dec. 1972
56%	71%	80%	79%

The PAAS data are not sufficient to show a trend about recruiting but in 1972, 3,475 rural respondents were asked: "Is the VCI presently able to recruit any new members in this village?"[27] Sixty percent answered no, 20 percent answered yes, and 19 percent did not know. Half of those who answered yes said that the VCI could recruit only with great difficulty.

Another criterion of VCI effectiveness was its ability to tax the population for funds to keep its organization and efforts going. The HES and PAAS both asked about the VCI ability to tax. Again, a trend is available from the HES but not from the PAAS. The HES asked if the VCI collected taxes from hamlet households in cash or in kind. By December 1971 the answer was no for 82 percent of the population.[28]

The PAAS rural survey asked 3,476 respondents in 1972: "Have VCI cadre been able to tax the people of this village in recent months?" Fifty-seven percent answered no; 19 percent said yes, a few times a month; and eight percent said the VCI taxed almost daily.[29] The PAAS rural data were again more conservative than the view from HES which included the cities. The HES trend indicates that the VCI were collecting taxes from fewer people each year.

A key facet of VCI effectiveness was to keep the identity of its members secret, particularly from the government. The HES asked: "Are the identities of members of the enemy infrastructure for this village known to friendly intelligence personnel?" The answers are interesting but troublesome because they contradict some of the HES data presented above. The trends are favorable to the government but these data from HES suggest that only 29 percent of the population in December 1972 lived where no VCI existed, in sharp contrast to the 55 percent figure from another HES question discussed above.

No explanation for the difference is available. The 55 percent version of the question asks about VCI in the hamlets and the 29 percent version asks about VCI in the villages. The village is an area like a township and it includes hamlets within its borders so the figures ought to agree.

It may be significant that the 29 percent answer agrees well with the 23 percent answer from the PAAS presented earlier in this chapter. The PAAS rural survey asked 851 respondents in March 1971 if they were aware of the present Viet Cong village/hamlet officials' identity (the HES asked if government intelligence personnel knew the identities of the VCI).[31] Since the VCI was supposed to be clandestine and this could be a dangerous question to answer, most respondents (68 percent) said they were not aware of the VCI officials. Another 24 percent said they were aware of a few of them.

The picture that emerges from the data is a subversive apparatus that was somewhat battered as a by-product of the war, not by an intense Phung Hoang effort. The VCI was still functioning among a significant portion of the South Vietnamese population in December 1972 just before the cease fire. There is no evidence in the data of a Phung Hoang Program of systematic political assassinations although people were specifically targeted and killed by Vietnamese action forces. Finally, the Phung Hoang Program was not very effective.

NOTES

1. Alan Dawson, "Thieu Regime Was Riddled With Vietcong," **The Washington Post**, (September 10, 1975), p. A9.
2. **Ibid.**
3. "Phoenix," **Analysis Report**, (June-July 1971), p. 2.
4. HES Question HQB-1 for July 1969 and June 1971.
5. PAAS Rural Survey, Question 38 asked in June 1971.
6. "Phoenix," **Analysis Report** (June-July 1971), p. 3.
7. "Phoenix Program: 1970 Results," **Analysis Report**, (September-October 1979), p. 23.
8. "Phoenix," **Analysis Report**, p. 2.
9. **Ibid.**
10. **Ibid.**
11. **MACV Measurement of Progress Report**, (December 1971), p. 68.
12. "Phoenix Program: 1970 Results," **Analysis Report**, p. 29.
13. PAAS Rural Question 202 asked in March, April, May, June and July 1971, and in June and July 1972.
14. PAAS Rural Question 203, asked in March, April, May, June and July 1971.
15. PAAS Rural Surveys. From published PAAS Reports in 1970, Question 32 in January 1970, Question 37 in June and December 1970, and other months shown.
16. PAAS Rural Survey, Question 37 asked in March, April, May, June, July and October 1971, and in August 1972.
17. PAAS Rural Survey, Question 82 asked in April, May, June and July 1971, and in January and August 1972.
18. PAAS Rural Survey, Question 88 asked in October 1971.
19. PAAS Rural Survey, Question 90 asked in October 1971.
20. PAAS Rural Survey, Question 74 asked in May, June and July 1971.
21. PAAS Rural Survey, Question 34 asked in March, April, May, June and July 1971, and in June, July and August 1972. Also, Question 83 asked in January 1972.
22. PAAS Rural Survey, Question 40 asked in March, April, May, June and July 1971, and in August 1972.
23. PAAS Rural Survey, Question 41 asked in March, April, May, June and July 1971, and in August 1972.
24. Hamlet Evaluation System, Question HQB-1.
25. PAAS Rural Survey, Question 38 asked in March, April, May and June 1971, and in January, June, July and August 1972.
26. HES Question HQC-4.
27. PAAS Rural Survey, Question 76 asked in January, June, July and August 1972.
28. HES Question HQB-2.
29. PAAS Rural Survey, Question 75 asked in January, June, July and August 1972.
30. HES Question VQD-5.
31. PAAS Rural Question 211.

Part Five

Civil Operations

18
The Enormous Refugee Burden

Vietnamese Government records suggest that about seven million people at one time or another were officially registered as refugees or war victims during 1965-1972. This means that one-third of South Vietnam's population were official refugees or war victims at some point during that period. More than a million were people whose homes were destroyed or damaged by the 1968 Tet Offensive. They were not displaced from their area of residence.

Many people undoubtedly registered as refugees or war victims more than once. Military Region 1 was hit hard in the 1968 Tet Offensive. In 1972, long after most of the Tet Offensive victims had returned to their homes, it was hit again even harder. Many of the 1968 refugees and victims were probably caught in the 1972 offensive and registered for government assistance again but no records exist to confirm this. Others who were displaced, injured or suffered property damage from the war never entered the official system for care and relief.

This does not mean that seven million people in South Vietnam were on the refugees or war victims rolls at the end of 1972. Most of them had passed through the system, received some benefits, and returned to their homes or resettled. The number of refugees in December 1972 was probably down to less than one million because the number living in official refugee camps and receiving government assistance was 650,000. An estimated 450,000 displaced by the 1972 Easter Offensive had already returned home and another 200,000 were believed to be living with relatives or otherwise caring for themselves.[1]

The Statistics

It is important to recognize the character of the refugee and war victim statistics. Their function was to identify numbers of individuals to whom payments were due,[2] not to count all refugees and war victims in South Vietnam. The statistics were a source of misunderstanding because outside observers believed they represented the total number of refugees, while the officials working in the refugee program considered them to be the current number of refugees or war victims to whom payments were due.

The nature of the figures meant that the case load might rise because of delays in paying benefits, even though the refugees might have found employment or returned to their homes. Or the case load might be too low because refugees weren't being registered although many existed. To compound the problem, the statistics weren't reported with a great deal of accuracy. In 1967 U.S. Senate investigators asserted that "...nothing resembling even remotely accurate information on the numbers of refugees has been made available."[3] The reporting improved, but General Accounting Office investigators observed in early 1970:

> Since February 1968 the refugee reporting system has undergone three major revisions but the information being reported is still conflicting, confusing, and inconsistent-- in part because it is compiled by untrained personnel.[4]

Despite their lack of precision, the refugee figures are fairly reliable in indicating the magnitude of the problem and they did fluctuate with the tempo of combat. When combat increased, so did the number of refugees. When it decreased the number of refugees did too.

Refugees, War Victims and Migrants

Three groups commonly called refugees are addressed here: war victims, refugees and migrants. War victims were civilians who suffered property damage or personal injury from the war but did not have to leave their homes or employment for an extended period of time.[5] They registered for government benefits. Refugees were people who were forced to move away from their homes and employment and who also registered for government benefits. These two terms are often very close in meaning in that most of the "refugees" from the 1968 Tet Offensive were really war victims because almost all remained in the same urban locales. Migrants were people who moved to the cities seeking work. They did not register for government benefits.

Some observers lumped migrants into the refugee totals:

> Presently there is high employment in the urban areas and most refugees have found means of support either directly because of the U.S. troops or indirectly by providing the troops with needed services, such as laundries and housekeeping.[6]

Dr. Gerald C. Hickey, a leading authority on Vietnamese society, stated the situation more accurately:

> ...a good percentage of the people who flocked to the cities are not actually refugees. What happened is that the American military build-up and the way we fought the war basically restructured Vietnamese society from predominantly rural to predominantly urban.

At one time we had 60,000 American troops in Saigon alone, living in about 500 different buildings. This created a huge demand for maids, cooks, drivers, all kinds of services. So people came in to get jobs, to earn more cash than they ever had in their lives. They have found an entirely new way of life. They like it and they hope to stay put.

Out in the country life is very quiet and isolated. In the cities you stay up late, it is lots of fun with all kinds of people around. Vietnamese are very gregarious; they like the feeling of living all together in a crowd with lots going on.

If you have just a little money in the city you have electricity. Even a 20-watt bulb is better than an oil lamp. There are services people do not find in the countryside.[7]

Results from the PAAS support Dr. Hickey's major points.

Urbanization

When asked if they were native to the area 75 percent of the urban respondents said no. Only 25 percent were native to the city they were living in.[8] The rest had come from somewhere else.

Many Vietnamese said they would move to another place to get a better job according to the PAAS results shown in Table 18.1. The data suggest that the urban resident was more willing to move to another province than the rural resident. This is probably because he assumed he would be moving to another city. He had already moved to the one he was in now so the idea of moving was not new. On the other hand, 22 percent of the rural respondents were willing to move to another district in the same province to obtain a better job, so there may not have been much difference between the two groups on this issue.[9]

TABLE 18.1
If You Can Get a Higher Paying Job But Have to Move To Another Province, Would You Accept The Job?

	Rural	Urban
Yes	13%	23%
No	86%	76%
Number of respondents	1,919	2,312

Source: PAAS Rural Question 422, asked in January and March 1972. PAAS Urban Question 5423, asked in January, February, March and September 1972.

TABLE 18.2
Did Your Last Job Change Require You
To Move Your Place Of Residence?

	Rural	Urban
No	45%	67%
Yes - to another		
Hamlet	13%	2%
Village	20%	4%
District	15%	3%
Province	5%	21%
Military Region	2%	3%
Total Yes	55%	33%
Number of respondents	146	131

Source: PAAS Rural Question 177, asked in December 1971. PAAS
Urban Question 5400, asked in December 1971 and September 1972.

Not only did significant portions of both groups say they would move to get a better job but a significant percentage of them actually did move. The data from small samples suggest that 55 percent of the rural respondents and 33 percent of the urban respondents moved in their last job change (see Table 18.2).

The differences suggest that it was easier for the urban respondent to find another job where he lived than it was for the rural respondent. When the urban respondent did move he tended to move to another province. This suggests that he probably moved to an urban area in another province, since most provinces had only one major urban center. It may be a coincidence, but 22 percent of the Table 18.1 rural sample said they would move to another district or farther to get a better job, and 22 percent of the Table 18.2 rural sample actually moved that far or farther to get one.

When asked "What do you like best about living in an urban area?" 48 percent of the respondents cited better security than in the countryside. This might suggest that security was the prime motive for living in the city. The rest of the sample cited better economic opportunities (19 percent), better educational and health facilities (10 percent), and better entertainment and atmosphere (four percent) as the best aspects of urban life.[10]

Only 12 percent of the respondents said they didn't like living in an urban area and would return to the countryside when security permitted. Another set of PAAS questions suggests that only 15 percent of the urban respondents would return to their native rural area "if the war were to end today and peace were permanent."[11] Finally, 92 percent of the urban respondents native to their area said that they planned to remain where they were if the war ended.[12] More significant, 62 percent of the non-urban residents said they also planned to stay put.[13] Most urban dwellers clearly planned to stay in the city even when security ceased to become a significant factor. Other research supports the notion that a great many migrants moved to the cities and towns for reasons other than security:

> Among the most striking findings of the research reported here were that the war was only one of a number of reasons why people migrated to Saigon, that once in the city it did not figure prominently in the lives of those interviewed, and that it had relatively little significance to migrants in deciding if Saigon was to be their permanent home. In sharp contrast to the portrait of the population advanced by many as one caught between the two fires of the war--the GVN and the PRG--the authors found little evidence that this was the case. Instead, the migrants studied appeared suspended between war and peace, responding to pressures and events associated with neither.[14]

The data also suggest that there was a good deal of mobility and aggressive job hunting in South Vietnam. It is simply not correct to say that the urban growth there was solely a product of refugee movements. Many of the rural families that moved to the cities went there to improve their lives and they planned to stay. Urbanization has been a worldwide phenomenom for some time so this should not be surprising.

Refugees

Refugees were people who were forced to move away from their homes and employment and registered for government benefits. If they didn't register they didn't show up in the statistics. Other large scale displacements of people have occurred in Vietnam's history. Two of them can be directly related to events in Vietnam since World War II.

The first occurred after the Geneva Agreement of 1954 which gave all Vietnamese people 300 days to choose whether they wanted to live in North or South Vietnam. Approximately 900,000 moved south and about 75,000 went north.[15] The Diem government and the French were swamped so the United States became a third party in the resettlement effort, providing $56.8 million in aid.[16] Resettlement of the refugees was difficult because there was little time for planning and little land available.

In spite of this the South Vietnamese Government and American officials could point with pride to their accomplishments over the next three years as some 660,000 of the refugees became nearly self-sufficient.[17] Work with the refugees continued through the late 1950's and into the 1960's with important assistance coming from a number of American volunteer agencies but for all practical purposes the refugee problem was solved by the late 1950's. A new and smaller crisis arose in 1962 and 1963 when Viet Cong harassment and terror drove approximately 150,000 Montagnards from their mountain homes, but this problem was quickly solved using the experience acquired in the 1950's.[18]

The second large scale displacement of people began as the war intensified in 1965 and the numbers of people shifting began to equal 1954 levels and beyond. The second wave had at least one important difference from the first   because most refugees moved only a few miles this time. The movement had little in common with the mass movements of refugees in Europe during World War II when people were driven from their homelands and remained homeless for years. The Vietnamese refugees remained nearby for the most part, and many of them were able to return home as security began to spread into the countryside in 1969.

The continuous stream of refugees throughout the country between 1965 and 1967 created widespread confusion and uncertainty about how to deal with the problem, particularly in the camps in the northern part of South Vietnam. The challenge of caring for so many people while fighting a war was great. Lacking an adequate program or the resources for one, the government response was slow and hesitant.[19] American concern about the problem mounted and American efforts to assist the refugees began to increase. In 1966 and 1967 the South Vietnamese and American efforts concentrated on developing an organization, recruiting people, finding resources, identifying the kinds of aid required in different refugee situations and building up the necessary logistic support.[20]

By the end of 1967 the stage was set for an all-out attack on the refugee problem. At this point the communists launched their large offensives in 1968, starting at Tet, and temporarily displaced more than one million additional people. South Vietnamese and American efforts had to concentrate on caring for them, so another year passed before efforts really got underway to return the long term refugees to their homes or resettle them.

The problems of trying to get organized while the flow of refugees continued led the refugee program to be concentrated on payments to individuals who qualified.[21] This ensured that refugees received some assistance but also led to complex bureaucratic procedures of registration, authentication and financial accounting which generated delays when the refugee flows were highest. The focus on the procedures also cut into the ability of the government to give much assistance to refugee communities and camps.[22]

In 1969 considerable progress was made in paying refugees their allowances (some long overdue), returning 200,000 of them to their homes,[23] and resettling others. The program continued to gain momentum until 1972 when the intense fighting leading up to the cease fire agreement dislocated an estimated 1.2 million people and the effort focused once again on short-term relief.

Table 18.3 shows summary statistics of the number of refugees who registered and to whom benefits were paid through

TABLE 18.3
Refugees And Benefits

	Thousands of Persons	
	Newly Registered[a]	Benefits Paid To[b]
Prior to 1967	1678	1082
1967	463	572
1968	494	576
1969	114 (+476 registered for out-of-camp benefits)[c]	1,277
1970	129 (+281 registered for return-to-village benefits[c]	925
1971	136 4,012 [sic][d]	450+ 4,882+

Source: [a] Nooter, p. 38. (See Chapter 18 Notes).
[b]Colby, p. 24 (See Chapter 18 Notes).
[c]Refugees generated in prior years but registered this year for out-of-camp or return-to-village benefits.
[d]Figures add to 3771 but 4012 total is shown in source document, so there may be a typographical or other error in the yearly figures shown.

the end of 1971. The reliability of the data is limited but the table does give some idea of the enormity of the problem and the 1972 offensive generated another 1.2 million refugees. The number of benefits exceeded the number of refugees because many refugees received more than one set of benefits. Refugees might receive temporary benefits at the time they were registered and then be paid resettlement or return-to-village benefits when they went off the rolls.

The South Vietnamese refugee program did not provide extensive assistance to any individual or family because the number of refugees was so large and the resources made available to help them so small.[24] The program worked somewhat as follows. Soon after refugee families reached secure areas those seeking assistance were housed in temporary camps. Each newly arrived family received emergency food commodities for seven days followed by a two-month temporary allowance[25] which was extended until the family could return home or begin to settle elsewhere at which time additional benefits were paid.[26]

Temporary benefits were designed to give interim assistance to people thrown into refugee status. Through the first quarter of 1971, 2.3 million refugees reportedly had received temporary benefits.[27]

The benefits were provided by the South Vietnamese Ministry of Refugees and Social Welfare after the individual or family registered. The registration was handled by local officials, by the Ministry staff, or by special teams sent to register refugees. For the first seven days the refugees would receive 500 grams of rice per person per day, three cans of condensed milk per family of at least five members, and 20 grams of salt per person per day, plus whatever shelter was available.[28] After the first week refugees received either 20 piasters or 500 grams of rice per day and temporary shelter was provided for the refugees in camp. These benefits lasted two months or until the refugees resettled or returned to their villages.[29] Added to these benefits was additional assistance in the form of PL-480 foods, aid from voluntary agencies, civic action assistance from military units that were located in the neighborhood, and assistance from international agencies and from other nations.

Temporary benefits were paid to refugees not housed in temporary camps if they lived in groups of 20 or more families and they were reported as out-of-camp refugees.[30] Out-of-camp refugees gained attention in November 1968 when the government began a program to find and register all refugees throughout South Vietnam. The initial results of the survey added approximately 500,000 refugees to the rolls.

Resettlement benefits were designed to assist refugees in settling somewhere other than their original homes. Before 1970 refugees receiving these benfits were reported as being resettled, although their problems were usually far from being over. From 1970 on they were reported as "resettlement benefits paid" in an attempt to reflect their status more accurately.[31]

Basic resettlement benefits consisted of a 3,600 piaster food allowance per person for six months, and 7,500 piasters and ten sheets of roofing per family. Montagnards received 20 grams of salt per person per day for six months in addition. Additional aid was available from the PL-480 and other programs. Through the first quarter of 1971 approximately 1.7 million refugees reportedly had received resettlement benefits.[32] The figure is a crude estimate although reported by South Vietnamese officials through the official reporting system. There were also allegations that some refugees reportedly receiving benefits did not receive them.

Senate Subcommittee investigators in 1967 asserted that one group of 13,000 refugees in Pleiku was counted as resettled but 10,000 of them had never received any part of a resettlement allowance.[33] In Binh Thuan U.S. officials reportedly told subcommittee members that 115,000 refugees reportedly received resettlement allowances but 65,000 received only part of their allowance or nothing at all.[34]. As to those who were paid, GAO investigators said that "many of the refugees paid allowances by the GVN were, in our opinion, only slightly better off than prior to receipt of payments."[35]

Return-To-Village Program

The return-to-village program began in 1968 as a reflection of the improving security situation and to help refugees move back to their original villages. It became a major aspect of the program to repopulate the countryside.[36] As a result of this program, benefits (the same as for resettlement) were paid to people who had already received resettlement benefits but now wanted to return to their villages. Eligibility for benefits was also extended to those who had moved to Saigon whether originally registered as refugees or not. It is estimated that over 800,000 refugees returned to their villages before this program began without receiving the benefits.

More than 600,000 refugees were reportedly paid return-to-village benefits 1969 through March 1971, and 280,000 were in the process of receiving the assistance at the end of that period.[38] The USAID/Vietnam Mission Director estimated in April 1970 that refugees returning to their villages under the program probably were about half as well off as before they were displaced.[39]

Two events independent of the war in South Vietnam during 1970 generated more than 500,000 refugees. The first event was Sihanouk's fall in Cambodia. The second was extensive flooding in six provinces of central Vietnam.

After Sihanouk's fall in Cambodia the new government's anti-communist stance spilled over to affect all Vietnamese living in Cambodia, communist or not. As a result some 210,000 Vietnamese residents of Cambodia moved to South Vietnam with GVN assistance.[40] Most refugees went into hastily erected camps where they received temporary benefits and were then released at their request or were given help in finding a resettlement area.

The extensive flooding in central Vietnam struck with little warning and rendered 325,000 people homeless within days. They also received aid from their government supported by American helicopters and other resources.

Two Issues: Refugee Camps and Relocation

The two issues that drew the most criticism about the refugee program were conditions in the refugee camps and the occasional practice of forcing people to leave their homes and relocate elsewhere. These problems were most evident in the northern areas of South Vietnam where the fighting was most intense and where it was tougher to make a living than in the delta.

The first issue was the refugee camps. Individual benefits have already been discussed but there were needs beyond food and shelter for the refugees. Special programs were developed to address the needs of refugee camps, resettlement centers and return-to-village communities. The Ministry of Social Welfare Refugee Site Development Program started in late 1966,[42] It was designed to help refugees establish themselves in resettlement sites by providing facilities and services such as wells, latrines, classrooms, simple health facilities and services, vocational training and, where land was available, vegetable seeds and other agricultural assistance.

Until 1970 the site-development program was impeded by the diversion of resources and emphasis to the higher priority needs of emergency relief and paying individual benefits. In 1970 reduced case loads, pacification momentum and the emerging effects of the return-to-village program began to eliminate the need for some refugee camps and freed resources to improve others. The Ministry of Social Welfare budget in 1971 included 538 million piasters specifically earmarked for development of resettlement sites and reconstruction of community facilities in the refugees' original villages.[43]

Special efforts were made in Military Region 1 which had the worst camps.[44] In the delta (Military Region 4) many people also fled from their homes but, given the relative ease of subsisting there, were quickly assimilated and never became the obvious problem represented by the people in northern refugee camps.[45]

The shortcoming of the refugee camps were well known to the people trying to correct them. There was no attempt to hide the problem. A monthly refugee report (March 20, 1970) for 402 occupied sites in South Vietnam said that 176 sites (42 percent) were overcrowded and 87 sites (21 percent) were deficient in medical support. In addition, 833 classrooms were needed and an undetermined number of sites had poor water supplies. Of the 383 sites assigned ratings by the South Vietnamese Ministry of Social Welfare, 91 (24 percent) were rated substandard.[46]

To sum up the problem, the USAID/Vietnam Mission Director estimated that most people in resettlement sites were only about one-third as well off as before being displaced.[47] It is important at this point to remember the people were refugees because of the war. The war caused the situation, not the refugee program.

The second criticism concerned relocations, forced and voluntary. During the height of the fighting in 1967 and 1968, and again in 1970 and 1971 (during the relocation of Montagnards in the Central Highlands and the South Vietnamese army operations in the U Minh Forest in Military Region IV) civilians were forcibly removed from their homes at the insistence of the South Vietnamese military. Compared to the refugee totals the numbers were relatively small. There are, in fact, relatively few documented cases of forced relocation.

The stated purpose of forced relocations was to move the people out of the way of military actions or to prevent their being used by the communists as sources of manpower, supplies or intelligence. Criticism of forced relocations mounted because of the hardships they imposed on the people who were moved. Therefore, in early 1970 the GVN adopted a formal policy that called for bringing "security to the people instead of bringing people to security."[48] The policy and guidelines for the exceptions where relocation was really considered necessary were incorporated in decrees issued by the South Vietnamese prime minister on March 2 and April 18, 1970.[49]

During the relocation of Montagnards from the Central Highlands in late 1970 and early 1971 South Vietnamese military and civilian authorities failed to comply with the directives.[50] American pacification advisors at all levels then made a concentrated effort to stop further forced relocations. These efforts resulted in another decree from the Prime Minister on May 12, 1971 reaffirming the government policy restricting relocation of people and tightening procedures by requiring on-the-spot inspection by regional and national pacification officials before approval of any relocation plan.[51] This reduced the problem.

In contrast to forced relocation designed to clear civilians out of an area until security could be established, voluntary relocation was designed to provide a new life for refugees who had little chance of returning to their original homes. As might be expected voluntary relocation got mixed up with forced relocation when the program surfaced and this raised an outcry.

A number of refugees from communities in Military Regions 1 and 2 had little or no hope of returning to their original homes or of supporting themselves where the refugee settlements were organized. Their plight generated the idea of voluntary relocation and the government established a Directorate of Land Development and Hamlet Building which drew up a plan to resettle people in need of land on land in need of people. The plan had two goals:[52]

1. To offer refugee communities with no future an opportunity to move of their own free will to areas where they could make a living.

2. To open up for productive use several hundred thousand hectares of idle government land and thereby aid the economic development of South Vietnam.

The goals were laudable and they could have benefited the people and the country. The danger was that the second aim could erode the voluntary nature of the first if heavy emphasis was placed on opening up and taking control of vacant land.

It was clear that South Vietnamese people were willing to move to other areas to improve their standards of living. The PAAS data have shown this. There is also the precedent of 900,000 people voting with their feet and moving south in 1954 to settle on vacant land. The 200,000 refugees from Cambodia also moved into some of the vacant land owned by the government.

Preparations for the first pilot project under the new program began in the summer of 1971. Ha Thanh hamlet in Quang Tri province was the first hamlet to be offered resettlement. Ha Thanh, two miles below the Demilitarized Zone (DMZ), was established as a temporary refugee camp in 1967 for 15,000 refugees but it never became self-supporting. Two-thirds of its population drifted away, leaving 5,000 people living in abject poverty.[53]

Following a process that included consultation with provincial and district officials, a presentation to the villagers, a request from them for more particulars, and a trip by hamlet representatives to Military Region 3 where they inspected various sites, the population of Ha Thanh and their personal belongings were taken by air or ship to various sites in Military Region 3. With the help of resettlement allowances and other government assistance they began to work the land allotted to them, build houses and settle down. By May 1972 the government had requests from another 12,000 refugees to relocate from Military Region 1 to Military Regions 3 and 4 during the remainder of 1972.[54]

War Victims

War victims were a separate category developed in 1968 to provide benefits to civilians who suffered personal injury or damage to property as a result of the war but did not have to leave their homes for a long period. The war victim benefits for property damage, death and injury were as follows.[55]

All families whose houses were damaged 20 percent or more were eligible to receive the following: two meters of cloth per person; one blanket and one mosquito net per family of two to four persons, and two mosquito nets for each family with five or more members. If money were paid in lieu of commodities the rates were 50 piasters per meter of cloth, 400 piasters per blanket and 400 piasters per mosquito net.

Families with houses damaged 20 to 50 percent received an additional 500 grams of rice per person per day for 15 days, or money at the rate of 40 piasters per kilogram of rice. A house-construction allowance of 3,000 piasters was also provided. Families with houses damaged more than 50 percent received the same rice allowance but for 30 days and a house-construction allowance of 7,500 piasters plus ten sheets of roofing.

Death benefits were 4,000 piasters if the deceased was 15 or over and 2,000 piasters if under 15. Injuries requiring medical treatment for at least seven days received a benefit of 2,000 piasters.

By the first quarter of 1971 approximately 1.6 million war victims had registered for benefits and 1.35 million (83 percent) had reportedly received them.[56] The total included approximately one million temporary victims of the Tet and May 1968 offensives. As already mentioned, most of the Tet 1968 "refugees" were actually war victims aided through Project Recovery and other civil programs.[57]

Table 18.4 shows that funding support for the refugee and social welfare programs in South Vietnam amounted to about $100 million per year until fiscal 1971 when it dropped to about $75-$80 million. The decline stemmed from reductions in our AID budget, PL-480 food and U.S. voluntary assistance, but it was attenuated somewhat by rises in counterpart funds and the South Vietnamese government budget.

TABLE 18.4
Refugee and Social Welfare Funding Summary

	Millions of U.S. Dollars						
	FY 68	FY 69	FY 70	FY 71	FY 72	Totals	%
AID Budget	17.9	9.5	5.9	3.8	1.7	38.8	9
Counterpart funds[a]	20.0	28.4	32.1	31.5	42.4	154.4	34
PL-480 Food (as programmed)	32.3	33.9	24.2	10.0	5.0	105.4	23
Ministry of Social Welfare (GVN Budget)[a]	4.3	3.6	7.6	8.7	10.2	34.4	8
U.S. Volunteer Agencies	22.4	25.9	22.4	19.4	16.8	106.9	23
Free World Assistance	3.1	3.1	3.1	3.1	3.1	15.5	3
Military Civic Action (estimated)	.2	.2	.2	.2	N/A	.8	–
Total	100.2	104.6	95.5	76.7	79.2	456.2	100

Source: Colby, Annex D, for FY 68 through FY 70. Nooter, P. 39 for FY 71-72. (See Chapter 18 Notes)
[a]Piasters converted to dollars at 118 piasters to one dollar.

For the period as a whole 80 percent of the funding support for refugee and social welfare programs came from three sources: counterpart funds (34 percent), PL-480 food (23 percent) and U.S. voluntary agencies (23 percent). The rest came from the South Vietnamese government. It should also be recognized that the much larger amounts of American and South Vietnamese funds spent on local economic revival, anti-inflation programs, and repair and maintenance of transport and communications also benefited refugees as well as the general population. Most refugees did earn some income on their own.

Given the billions of American dollars spent on the war effort it is difficult to understand why the United States didn't spend more on assistance for refugees and war victims. It is also surprising that Congressional critics of the refugee conditions did not push harder to appropriate or earmark more funds for this purpose.

NOTES

1. **Message Saigon 00431, 121255Z, from American Embassy Saigon To Secretary of State,** Subject: Refugees, Weekly Summary Report, p. 1.

2. Statement of Ambassador William E. Colby, Deputy to COMUSMACV for CORDS, to Senate Subcommittee on Refugees and Escapees, April 21, 1972, p. 6. (Hereafter cited as "Colby".)

3. Civilian Casualty and Refugee Problems in South Viet-Nam, Findings and recommendations of the Subcommittee to Investigate Problems connected with Refugees and Escapees of the Committee on the Judiciary, United States Senate, May 9, 1968. U.S. Government Printing Office, p. 10. (Herafter cited as "Senate".)

4. "Continuing Difficulties in Assisting War Victims in Viet-Nam," By the Comptroller General of the United States (B-13301), November 20, 1970, p. 2. (Cited hereafter as "GAO Report".)

5. Statement of the Honorable Robert H. Nooter, Deputy Coordinator, Bureau for Supporting Assistance, Agency for International Development, before the Judiciary Sub-Committee on Refugees, U.S. Senate, May 8, 1972, p. 5. (Cited herafter as "Nooter".)

6. GAO Report, p. 26.

7. "Can South Viet-Nam make it on its Own?" U.S. News and World Report, (August 13, 1973), p. 7.

8. PAAS Urban Question 5516, asked in October 1971 and June, July and October 1972. Cumulative number of respondents was 2526.

9. PAAS Rural Question 421, asked in January and March 1972. Cumulative number of respondents was 1919.

10. PAAS Urban Question 5102, asked in March, April, May, June, July, October and November 1971. Cumulative respondents numbered 2905.

11. From PAAS Urban Questions 5517 and 5518 asked in April, June, July and October 1972. The two questions were identical but 5517 as asked of 744 respondents native to the area, and 5518 was asked of 2035 non-natives. Of the combined sample, 422 non-native respondents indicated they would return to their native rural area if peace became permanent.

12. PAAS Urban Question 5517.

13. PAAS Urban Question 5518.

14. Allan E. Goodman and Lawrence M. Franks, "Between War and Peace: A Profile of Migrants to Saigon," The Asia Society—SEADAG, New York, N.Y. p. 1.

15. Opening statement by William K. Hitchcock, Director, Refugee Directorate, CORDS. Senate Foreign Relations Committee Hearings on Viet-Nam. February 17-20, 1970. (Cited hereafter as "Hitchcock".)

16. Senate, p. 1.

17. Ibid.

18. Ibid., p. 2

19. Hitchcock, p. 5.

20. Ibid., p. 7.

21. Colby, p. 6.

22. Ibid.

23. Nooter, p. 6.

24. Hitchcock, p. 8.

25. **Colby,** Annex A.
26. **Hitchcock,** p. 8.
27. **GAO Report,** p. 23.
28. **Colby,** Annex A.
29. **Ibid.**
30. **GAO Report,** p. 23.
31. **Colby,** p. 19. Also, **GAO Report,** p. 11.
32. **Ibid.**
33. **Senate,** p. 10.
34. **Ibid.**
35. **GAO Report,** p. 20.
36. **Colby,** p. 20.
37. **Ibid.,** p. 21.
38. **Ibid.**
39. **GAO Report,** p. 22.
40. **Colby,** P. 26.
41. **Ibid.,** p. 27.
42. **Colby,** p. 28.
43. **Ibid.,** pp. 29-30.
44. **Ibid.,** p. 29.
45. **Hitchcock,** p. 4.
46. **GAO Report,** pp. 32-33.
47. **Ibid.,** p. 21.
48. This was always the policy of American pacification advisors and they protested several military relocations schemes.
49. **GAO Report,** p. 21.
50. **Ibid.,** p. 10.
51. **Ibid.**
52. **Ibid.,** p. 11.
53. **Ibid.,** p. 13.
54. **Ibid.,** p. 14.
55. **Colby,** Annex A 1.
56. **Ibid.,** p. 22.
57. **Ibid. Hitchcock,** p. 7; **Nooter,** p. 6.

19
Land Reform:
Best of This Century?

Sixteen years of broken promises on land reform provide warrant for skepticism about the new legislation President Thieu has signed....

...The far-reaching nature of the legislation-- probably the most ambitious and progressive noncommunist land reform of the twentieth century--provides built-in safeguards against evasion.

New York Times Editorial,
April 1970[1]

In fact, the land distribution programme implemented by Saigon has effectively taken place; it does not exist only on paper.

Oliver Todd,
September 1973[2]

A key communist strategy in South Vietnam was to concentrate on the rural population. Perhaps their most powerful appeal was the promise of land. When the communist forces took over a village, they told the farmers that the landlords would be chased out or killed and that the tenant farmers would be given the land they were farming. But they didn't tell them that land would be given only to those who actively supported communists. No title would be issued. If the tenant farmer died the land would not be left with the widow and children but would be given to another farmer who was friendly to the communists. Finally after an interval of five or ten years the farmers would surrender their lands to a commune of which they would be a part.[3]

The promise of land had powerful appeal in South Vietnam and land reform was a constant government theme from the early 1950's. Little land was distributed to landless peasants until the Land-to-the-Tiller program began in 1970.

Land Reform Before 1970

South Vietnam had one of the world's highest tenancy rates before the Land-to-the-Tiller Program began in 1970. The government estimated that approximately 60 percent of all the rice and secondary crop land was being farmed by tenant farmers who did not own the land.[4] An American consultant to the 1967-1968 study of South Vietnam's land tenure situation stated that: "In its percentage of landlessness, the Mekong Delta...qualified as one of the five worst areas of the world."[5]

A tenant farmer in southern South Vietnam cultivated two hectares (one hectare = 2.47 acres) on average, paying a rent that averaged about 35 percent of his crop. In the Central Highlands of South Vietnam the plot averaged about one hectare.[6] The farmer was a manager because the landlord normally did not participate in the production process. He did not furnish seed, credit, farm implements or marketing outlets. He simply collected the rent.

Land tenancy had been high for a long time particularly in the southern portion of South Vietnam. In 1945 about 6,000 landowners held 1.2 million hectares (nearly three million acres) of cultivated land there, while 430 French nationals owned 250,000 hectares of land in the Mekong Delta. Eighty percent of the land in that area was farmed by tenants who were paying rents as high as 50 percent of the crop.[7]

Early in 1951 Emperor Bao Dai proclaimed a land tenure reform program but the committee to carry it out was not organized until late 1952. By then political difficulties and the deteriorating military situation prevented execution of the program.[8]

In 1956, under U.S. pressure, President Ngo Dinh Diem decreed a 100 hectare limit (247 acres) to riceland ownership (Ordinance 57). Any excess was to be expropriated and sold to the farmers. The owners received ten percent of the land price in cash and the remaining 90 percent in government bonds redeemable over 12 years.[9]

Redistribution of land to the farmers proceeded slowly. The 100 hectare ownership limitation freed only 453,000 hectares for redistribution. There were also another 230,000 hectares of French owned land bought by the GVN in 1958. By the end of 1962 some 428,000 hectares had been expropriated.[10] But a year later only about half of that land (246,000 hectares) had been sold to the farmers, benefiting 115,000 families.[11] Only 45,000 additional hectares of land were distributed to 21,000 families during the five years between the end of 1963 and the end of 1968.[12] None of the former French land was distributed until 1966 and most of it was still in government hands at the end of 1968.[13]

The new constitution for South Vietnam promulgated in April 1967 emphasized in Article 19 that "The State advocated a policy of making the people property owners," and in Article 21,"The State advocates raising the standard of living of rural citizens and especially helping farmers to have land for cultivation." No effects were seen until 1969 when land reform began to gather momentum. Land distribution skyrocketed by previous standards when 310,000 hectares were distributed to 232,000 tenant families under the various programs in existence.[14]

In April 1969 the government froze land occupancy and rents for one year to prepare for the new land reform. This prevented landlords from changing tenants before the new program could go into effect, and the rent freeze permitted tenants to keep the increased returns from using fertilizers and new seeds.[15] In June 1969 the Land-to-the-Tiller bill was approved by the Cabinet and sent to the National Assembly the following month.[16]

The stage was set for a major land reform program and the South Vietnamese tenant farmers were ready for it. Surveys of Vietnamese attitudes in Military Regions 3 and 4 toward land ownership and reform indicated that strong antagonism between landlords and tenants was rare (some were relatives), even though the average rent being charged was 35 percent of the crop, above the 25 percent maximum fixed by law.[17]

Landlords were not meeting their obligation to reduce rents in case of total or partial crop failure. More than half of the tenants eligible for reductions in 1966 did not get them. Eighty percent of the tenants said they would be willing to buy the property they rented and would pay its current market value if the purchase was divided into 12 annual installments.

Offered a choice between permanent guaranteed occupancy and purchase, 85 percent preferred purchase. When asked what was needed to improve life in the village, 37 percent of the respondents mentioned land ownership. The need for credit was a close second with 36 percent. Only six percent of the respondents had received land under President Diem's Ordinance 57, and 84 percent of them said the plots were too small.

On the other hand, 91 percent of the landlord respondents who had held more than 100 hectares had lost the surplus hectares. Eighty-three percent of the landlords interviewed said they had approved of Ordinance 57 in principle because they were aware of the need for it. Landlord complaints about Ordinance 57 centered on the administration of it, including compensation and the fact that the government held on to the expropriated lands and rented them out for years.

Absentee landlords were asked about future land reform. Twenty percent said they favored it, 32 percent would not oppose it and 25 percent would abide by the government's decision. Some of those most favorably inclined held land in areas that were not secure so the idea of government payment for land they couldn't use anyway probably had considerable appeal.

The results suggest that the tenant farmers were eager to own their land--even at full current prices--and most of the landlords said they were not opposed to a land reform program.

Land-To-The-Tiller Law

On March 26, 1970 after passage by the legislative bodies President Thieu, who had "fought a bitter battle to get the reform adopted without crippling amendments,"[18] signed the Land-to-the-Tiller bill into law. Its stated purpose was to abolish farm tenancy and create a nation of landowners. Title was to be given, free of charge, to all persons farming rice land as tenants, share-croppers, squatters, or Viet Cong appointed cultivators. The bill was expected to affect approximately 800,000 farm families who were farming 1.3 million hectares of rice land[19] and the the 16,000 landlords who owned the land.[20]

The main features of the program resulting from the bill were:[21]

1. Land holdings were limited to 15 hectares (37 acres). All other land would be redistributed free to the farmers, a significant departure from past programs.
2. Titles were to be issued by the village Administrative Committee and registered with the Province and Central Governments. Only ten percent of people on the village committees were landlords, and 30 percent of the village officials would benefit from the program.
3. Landlords were to be paid a price equal to 2.5 times the annual paddy yield of the land, 20 percent in cash immediately, the balance in negotiable bonds redeemable over eight years and bearing ten percent interest.
4. Farmers would receive a three hectare plot in the delta and one hectare in central Vietnam. They would not be liable for back taxes or back rent but would pay taxes in the future after they had held the land for one year.
5. Farmers had to till the land to keep it.

The Program

In signing the new law, President Thieu announced that the government would distribute one million hectares (2.5 million acres) of land to tenant farmers within three years.[22] They did it. By April 1973 the government had printed the new titles for 2.5 million acres and had distributed about 75 percent of this land to farmers. It had issued 60,700 checks for 14.8 billion piasters and 506,600 bonds valued at 82 million piasters.[23] Several key elements combined to enable the program to meet its goals. First, it had the advantage of top level leadership and ability. President Thieu gave clear, unwavering support to the program and put good leaders in charge of it.

Second, and perhaps more important, the program was decentralized to the villages. A Land Distribution Committee was established in each village with the authority to make the decisions about who received the land. It also made the decisions about compensation, particularly determinations of true owners and plot yields. The typical province administration (with 40 to 50 villages) simply could not have handled the volume and met the deadline.

Third, aerial photography instead of land cadastral surveys was used to locate and identify the plots of land to be distributed.

The entire process of registering the land, issuing it and paying for it was done with assistance of computers. The semi-automatic system created was instrumental in overcoming bureaucratic delays in title preparation and distribution.

Fourth, the government focused sharply on two main tasks, distributing land and paying for it. As soon as the land wasidentified and allocated by the village committee, it was issued even though precise records often were not available. In this manner, and with the assistance of the aerial photography and computers, the South Vietnamese avoided a long tooling up period and got the program moving right away. This contrasted sharply with their previous land reform programs.

Finally, the program received massive publicity. During 1970 the PAAS suggested that 70 to 80 percent of the rural population had some awareness of the Land-to-the-Tiller Law[24] with approximately 45 percent of them having heard about it from the radio.[25] It was a popular topic with the people. When asked what kind of people's information should be emphasized and which they liked best, Land-to-the-Tiller was a favorite topic.[26]

The farmers were willing to pay for the land, but the government, possibly to counter the communist program of "free" land, decided to give the land away and have the government pay the landlord. The payments were estimated at the equivalent of $537 million through 1981.[27] This placed a serious financial burden on the government and U.S. assistance was expected to be necessary to help meet the expense.

The Results

Table 19.1 displays the basic statistics of the Land-to-the-Tiller Program through March 31, 1973. The table implies that the average plot of land involved with each application and title was 1.16 hectares, or 2.9 acres. In a PAAS survey of 938 rural respondents in January 1972,[28] seventy-two percent said their family owned less than two hectares of land and 55 percent owned less than one hecatare, so the plot sizes don't seem to be too small.

When the 495,000 hectares distributed by other land reform efforts were added to the Land-to-the-Tiller Program, the total land distributed was 1.5 million hectares.[29] The total amount of rice land in South Vietnam was 2.3 million hectares. Between 1956 and 1973 sixty-five percent of all the rice land was redistributed. Nonetheless, the government continued to distribute the remaining land under the Land-to-the-Tiller Law, estimated at approximately 295,000 hectares.[30]

In central Vietnam the program was not very effective mainly because the land plots already were small and there was little absentee ownership.[31] The other main weakness was that the land reform program for montagnards was poorly executed and did not receive adequate government support.[32]

The data are probably fairly reliable because monitoring and inspection of the Land-to-the-Tiller Program were pretty good. The key decisions were made in the village and this did much to

TABLE 19.1
Land Reform

	Number of Applications & Titles	Hectares Covered
Applications Approved	910,915	1,067,512
Titles Issued	867,592	1,007,217
Titles Distributed	680,136	792,491

Source: Muller: Willard C., The Land-to-the-Tiller Program: The Operational Phase, April 1973, USAID/Viet-Nam, p. 37.

ensure the fairness of the program because the local people knew the plots, who owned them and who was tilling them.

The program appeared to be quite clean given the large potential for corruption. There are reports of "tea money" being paid by landlords to get officials to expedite payments, but the complaints from farmers were low. Few, if any, scandals surfaced in the American press and the U.S. General Accounting Office seemed satisfied with the program.

The Vietnamese peasant, as usual, wasn't as impressed as the outsiders. Six rural PAAS surveys asked 5,900 rural respondents if they believed the Land-to-the-Tiller Law was being fairly administered in their village. Of the 3,500 who had an opinion 47 percent said yes, 28 percent said no.[33]

The communists never mounted much of an attack against the program. Isolated critical statements were issued from time to time, but they did not amount to much.[34]

Impact Of The Program

The Land-to-the-Tiller Program dropped land tenancy in South Vietnam from 60 percent of cropland down to ten percent in three years and the government still continued to distribute land.[35] Data from the PAAS support the contention that the number of landowners increased dramatically. In December 1970 and in December 1972 seventy-three percent of the PAAS rural respondents said they were farmers. The shift from tenant to landowner is shown in Table 19.2. Twenty-nine percent said they were landowners in 1970 and 56 percent said so two years later.

The results vanished into the communist version of land reform so we shall probably never know whether the peasants receiving land provided real support to the South Vietnamese Government. But the short-term results appeared favorable. A study in 1972 concluded that the program had hurt the communists politically, reduced peasant neutrality, helped unify the village as a local government and community, created an appetite for land

TABLE 19.2
What Is Your Occupation?

	Percentage of Respondents	
Occupation	1970	1972
Farm Laborer	16	10
Tenant Farmer	28	7
Landowner	29	56
Total:	73%	73%
Number of Respondents (100%)	3,307	4,032

Source: PAAS Rural Survey, Question 15 for December 1970, and Question 16 for December 1972.

among the landless, and received credit for more changes than it probably should have.[36] A General Accounting Office team reported: "Most farmers we talked to were pleased to be landowners and believed they were better off now economically."[37]

Before land reform Japan's tenancy rate was 65 percent, Taiwan's was 50 percent and South Vietnam's was 60 percent. Approximately 3.8 million acres were distributed in South Vietnam compared to Japan's 4.2 million acres and Taiwan's 600,000 acres.[38] Land tenancy in Vietnam dropped to ten percent. The **New York Times** was right. It probably was "the most ambitious and progressive noncommunist land reform of the twentieth century." The land reform program carried out in South Vietnam in the midst of a war was a remarkable accomplishment.

NOTES

1. "Viet-Nam Land Reform," **New York Times,** (April 9, 1970), p. 22.
2. **Congressional Record** - Senate, April 23, 1974, p. 56126, quoting an article by Oliver Todd entitled "How I Let Myself Be Deceived By Hanoi," published in **Realites,** (September 1973). Mr Todd, a British-born writer, had closely observed Vietnam for almost two decades. He was a long-time associate of **Le Nouvel-Observateur,** a leading left-of-center French weekly.
3. Willard C. Muller, **The Land-to-the-Tiller Program: The Operational Phase,** (April 1973, USAID/Viet-Nam), p. 1
4. **Ibid.**
5. **Ibid.,** quoting from Roy L. Prosterman, "Land Reform in Viet-Nam," **Focus,** Vol. 22, No. 5, (January 1972), p. 2.

6. MacDonald Salter, **Land Reform in South Viet-Nam,** (AID/Washington, June 1970), p. 2.

7. "Land Reform in Viet-Nam," **Viet-Nam Bulletin,** Embassy of Viet-Nam, (Washington, D.C., March 1970), p. 1.

8. **Ibid.,** For an account of earliest land reform efforts in Vietnam, see "Land Reform of Viet-Nam Through History," by Phuong Anh Trang, in **Viet-Nam Bulletin** (March 22, 1971), pp. 2-4.

9. **Ibid.**

10. Comptroller General of the United States, **Progress and Problems of U.S. Assistance for Land Reform in Viet-Nam,** (June 22, 1973), p. 6.

11. "Land Distribution 1963-71," **Viet-Nam Bulletin,** (March 20, 1972), p. 10.

12. **Ibid.**

13. **Ibid.**

14. **Ibid.**

15. Prosterman, "Land Reform in Viet-Nam," **Focus,** p. 2.

16. **Ibid.**

17. Roger Juedtke, "Land Reform: Summary of SRI Attitudinal Surveys in South Viet-Nam," **CORDS XIII,** (September 10, 1969).

18. "Viet-Nam Land Reform," **New York Times,** (April 9, 1970), p. 22.

19. Don Hoang, "Technical, Economic and Social Aspects of Land Reform in Viet-Nam," **Viet-Nam Bulletin,** Embassy of Viet-Nam, Washington, D. C., (March 22, 1971), p. 9.

20. Prosterman, "Land Reform in Viet-Nam," **Focus,** p. 7.

21. **Ibid.**

22. Muller, **Land-to-the-Tiller,** p. 3

23. **Ibid.**

24. PAAS Rural Survey, Question S37, asked in April, May, July, October and December 1970.

25. PAAS Rural Survey, Question S38, asked in April and May 1970.

26. PAAS Rural Survey, Questions 220 and 221, asked in March 1971 of 835 respondents.

27. Comptroller General, "Progress and Problems," p. 13.

28. PAAS Rural Question 431.

29. Dong, "Technical,", p. 12.

30. Muller, **Land-to-the-Tiller.,** p. 36.

31. See Comptroller General, "Progress and Problems," p. 11, and Muller, **Land-to-the-Tiller,** P. 19.

32. **Ibid.,** Comptroller General, p. 17 and Muller, p. 23.

33. PAAS Rural Question 104 asked in March, April, May, June, July and November 1971, and in April 1972. 5863 respondents; 3488 had an opinion.

34. Muller, **Land-to-the-Tiller.** p. 32

35. **Ibid.,** p. 33

36. Comptroller General, "Progress and Problems," p. 12, summarizing: **The Impact of the Land-to-the-Tiller Program in the Mekong Delta,** by Henry C. Bush and Staff, Control Data Corporation, 1972.

37. **Ibid.,** p. 13

38. Muller, **Land-to-the-Tiller,** p. 4.

20
Inflation:
War-Fueled but Well-Controlled

Until recently so much American money was available in one form or another that Vietnamese who were not actually killed, wounded or made homeless by the war stood a good chance of improving their standard of living even while their country was fighting for its life.

The Economist[1]

Inflation is a by-product of war and the war in Vietnam was no exception. In this case increased government spending for national defense, coupled with allied spending (mostly by Americans), generated excessive demand for a limited supply of local goods.

The analysis here does not attempt to deal with the economics of Vietnam during the war. The subject is much too complex for the author to address. This inquiry is limited to a simple presentation of the inflation problem in South Vietnam during 1965-1972, a comparison with wartime inflation in South Korea 1950-53, and some views of the South Vietnamese people about inflation and their economic situation.

Inflation is expressed here by consumer price indexes. Table 20.1 displays them for South Vietnam, three other Southeast Asian countries, South Korea and Brazil from 1963 through 1972. It suggests that consumer prices in South Vietnam rose more than four times as fast as they did in the other Southeast Asian countries, almost three times as fast as in South Korea but not as fast as in Brazil. According to the International Monetary Fund, South Vietnam's inflation problem was worse than 65 other countries listed.[2] Only Uruguay, Brazil and Chile had faster price rises.

The data suggest that inflation during the American presence was not contained very well because inflation in South Vietnam was bad compared to other countries. However, to add perspective to the comparison, we need to find a country that suffered a war and relied heavily on outside forces to fight it. South Korea during the Korean War (1950-1953) fits into that category.

TABLE 20.1
South Vietnam's Prices Rose At Least Four Times As
Fast As Prices In Other Southeast Asian Countries[a]

End of Year:	South Vietnam	Commercial Price Indexes Thailand	Malaysia	Philippines	South Korea	Brazil
1963	100	100	100	100	100	100
1966	194	107	101	117	163	445
1967	279	111	105	124	180	591
1968	358	113	105	127	201	723
1969	431	116	104	130	221	886
1970	590	117	106	148	249	1082
1971	698	119	108	170	280	1300
1972	875	124	112	188	313	1514

[a]Source: International Monetary Fund, "Changes in Consumer Prices",
International Financial Statistics, Vol. XXVI, Number 9, September
1973, p. 35.

There are many differences between the situations in South
Vietnam and Korea, including the kind of war being fought, the
stability of the regimes, and many other factors, so care must be
taken not to overstate the comparison or to draw far-reaching
conclusions from it. Nonetheless, it is interesting and useful to
compare the effects of the respective wars on price increases in
the two economies.

In Korea and Vietnam, war brought inflation, with the
inflation in Korea being much more severe than the inflation in
South Vietnam as shown in Table 20.2. In the first year of the
Korean War retail prices in Seoul rose nearly 300 percent. Before
the war was over prices were more than 20 times higher (1,980
percent) than they were before it started. By 1956 they were 57
times higher (5,723 percent), although they fell the following
year.

In South Vietnam prices rose less than 100 percent during
the first year that American troops were committed to the war.
By the time of the cease fire agreement in January 1973 prices had
risen to a level ten times higher than before American forces went
into combat. This amounts to an average price increase of 33
percent per year.

Inflation was a greater problem in Korea even before the war
began there. From 1946 through 1950 Korean prices increased
more than sixfold (500 percent). In the four years before 1965
South Vietnamese prices increased about 50 percent.[3] In both
countries the pace of inflation increased with the arrival of

TABLE 20.2
Korean War Inflation Was Much Worse
Than Vietnam War Inflation

South Vietnam		South Korea	
End of Year	Retail Price Index - Saigon[a]	Retail Price Index - Seoul[b]	End of Year
1964	100	100	Mid-1950
1965	N/A	189	End-1950
1966	216	607	1951
1967	305	1,268	1952
1968	408	2,080	1953
1969	539	3,077	1954
1970	698	3,920	1955
1971	798	5,723	1956
1972	981	5,209	1957

[a]Source: **Viet-Nam Economic Data - December 1972,** Office of Economic policy,Viet-Nam Programs, Agency for International Development, p. 1.
[b]Source: Table 43: **Development of the Korean Economy,** 1958. Ministry of Reconstruction, Republic of Korea. The index series was constructed on the basis of yearly percentage changes in the Bank of Korea Seoul Retail Price Index, June 30, 1950 = 100.
NOTE: These indexes are based on a January 1, 1965 base for South Vietnam and a June 30 1950 base for South Korea so the numbers are different from those in Table 20.1 which is based on a 1963 base.

allied forces. According to the crude quantity theory of money, an increase in the money supply, all other things being equal, brings about a proportionate increase in prices. Loss of confidence in the currency, however, can generate exaggerated price rises in reaction to large and continued increases in the money supply. This happened in Korea but not in South Vietnam. Table 20.3 shows that the Korean money supply was 290 times higher at the end of the period shown, while the Vietnamese money supply was only 11 times higher.

Comparing Wartime Inflation In Korea and Vietnam

In Korea the relationship between money-supply increases and price increases passed through three phases. In the first phase (the prewar years), prices rose at a slower rate than the increase in money supply. From the end of 1947 to the end of 1949 the money supply almost tripled and prices doubled. In the second phase (the first two years of the war, 1950 and 1951), prices rose much faster than the money supply. Money supply was up sixfold,

TABLE 20.3
The Money Supplies rose

End of Year	South Vietnam Money Supply[a] Billions of Piasters	South Korea Money Supply[b] Billions of Hwan	End of year
1962	19.5	0.5	1947
1963	22.3	0.7	1948
1964	27.4	1.2	1949
1965	47.6	2.8	1950
1966	65.4	7.3	1951
1967	82.2	14.3	1952
1968	124.1	30.3	1953
1969	140.7	58.1	1954
1970	162.9	93.5	1955
1971	208.4	120.9	1956
1972	220.6	145.2	1957

[a]Source: For 1962-1965: Table C-3: Annual Statistical Bulletin, Number 11 and Supplement, Office of Joint Economic Affairs, USAID/VN. For 1966-1972: **Viet-Nam Economic Data – December 1972**, Office of Economic Policy, Viet-Nam Programs, Agency for International Development, p. 5.
[b]Source: Table A-35 and A-43: **Development of the Korean Economy, 1958,** Ministry of Reconstruction, Republic of Korea.

prices up nearly twice as much. In the third phase (from the end of 1951 to the end of 1953), prices again rose at a slower rate. While the money supply quadrupled, price increases tripled.

In Vietnam price rises were slower than money supply increases until 1966. From 1961 through the end of 1965 price rises were less than money supply increases in every year.[4] The prime reason for this was that the economy was not yet fully employed. In addition, the increasing monetization of the rural areas was absorbing some of the increase in the money supply.

In 1966, with the advent of full employment, prices rose faster. While the money supply increased by slightly less than 50 percent, prices increased by slightly more than that. American stabilization policies after 1966 acted to limit inflation to an average of 30 percent per year until the end of 1972. The addition of effective Vietnamese economic reforms and American troop withdrawals helped hold price rises to 14 percent in 1971 and to 23 percent in 1972, despite extremely heavy fighting and disruption most of that year.

War almost invariably brings sharp increases in the money supply. Government expenditures increase while revenues decline because of war disruption. The government usually resorts to printing money to finance the deficit. Controlling inflation must involve measures which either increase revenues, reduce costs (of the local government and of the allied forces), reduce extensions of credit, or increase imports (that is, offsetting increasing demand through increasing imports). These factors were controlled better in Vietnam than in Korea with the result that inflation was not as bad there.

In the first place, there was a much larger and more consistent import program in Vietnam. Imports more than absorbed the money created by allied spending in every year from 1963 through 1967. In Korea imports never offset allied spending and in the first phase of the war imports were pitifully low.

Second, allied spending was much more carefully controlled in Vietnam. In Korea there were various recommendations to reduce local hire and to increase offshore purchases, but no control mechanism such as the "piaster ceiling" was introduced. Although the ceiling in Vietnam was useful in 1966-1967, when the Saigon port was clogged, it eventually contributed to the problem by withholding U.S. dollars from the South Vietnamese government.

Third, credit expansion in Korea was much greater and much more erratic. Until 1966 credit expansion in Vietnam was negligible and the increases after that were primarily associated with the rising flow of imports.

Finally, in both Korea and Vietnam, controlling the government budget and increasing the revenues were difficult to achieve. The Korean government was able to balance its budget after March 1951 only by shifting the financial care of refugees and prisoners of war from its own account to the United Nations account. The South Vietnamese budget did not balance either.

It is clear that, by Korean War standards, the U.S. helped the South Vietnamese to contain their inflation fairly well. But the South Vietnamese people didn't think so.

What Did The People Think About The Economic Situation?

The PAAS offers some insights into what the South Vietnamese people thought about their economic situation. Remember, they were caught in one of the worst inflations in the world although not as bad as the Brazilians or as the Koreans during the Korean War.

Urban respondents believed that the government performance in handling economic problems was poor. The results of urban and rural PAAS surveys are shown in Table 20.4. The rural respondents were happier with their government's economic performance than were the urban respondents who had to bear the full brunt of inflation. Actually, considering the rate of inflation, the results can be viewed as mild.

Urban and rural respondents agreed about which area of the economic sector had been hit hardest by rising prices, namely, everything (urban, 50 percent; rural 56 percent). Most of the rest cited food (urban, 36 percent; rural 31 percent).[5] But their views of who suffered the most from inflation varied in an expected way. Both sets of respondents agreed that soldiers, civil

TABLE 20.4
How Do You Rate GVN Peformance In
Handling Economic Problems?

	Urban	Rural
Poor	63%	36%
Successful	23%	42%
Doesn't Know	11%	22%
Number of Respondents	5,096	8,300

Source: PAAS Urban Question 5109, asked in March, April, May, June, July and October 1971, and in May, June, July, August 1972. PAAS Rural Question 101, asked in the same months except May 1972.

servants and workers were suffering, but the rural respondents emphasized farmers, while the urban respondents emphasized workers. Neither believed that the merchant suffered most.[6] In 1971 and 1972 sixty-five percent of the urban and rural respondents agreed that "prices increased faster this year than they did last year" (64 percent urban; 66 percent rural). About 15 percent said that the increase was the same, and another 15 percent said that it was slower.[7] These responses clearly bear little relationship to the actual movements of the price indexes shown earlier because the 1971 increase was much less than the 1970 increase, but they do convey a mood of dissatisfaction.

When asked about the causes of the inflation, urban and rural respondents most often blamed natural conditions of war and exploitation by merchants. Urban respondents also cited "heavy spending by U.S. troops and the government budget," showing more sophistication than rural respondents, many of whom simply cited high prices as the cause of inflation.[8]

Urban and rural respondents were also asked what could be done to control inflation. Price controls, more production, and reducing government expenditures were the measures mentioned most often. Rural residents tended to favor price controls (39 percent) while urban respondents split about evenly for price controls (22 percent) and higher production in Vietnam for sale outside the country (20 percent).[9]

The Vietnamese people were acutely aware of the inflation and urban and rural respondents were in fair agreement that:

1. The government's economic performance left something to
    be desired.
2. Rising prices affected everything, particularly food.
3. Salaried people suffered the most.
4. Prices were always increasing faster than they did last year (even when they weren't).

5. Inflation was caused by natural conditions of war, exploitation by merchants, and heavy U.S. and government spending.
6. Price controls, higher production and reduced government spending would help solve the inflation problem.

In addition to asking about inflation, the PAAS covered other economic matters. One question asked about general economic conditions now compared to five years ago.[10] The rural respondents generally felt they were better off despite inflation, but the urban respondents did not. The pattern of their responses was exactly the opposite. This fits the situation because the farmers were able to cope with inflation better than the city dwellers.

Farmers could raise the prices of their crops or even hold them off the market while prices rose because the radio had ended the dominance of the Chinese rice merchants by telling everyone the wholesale and retail prices of rice in Saigon and other cities. The farmers could bargain with the local rice dealer accordingly, knowing that inflation would continue to increase the price of rice if they had to hold their crops for awhile. Also, many farmers were benefiting from land reform, becoming landowners for the first time.

When rural respondents were asked what they liked best about living in a rural area, 40 percent cited the lower cost of living.[11] City dwellers had fewer ways to protect themselves. When asked what they disliked most about living in the city, 42 percent cited the high cost of living.[12] Those in both groups who felt that economic conditions had improved thought the merchants had benefited most. Fifty-six percent of the 347 urban respondents felt this way, compared to 36 percent of the 1,501 rural respondents. Twelve percent of the latter felt that poor farmers who owned their land had benefited most, perhaps an effect of land reform.[13]

Despite their complaints, it seems clear that the standard of living of most Vietnamese rose during the war. Refugees and others hard hit by the war were obvious exceptions. More people went to work and earned more money to buy more goods than ever before, and the import program kept the markets supplied with consumer goods of all types, bringing on the Honda and transistor revolutions. In the countryside farmers took advantage of miracle rice, fertilizers, tractors, the ability to hold rice off the market to raise prices, and a variety of other techniques to increase their incomes.

Some clue to the standard of living can be gleaned from answers to the question: "If you had extra money, what would be the first thing you would do with it?"[14] Both urban and rural respondents would either have fixed up their houses or invested the money, hardly the response of people who were destitute. Vietnamese interest in fixing up their homes was cited by a hardware dealer in the town of Gia Nghia, who bemoaned the lack of business since the communists had begun an effort to cut off the town. "In peacetime people want to fix up their houses. But who wants to repair anything at a time like this?"[15]

How well was inflation contained? The Korean experience, the substantial reduction in inflation during 1971 and 1972, and the rising standard of South Vietnamese living during the war all suggest that the effects of inflation were contained well, under the circumstances. After the January 1973 cease fire, however, inflation became a serious problem again as American levels of assistance declined markedly.

NOTES

1. "Vietnam--Squeezed Artery," **The Economist,** (August 31, 1974),.

2. International Monetary Fund, "Changes in Consumer Prices," **International Financial Statistics,** Vol. XXVI, Number 9, September 1973, p. 35.

3. "Economic Impact--Korea and South Viet-Nam Buildups," **Analysis Report,** (February 1967), p. 49.

4. **Ibid.,** p. 50.

5. PAAS Urban Question 5151, asked of a total of 2685 respondents in July and October 1971 and in June, July and August 1972.

6. PAAS Urban Question 5132, asked in May and October 1971, and in May, June, July and August 1972. PAAS Rural Question 132, asked in April, May and October 1971, and in June, July and August 1972.

7. PAAS Urban Question 5150, asked of a total of 2762 respondents in July and October 1971, and in June, July and August 1972. PAAS Rural Question, asked of a total of 4704 respondents during the same months.

8. PAAS Urban Question 5131, asked in May and October 1971, and in May and June 1972 of 1962 respondents. PAAS Rural Question 131, asked in March, May and October 1971, and in June 1972 of 3622 respondents.

9. PAAS Urban Question 5133, asked of a total of 1962 respondents in May and October 1971 and in May and June 1972. PAAS Rural Question 133, asked of a total of 2682 respondents in March and May 1971, and in June 1972.

10. PAAS Urban Question 5147, asked of 1375 respondents in June and July 1971, and in March 1972. PAAS Rural Question 147 asked in July and October 1971, and in March 1972, for a cumulative total of 2884 respondents.

11. PAAS Rural Question asked of 922 respondents in January 1972.

12. PAAS Urban Question 5103, asked in March, April, May, June, July, October and November 1971, and in April and May 1972. total of 4010 respondents.

13. PAAS Urban Question 5148, asked in October 1971, and PAAS Rural Question 148 asked in July and October 1971.

14. PAAS Urban Question 5149, asked in June, July and October 1971 and in March 1972; 1920 respondents. PAAS Rural Question 149, asked in July, October and November 1971, and in March 1972; 3834 respondents.

15. **Baltimore Sun,** (November 13, 1973) p. 5.

Part Six

A Summing Up

21
Epilogue: 1975

The United States committed its military forces to battle in July 1965. Almost eight years later--at the end of 1972--after one final surge of bombing, they were gone and a "cease fire" agreement was signed with the communists in January 1973. All American ground, air and naval forces were out of the war and so were virtually all of the military advisors.

South Vietnamese forces appeared to be doing a good job. They had repulsed the 1972 offensives without the help of American ground forces but with the aid of heavy American air and logistical support. However, they had not moved forcefully to solve their critical problem of poor leadership. Without better leadership, they could not improve their training, clean out their staffs and fill their combat units to full strength. The departure of American and South Korean forces left the anti-communist side weaker than before the cease fire.

Pacification had been successful. There was widespread evidence and agreement that the GVN exercised a predominant influence over the vast majority of South Vietnamese people, although the HES and other figures reflected setbacks during the heavy fighting of 1972.

But the communist troops and infrastructure were still intact and in place despite the tremendous allocation of allied resources, effort, and lives to the strategy of attrition. At the end of 1972 the communist forces were battered, to be sure, but they were still in the fight and they had improved their ability to wage large scale conventional warfare. The cease fire agreement was signed in January, which traditionally ushered in their peak combat effort of the year. Although it was not recognized at the time, the military balance was already shifting in their favor.

The South Vietnamese collapse and communist victory of 1975 are now history. They happened with a speed that startled the world including the victors, the vanquished, the American people, and their leaders. How could it have happened so fast? Military scholars and others may argue about the causes for years. No definitive answers are attempted here but some clues from the so-called "cease fire" period are worth examining.

First, there never was a cease fire. This is not news. Everyone recognized that some fighting continued but no one in Washington realized how intense it was until October 1974, near the end. This state of affairs resulted from poor reporting of South Vietnamese casualties.

Chapter 2 says that friendly combat deaths are the single best measure of the intensity of combat. After the cease fire agreement, the South Vietnamese were the only friendly troops still fighting so their combat deaths became the measure of combat intensity. The figures for South Vietnamese deaths reported to Washington indicated that combat during the year following the cease fire was 75 percent below the 1972 level. This was duly reported to Congressional committees as evidence that the cease fire was having a beneficial effect. In turn, the fact was used as part of the rationale for slashing aid to South Vietnamese forces during the summer of 1974.

The problem was that the official South Vietnamese figures for battle deaths once again turned out to be twice as high as the figures reported to Washington in the operational messages.[1] For RVNAF the war in 1973 was only 30 percent less intense than in 1972, the worst year for casualties that the South Vietnamese ever had.

In short, the war during the cease fire period continued on for RVNAF at a level of intensity above their losses during 1968, the year of the Tet Offensive. RVNAF took more casualties during 1974 than it did in any prior year except 1972. By December 1974 the South Vietnamese Army was a badly battered force. The effects of the beating showed in the pacification statistics, as HES ratings slipped to 1969 levels.

The communist forces, on the other hand, were getting stronger. They moved their logistics support into areas of South Vietnam they now controlled and protected it with strong anti-aircraft defenses. They built roads, bridges, pipelines, and they introduced several thousand more troops. By the end of 1974 they were in the strongest position they had been in since 1964. They launched their offensive, the conflict took on some of the characteristics of a war with fronts and the rest is history.

NOTES

1. With the changeover of American personnel in Washington after the cease fire agreement, the South Vietnamese casualty reporting system to Washington slipped back into a reliance on daily and weekly operational reports which didn't pick up the late RVNAF reports covering about half of their combat deaths. See Chapter 10 for a description of the problem as it existed circa 1967.

22
Some Conclusions

The Americans couldn't win in Vietnam but they couldn't lose either as long as they stayed. A stalemate was achieved with South Vietnamese strength continually building until the Americans left. The South Vietnamese failed to develop the ability to win, although they had years of protection behind an American shield to do so. They simply never faced up to their peril or made the extraordinary efforts needed to pull themselves together and keep the communists from winning.

On the military side, we simply did not do the job with the South Vietnamese that we did with the South Koreans because we had always assumed that we would win the war for them. On the other hand, we did not have command of their army or the support of a strong leader like Syngman Rhee. Even if these had both existed in South Vietnam, we could debate whether it would have made much difference because it was the American attrition strategy and tactics that failed to win this war, which was quite different from the one in Korea.

In contrast, the advisory effort for pacification apparently had some success. The American pacification advisors, many of them with years of experience in Vietnam, worked with the South Vietnamese (they had no American troops) and constantly put pressure on them to perform. They also did not feel the need to train a generation of American combat commanders for possible future wars, and therefore tended to keep people in their jobs instead of rotating them through the system to gain experience. The advisors also did something to improve the South Vietnamese leadership they had to work with.

If the United States ever again gets involved in a war without fronts, our top leaders and commanders could do worse than to demand systematic analysis of the situation with a strong emphasis on the patterns that emerge. It won't win the war by itself but it won't hurt the effort either.

Appendix:
The Southeast Asia Analysis Report

Fifty issues of the **Southeast Asia Analysis Report** were published from January 1967 through January 1972 by the Southeast Asia office under the Asistant Secretary of Defense (Systems Analysis). The Report had two purposes. First, it served as a vehicle to distribute the analyses produced by Systems Analysis on Southeast Asia. It also provided other agencies an oppportunity to tell us if we were wrong and to help prevent research duplications. We solicited and received frequent rebuttals or comments on our analyses, which sharpened our studies and stimulated better analysis by other agencies. Second, it was a useful management tool for getting more good work from our staff. They knew they must regularly produce studies which would be read critically throughout the Executive Branch.

The first page of the Report stated that it "is not an official publication of the Department of Defense, and does not necessarily reflect the views of the Secretary of Defense, Assistant Secretary of Defense (Systems Analysis), or comparable officials." The intent was solely to improve the quality of analysis on Southeast Asia problems, and to stimulate further thought and discussion. The report was successful in doing precisely this.

The Report also generated a hostile reception from some readers. The JCS twice tried to stop its distribution to the military departments and other government agencies. General Westmoreland, the U.S. Commander in Vietnam, included us among those who "constantly sought to alter strategy and tactics with naive, gratuitous advice."[1]

We distributed about 350 copies of the Report to the Office of the Secretary of Defense (OSD), the Military Departments, CINCPAC, MACV and to other interested agencies such as the Paris Delegation, AID, State Department, CIA, and the White House Staff. Most copies circulated outside OSD were in response to specific requests from individual persons or agencies. Our readership included many of the key commanders, staff officers, and analysts in Washington and in the field. Their coments were usually generous and complimentary, even when they disagreed with our conclusions. Some excerpts appear below:

"Ambassador _____ has asked me to tell you that he has much appreciated and benefited from the studies and analyses of this publication." (White House, 24 January 1969)

"One of the most useful Systems Analysis products we have seen is the monthly **Southeast Asia Progress Report....** Indeed it strikes many of us as perhaps the most searching and stimulating periodic analysis put out on Vietnam." (President of the RAND Corporation, 22 October 1969)

"In general, I think it is becoming the best analytical periodical I've seen yet on Vietnam (though there is not much competition)." (MACV-DEPCORDS, 21 April 1967)

"I believe the **SEA Analysis Report** serves a useful purpose, and I would like to see its present distribution continued." (Deputy Secretary of Defense, 31 May 1968)

"Statistical extrapolations of this type serve an extremely useful purpose in many facets of our daily work." (CIA, 6 February 1967)

"We were all most impressed with your first monthly **Southeast Asia Analysis Report.** Not only do we wish to continue to receive it, but we would appreciate it if we could receive 4 (four) copies from now on." (White House, 9 February 1967)

"We used a highly interesting item in your May **Analysis Report** as the basis for a note to the Secretary, which I've attached." (State Department, 28 June 1967)

"The SEA Programs Division is to be commended for its perceptive analysis of topics that hold the continuing concern of this headquarters....The approach was thoughtfully objective throughout and it was particularly pleasing to note a more incisive recognition of factors that defy quantified expression." (Commander, U.S. Army Vietnam-USARV, 29 November 1967)

"As an avid reader (and user) of the **SEA Analysis Report,** I see a need for more rounded analyses in the pacification field and fewer simplistic constructs." (MACV-DEPCORDS, 17 April 1968)

"I let Ambassador_____take a swing at the paper. He made several comments which may be of interest to you. Many thanks for putting us back on distribution for your report. Also, despite the return volley, I hope you will continue sending your products." (MACV-CORDS, 17 June 1968)

"Congratulations on your January issue. The 'Situation in South Vietnam' article was especially interesting and provoking." (State Department, 24 January 1969)

In November 1968, fifty-five addressees answered a questionnaire about the Report: 52 said the report was useful, two said it was not, and one said, "The report does not meet an essential need of this headquarters," but "it desired to remain on distribution" for seven copies. From 48 questionnaires with complete responses, we found that an average of 4.8 people read each copy—a projected readership of 500 to 950, depending on whether we assumed one or 2.4 readers of copies for which no questionnaire was returned.

As noted, there was some negative reaction to the Report. Concern was expressed about "the distorted impressions" the Report left with the reader and its wide dissemination which "implies its acceptance by the Secretary of Defense, giving the document increased credibility."

Articles from the **SEA Analysis Report** served as the most important source for this book. All articles printed in the **Report** have been collected and indexed in twelve volumes titled **A Systems Analysis View Of The Vietnam War 1965–1972, Vol. 1–12**, Thomas C. Thayer, Editor. All twelve volumes are available as a group or individually from The National Technical Information Service (NTIS), 5285 Port Royal Road, Springfield, VA. 22161. Telephone: 703-487-4650.

The titles to the twelve volumes are listed below, each with its individual NTIS reference number which must be included in any inquiry about the publications.

Vol. 1. The Situation In Southeast Asia, ADA 039313
2. Forces And Manpower, ADA 051609
3. Viet Cong - North Vietnamese Operations, ADA 039314
4. Allied Ground And Naval Operations, ADA 051610
5. The Air War, ADA 051611
6. Republic Of Vietnam Armed Forces (1), ADA 039315
7. Republic Of Vietnam Armed Forces (2), ADA 051612
8. Casualties And Losses, ADA 051613
9. Pacification Security, ADA 039316
10. Pacification And Civil Affairs, ADA 039317
11. Economics, War Costs And Inflation, ADA 051614
12. Construction And Port Operations In South Vietnam, ADA 051615.

NOTE

William C. Westmoreland, **A Soldier Reports,** (Garden City, N.Y., 1967), p. 147.

Glossary

ARVN	–	Army of the Republic of Vietnam. South Vietnamese Army.
CIA	–	U.S. Central Intelligence Agency.
CIDG	–	Civilian Irregular Defense Group.
CICPAC	–	Commander-in-Chief, Pacific Command.
CORDS	–	MACV Civil Operations and Revolutionary (Rural) Development Support U.S. Pacification Advisors.
COMUSMACV	–	Commander U.S. Military Assistance Command Vietnam.
COSVN	–	Central Office South Vietnam. The Communist headquarters command.
DIA	–	U.S. Defense Intelligence Agency.
DMZ	–	Demilitarized Zone between North and South Vietnam.
FWMAF	–	Free World Military Assistance Forces.
GVN	–	Government of (South) Vietnam.
HES	–	Hamlet Evaluation System.
HES/70	–	Hamlet Evaluation System - 1970.
Iron Triangle	–	A large communist base shaped like a triangle with underground fortifications 20 miles north of Saigon in Binh Duong Province.
J-2	–	Director of Intelligence.
JCS-J3	–	U. S. Joint Chiefs of Staff-Director of Operations.
JGS	–	Joint General Staff (South Vietnamese)
JUSPAO	–	Joint U. S. Public Affairs Office.
KIA	–	Killed In Action
KITS	–	Key Interteams of the Combat Peoples Self Defense Forces.
LOC	–	Line of Communication, roads, canals etc.
MACV	–	U.S. Military Assistance Command Vietnam.
MACV DEPCORDS	–	Deputy to COMUSMACV for CORDS.
MR	–	Military Region of South Vietnam.
NTIS	–	National Technical Information Service Center.

NVA	–	North Vietnamese Army.
OASD/SA	–	Office of the Assistant Secretary of Defense (Systems Analysis).
OB	–	Order of Battle.
OSD	–	Office of The Secretary of Defense.
PAAS	–	Pacification Attitude Analysis System.
Paris Delegation	–	The U.S. delegates to the peace talks with North Vietnam in Paris.
PF	–	South Vietnamese Popular Forces who operated in a village or hamlet.
PHOENIX	–	English name for the Phuong Hoang Program against the communist infrastructure.
PL-480	–	U.S. Public Law 480.
POW	–	Prisoner of War
PRU	–	Provincial Reconaissance Unit.
PSDF	–	Peoples Self Defense Forces.
RD Cadre	–	Revolutionary Development Cadre.
RVNAF	–	Republic of Vietnam (South Vietnam) Armed Forces.
RF	–	South Vietnamese Regional Forces who operated in a province.
SA	–	Systems Analysis.
SEA	–	Southest Asia.
SEAPRS	–	Southeast Asia Provincial Summary File.
Sortie	–	An operational flight by one aircraft.
SEER	–	MACV System for Evaluating the Effectiveness of RVNAF
SVN	–	South Vietnam.
TFES	–	Territorial Forces (RF & PF) Effectiveness System.
TIC	–	Troops In Contact.
TIRS	–	Terrorist Incident Reporting System.
USAID	–	U.S. Agency for International Development.
VC	–	Viet Cong were the South Vietnamese communists, as distinct from the NVA.
VCI	–	Viet Cong Infrastructure.
Viet-Nam	–	The technically correct way to refer to "Vietnam," but time has eroded that practice in the U.S. so it is written as "Vietnam" in this book.
VNAF	–	South Vietnamese Air Force.
VNMC	–	South Vietnamese Marine Corps.
VNN	–	South Vietnamese Navy.

Bibliography

PRIMARY SOURCES

Army Activites Report: Southeast Asia - Final Issue, Washington, D.C.: U.S. Army Center For Military History, 1972.

Army Concept Team In Vietnam. Hamlet Evaluation System Study (HES), A report prepared by the Simulmatics Corp., Cambridge, Mass., May 1968.

U.S. Department of the Army. Viet-Nam Studies: Medical Support of the U.S. Army In Viet-Nam, 1965-1970. Washington, D.C.: U.S. Army Center For Military History, 1973.

Carrier, J. M., A Profile of Viet Cong Returnees: July 1965 To June 1967. RM-5577-ISA/ARPA, Santa Monica, CA: The RAND Corporation, October 1968.

Comptroller General of The United States. Continuing Difficulties in Assisting War Victims In Viet-Nam (B-13301). Washington, D.C.: 1970.

U.S. Congress, Senate Committee on Foreign Relations, Vietnam: Policy and Prospects, 1970. Hearings 91st Cong., 2nd Sess., February and March 1970, p. 40.

U.S. Congress, Senate Foreign Relations Committee, Statement by William K. Hitchcock, Director, Refugee Directorate, CORDS, February 17-20, 1970.

U.S. Congress, Senate Committee on The Judiciary, Subcommittee to Investigate Problems Connected with Refugees and Escapees, Casualty and Refugee Problems in South Vietnam, May 9, 1968. p. 17.

U.S. Congress, Senate Judiciary Subcommittee on Refugees, **Statement of Robert H. Nooter, Deputy Coordinator, Bureau of Supporting Assistance,** AID, May 8, 1972, p. 32.

U.S. Congress, Senate Judiciary Subcommittee on Refugees, **General Accounting Office, Supplemental Inquiry Concerning the Civilian Health and War-Related Casualty Program In Vietnam (B-133001),** May 9, 1968, p. 40.

U.S. Congress, Senate Subcommittee on Refugees and Escapees, **Statement of Ambassador William E. Colby, Deputy to Commander, U.S. Military Assistance Command, Viet-Nam (COMUSMACV) for Civil Operations and Rural Development Support,** April 21, 1972, p. 6.

U.S. Congress, Senate **Subcommittee on United States, Security Agreements and Commitments Abroad Hearings,** October 20, 21, 22 and 28, 1969, p. 713.

Cooper, L. and Legere L. **The American Experience With Pacification in Vietnam.** Washington, D.C.: Institute For Defense Analysis R-185, 1972.

Croizat, V. J. A Translation from the French: **Lessons of the War in Indochina.** Santa Monica, CA: The RAND Corporation, RM-5271-PR, 1967.

U.S. Department of Defense, Office of the Assistant Secretary of Defense (Comptroller). **Southeast Asia Statistical Summary.** Washington, D.C., 1965-1973.

U.S. Department of Defense, Office of the Assistant Secretary of Defense (Systems Analysis). **The Southeast Asia Analysis Report.** Washington, D.C. November 1965 through January 1972. For details on how to obtain the **Analysis Report** articles, see the Appendix.

U.S. Department of Defense, Assistant Secretary of Defense (Systems Analysis). **Memorandum for The Secretary of Defense, Subject: "RVNAF Leadership,"** October 7, 13, 1970.

U.S. Department of Defense, Secretary of Defense. **Memorandum for the Chairman of the Joint Chiefs of Staff, Subject: "RVNAF Leadership,"** October 13, 1970.

Ginder, Samuel P. "Moral Imperatives In Foreign Policy." Final Seminar Paper, Georgetown University, 1983.

Development of The Korean Economy, 1958. Ministry of Reconstruction, Republic of Korea.

Hamlet Evaluation System (HES) Computer Files were released to the National Archives in 1975 on recommendation of the author for listing in the Catalog of Machine Readable Records in the National Archives of the United States.

Hollis, Harris W. Commanding General, 25th Infantry Division, U.S. Army. MACV Senior Officer Debriefing Report September 1969 to April 1970. Washington, D.C.: U.S. Army Center of Military History.

International Monetary Fund. "Changes in Consumer Prices." International Financial Statistics. Washington, D.C., 1973.

Kenny, Henry James. "The Changing Importance of Vietnam in United States Policy: 1949-1969." Ph.D. dissertation, The American University, Washington, D.C., 1957.

Koch, J. A. The Chieu Hoi Program in South Vietnam, 1963-1971, R-1172 ARPA, Santa Monica, CA: The RAND Corp., 1973.

Komer, Robert W. Bureaucracy Does its Thing: Institutional Constraints on U.S. Performance in Viet-Nam, R-967-ARPA. Santa Monica, CA: The RAND Corporation, 1972.

Komer, Robert W. The Malayan Emergency in Retrospect: Organization of a Successful Counterinsurgency Effort, R-957-ARPA, Santa Monica, CA: The RAND Corporation, 1972.

MACV "Capability Study of U.S. and ARVN Infantry Battalions." MACEVAL Study No. 2-68, Washington, D.C.: U.S. Army Center of Military History, 1968.

MACV Measurement of Progress Reports, Washington, D.C.: U.S. Army Center for Military History, April 1968 through December 1972.

MACV. Monthly Order of Battle Summary, Washington, D.C.: U.S. Army Center of Military History. 1965 through 1972.

MACV. Report of the MACV Information and Reports Working Group. Washington, D.C.: U.S. Army Center for Military History, 1963.

MACV. The System for Evaluating the Effectiveness of RVNAF(SEER), Washington, D.C.: U.S. Army Center for Military History, 1969.

Marshall, G. W. Proposed Research Paper: Preliminary Examination of the Hamlet Evaluation System (A Methodological Study). Institute for Defense Analysis. (Log. no. HQ 67-6959)3, 1968.

The Pacification Attitude Analysis System (PAAS) computer files were released to the National Archives in 1975 on recommendation of the author for listing in The Catalog of Machine Readable Records in the National Archives of The United States.

"Pentagon Defends the Air War," The Washington Star. Washington, D.C., April 25, 1971, p. 4.

Schwartz, A. I. Selected Characteristics of VC Incidents. Washington, D.C.: Weapons Systems Evaluation Group (WSEG) Staff Study N. 137, 1967.

Sterba, James B. "Hiepduc: One Man's Victory is Anothers Defeat," New York Times, September 7, 1969.

The Terrorist Incident Reporting System (TIRS) computer files were released to the National Archives in 1975 on recommendation of the author for listing in the Catalog of Machine Readable Records in the National Archives of The United States.

"U.S. Officials See a Viet-Nam Stalemate," New York Times, May 7, 1974.

"Viet Journal: In Defense of the U.S. Army," Washington Star-News, May 9, 1974.

"Vietnam--Squeezed Artery." The Economist. London: August 31, 1974.

Westmoreland, William C. Lecture. Medford, Mass: Tufts University, 1973.

SECONDARY SOURCES

Enthoven, Alain C. and Smith, K. Wayne. How Much Is Enough? New York: Harper & Row, 1971.

Fall, Bernard. Street Without Joy. Harrisburg: Stackpole Co., 1964.

_____. The Two Vietnams. New York: Praeger, 1966.

_____. Viet-Nam Witness 1953-1966. New York: Praeger, 1966.

_____. Last Reflections on a War. New York: Praeger, 1967.

Goodman, Allan E. and Franks, Lawrence M. "Between War and Peace: A Profile of Migrants to Saigon." **The Asia Society--SEADAG.** New York, p. 1.

The Senator Gavel Edition. **The Pentagon Papers.** Boston: The Beacon Press, 1971.

Halberstam, David. **The Best and the Brightest.** New York: Random House, 1972.

Mallin, Jay. **Terror In Vietnam.** Princeton: D. Van Nostrand, 1966.

O'Ballance, Edgar. **The Indochina War 1945-1954.** London: Faber and Faber, 1964.

The Royal United Service Institution, **Lessons from the Vietnam War.** Whitehall, London 1969.

Schram, Stuart R. **Mao Tse-Tung: Basic Tactics.** New York: Frederick A. Praeger, 1966.

Shaplen, Robert. "Letter from Saigon." **The New Yorker,** January 6, 1975, p. 104.

Taylor, Maxwell D. **Swords and Plowshares.** New York: W. W. Norton and Co., 1972.

Thompson, Sir Robert. **No Exit From Vietnam.** New York: David McKay Co., 1969.

Walt, Lewis. **Strange War, Strange Strategy.** New York: Funk & Wagnells, 1970.

Index

271